THE RED QUEEN AMONG ORGANIZATIONS

THE RED QUEEN
AMONG ORGANIZATIONS

HOW COMPETITIVENESS EVOLVES

William P. Barnett

PRINCETON UNIVERSITY PRESS   PRINCETON AND OXFORD

Copyright © 2008 by Princeton University Press
Published by Princeton University Press, 41 William Street,
Princeton, New Jersey 08540
In the United Kingdom: Princeton University Press, 6 Oxford Street, Woodstock,
Oxfordshire OX20 1TW
Library of Congress Cataloging-in-Publication Data

Barnett, William P.
The red queen among organizations : how competitiveness evolves / William P. Barnett.
p.   cm.
Includes bibliographical references and index.
ISBN 978-0-691-13114-6 (cloth : alk. paper)
1. Competition. I. Title.
HB238.B37 2008
338.6'04801—dc22   2007040835

British Library Cataloging-in-Publication Data is available

This book has been composed in ITC Galliard

Printed on acid-free paper. ∞

press.princeton.edu

Printed in the United States of America

10 9 8 7 6 5 4 3 2 1

To my parents, Burton and Dorothy Barnett

Contents

Preface

IT IS SAID that you know a person once they have shared with you their story. After that, so much more is clear about why they act as they do. Talking about the person to another, you may then say something like "Did you know what he spent the last ten years doing?" or "I thought that too, until I learned about his time in the service." Even when wondering about why we, ourselves, act as we do, we likely will look first to the experiences of our life that make us as we are. And when it is time to hire someone for an important job, like coaching a professional sports team (or perhaps running a large firm), who is most capable will likely be decided by looking to see who is most experienced. To know the qualities that make a person unique, we need to know the road they have traveled.

The same can be said for understanding the organizations we see around us. Organizations differ profoundly, and scholars routinely observe how these differences make some organizations more or less capable than others. But to really know an organization, to be an expert, we have to spend some time there. Presumably, this gives us a chance to get to know the organization's "story." So it is that stories of individual organizations are popular reading. Wanting to know an organization, I might at least hear about its story—the experiences that make it what it is. Only then will I understand the qualities that make the organization uniquely capable or especially fallible in certain ways.

To nonacademics, it may be surprising that this starting point is considered dangerous ground among academics. There remains, unresolved, an ancient debate about how we explain the world around us. Do we look at each individual's unique qualities as the "reason" for what they do, or do we look for general patterns that help us to understand whole groupings of individuals? In order to generalize about organizations, many favor the grouping approach. Popular books and academic theories alike typically describe types of organizations and predict that certain qualities can be used to separate organizations into such groupings. Consulting firms are paid handsomely to help organizations take on some qualities, or lose other qualities, in order to shape how these organizations behave. The alternative of looking for the unique qualities of each organization, it is feared, will degenerate explanation into the telling of stories. What good would explanations be if we end up with as many explanations as there are organizations?

A middle approach, and the one I take in this book, is to group organizations according to their "stories." Certainly each organization has a unique history, and to know that history would give us an intimate and more complete understanding of the organization's qualities. But it is likely that other organizations may have similar stories, and if our intuition about experience is correct, then similar experiences should produce similar qualities. Grouping by experience is common in everyday life. Often you will hear "Yes, but they were children of the Depression," or some similar generalization to make sense of whole groupings of individuals. Behind such explanation is the idea that some have stories in common and consequently share common qualities. Of course, if we could easily observe those qualities, we could forget about the stories. But often one's story is more observable than the qualities it produces.

Many of the stories behind the organizations we see around us feature competition in one way or another. Organizations in competition are challenged in many ways. Whether they realize it or not, people routinely confront problems in organizational life that were brought on by competition. Competition increases scarcity, triggers change, and imposes penalties for our failings; so it is that competition is at the root of many of the challenges we face on a day-to-day basis in organizations. In this book, I will group organizations according to whether their stories feature competition. These stories likely created a variety of unique qualities in the thousands of organizations studied in this book, but it would be beyond me to feature all these stories. Whatever these individual qualities, I propose to group them according to whether they resulted from the experience of competition. Generalizing from their stories in this way, I help to explain differences in the fates of these organizations going forward.

It may seem painfully obvious that organizations with a history of competing are different from organizations that lack such experience. I confess at the start that I often wonder why I have spent so much time and trouble belaboring this point. I do get more from this analysis, however, than the cliché "competition makes you strong." Certainly that saying is at the heart of the book, and it will not surprise readers to know that this statement will find (qualified) support in my study. But sometimes the consequences of competition will cut the other way. Lessons well learned often turn maladaptive as times change, or as organizations enter into new contexts. Other times, the costs of enduring competition may outweigh the benefits. Although I cannot escape the cliché that competition makes you strong, by thinking it through explicitly I can show when it applies and when it does not in a systematic, predictable way.

Acknowledgments ————————————————————

THIS BOOK was conceived and written at the Center for Advanced Study in the Behavioral Sciences in Palo Alto, California. In 1995, as a Fellow there, I wrote my first papers on Red Queen competition, and after collecting more data I returned to the Center to write this book during the 2004–2005 academic year. My thanks to the colleagues I got to know at the center during those special years, especially Keith Krehbiel, Doug McAdam, Bob Scott, and David Stark.

I thank my friend and advisor Glenn Carroll for doing his best to guide me over the years, and thanks also to John Freeman, Mike Hannan, and James March for their instruction and advice. I appreciate the many colleagues who have helped me to develop the ideas in this book: Terry Amburgey, Jim Baron, Jon Bendor, Robert Burgelman, Jeff Chambers, Jerker Denrell, Bill Durham, Bob Frank, Pam Haunschild, Dave Hitz, Paul Ingram, Theresa Lant, Dan Levinthal, Dave McKendrick, Anne Miner, Gabor Peli, Joel Podolny, Laszlo Polos, Woody Powell, John Roberts, Martin Ruef, Garth Saloner, Jesper Sorensen, Toby Stuart, Mayer Zald, and Ezra Zuckerman. Several colleagues played a role in this project as Ph.D. students: Mi Feng, Lee Fleming, Henrich Greve, Morten Hansen, Xiaoqu Luo, Doug Park, Thekla Rura-Polly, Daniel Stewart, Nick Switanek, Jane Wei-Skillern, and Deborah Yue. Special thanks go to Elizabeth Pontikes, Olav Sorenson, and Aimee-Noelle Swanson for conducting most of the data collection and coding in the computer industry study. I appreciate Glenn Carroll, Ming Leung, Elizabeth Pontikes, and Huggy Rao for providing detailed comments on early drafts. Tim Sullivan of Princeton University Press provided extremely valuable advice throughout this project.

Thanks to the Graduate School of Business at Stanford University for generously supporting my research. I appreciate the hard work of the staff at the GSB, especially Bryan McCann, Marcelino Clarke, and Paul Reist. Most of all, I am grateful for the patient support of my wife, Yvette Bovee, and my children, Julia, Jessica, Burton, Ian, James, Louise, Willie, and Lillian.

THE RED QUEEN AMONG ORGANIZATIONS

ONE

Why Are Some Organizations
More Competitive than Others?

FORMAL ORGANIZATIONS OPERATE in every aspect of modern life, and in each domain some organizations become remarkably successful while most others do not. Popular magazines feature thriving businesses, describing these most competitive organizations and their leaders as models to be emulated. Meanwhile, thousands of other businesses flounder, and many fail outright. Winning and losing organizations appear in many other walks of life as well. Think of charitable organizations, research and development consortia, churches, sports leagues, social movement organizations, schools, political parties, or any other kind of organization, and you will likely know of a few stand-outs. Look deeper into any of these domains, however, and you will see many other organizations that have fallen short of success. How can we explain why some organizations are more competitive than others?

This question may seem straightforward, answerable simply by looking at what distinguishes the winners and losers we see around us. What makes the question tricky, however, is how quickly its answer changes over time. Even as our attention is fixed on today's champion organizations, most champions of the past have fallen, and many are gone entirely. This is true, of course, when industries rise and fall, as was the case for the U.S. rail, textile, and steel industries, among others. But the same pattern of ascendance and failure appears as well in growing, vital industries. Not long ago, it was unthinkable that the likes of Bethlehem Steel or PanAm would become history even as their industries continued to grow. So the champions of each new organizational generation seem invulnerable in their times. But with the passage of time, the cycle of winning and losing among organizations replays, with yesterday's champions falling away as new winners ascend.

Seeing our most successful institutions rise and fall can be perplexing, and as people search for answers academics have responded in force. Looking back over a century, one can find shelves of possible explanations, most of which point to a particular solution as pivotal for organizations if they are to sustain their competitive advantage. If you are young, you might not realize how many times the "new new thing" has come and gone. Those who have repeatedly witnessed mighty institutions rise and fall know that if there is a way to gain an enduring advantage, we do not seem to have found it. Our libraries are full of possible explanations, just as our organizations are stockpiles of experience. Yet we seem unable to stop the cycle; organizations rise and fall today as they always have, taking with them not only yesterday's livelihoods but also yesterday's explanations. History repeating itself seems to imply that we have been unable to learn.

Here I offer a theory of why some organizations are more competitive than others, and why it is that such competitive advantage is fleeting. The basic idea is simple. If today your organization encounters competition, it will not perform as well as it might have otherwise. To meet this challenge, you will likely attempt to improve; you may even experiment with new ways of approaching the job at hand. If you succeed, now your rivals face stronger competition from you, as your solutions have become their problems. To perform as well as they might have hoped, now your rivals are challenged to improve. As they come up with new solutions, you in turn are again faced with new challenges, and the cycle starts again. Competing organizations engage in an ongoing cycle of cause and effect, becoming stronger competitors—but in so doing making their rivals stronger, too.

By this account, we do learn over time, but it is precisely this learning that prevents successful organizations from sustaining their advantage. Rather, even as organizations often are improving, relative to one another they appear to be standing still—or sometimes even falling behind. In evolutionary theory, this process is known as "Red Queen" evolution,[1] a reference to Lewis Carroll's *Through the Looking Glass*, in which the running Alice comments on her relative stability, "Well, in our country, you'd generally get to somewhere else—if you ran very fast for a long time as we've been doing." To this the Red Queen responds, "A slow sort of country! Now, here, you see, it takes all the running you can do, to keep in the same place." In an ecology of learners, relative stability masks an absolute dynamic. Organizations learn and sometimes pull ahead, but in so doing they sow the seeds of their rivals' improvements. In Red Queen competition, learning does not lead to sustained advantage; to the contrary, learning is the reason that advantage repeatedly is lost.

My objective here is to make explicit a theory of Red Queen competition among organizations. Many aspects of Red Queen competition are well understood by managers of organizations, industry experts, and academics. But I have tried to develop these ideas into a theory that goes beyond the common-sense notion conveyed in the Lewis Carroll quote. By working through each aspect of the process as it is likely to unfold among organizations, I develop an empirically testable model of Red Queen competition. The first step is to conceive of competitiveness not as a property of markets, but rather as a property that can vary from organization to organization.

"Competitiveness" Varies from Organization to Organization

Individual organizations differ remarkably in how competitive they are. Consider, for instance, the makers of candy canes. Striped, peppermint, cane-shaped hard candies probably do not strike most of us as a remarkable achievement. But, in fact, over the twentieth century, hard-candy manufacturers in the United States developed formulas and production technologies to pull, twist, and harden sticks of candy—including techniques for putting a "hook" at the end. Along the way, these organizations dealt with problems of melting and breaking candy from production through to distribution. One of these pioneering organizations was Bobs Candies. Many hundreds of organizations came and went in the candy industry over the life of Bobs, but this company managed to adapt to this competition over time and eventually became a leader in the candy cane market. Bobs had qualities that other organizations lacked. We might debate what those qualities were, but the bottom line is that these qualities allowed Bobs to survive in a market where most who tried failed.

Thinking of individual organizations like Bobs focuses attention on "competitiveness" as varying from organization to organization. In contrast, most prevailing theories on the subject conceive of competition as a property of markets, or of market segments. When competition exists, it is thought that anyone engaging in that particular market is subject to the force of competition, as when one joins into an auction. Yet we know that organizations vary in their ability to compete, and so some organizations are more formidable competitors than others. To see this, consider figure 1.1. The figure portrays two hypothetical organizations, denoted by j and k. Because these two organizations have different qualities, we would expect that they would differ in terms of their viability. For instance, j might have capabilities that make it especially viable compared to k. In terms of figure 1.1, this would imply that β_j is greater than β_k—that is, organization j's characteristics make it more viable than organization k. In the same way, I propose that we allow for the competition generated by organizations to differ in strength as well. Just as j's characteristics make it more viable, so might they make it a stronger competitor. In figure 1.1, this would mean that j's competitive effect on k (w_j) is greater than k's competitive effect on j (w_k). Just as some organizations are more viable than others because of their different qualities, so do some organizations generate stronger competition than others.

The theory of Red Queen competition explains the differences we observe in β and w among organizations as resulting from the different competitive histories of these organizations. Often, exposure to competition will make organizations more viable and stronger competitors. In other cases, however, such a history will backfire, making organizations espe-

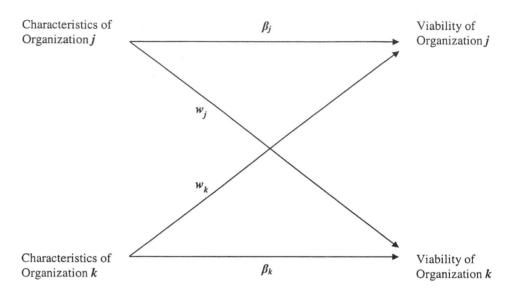

Figure 1.1. Competitiveness varies from organization to organization. Organization **j**'s characteristics affect its own viability according to β_j and affect its rivals' viability according to $\mathbf{w}_j$, the competitive intensity of organization **j**. Source: Barnett (1997).

cially well adapted to contexts that no longer exist. In still other cases, organizations will attempt to avoid or prevent competition entirely. To understand when these different outcomes will arise, it is necessary to make some assumptions about what is known by people in organizations, how organizations behave given what their members know, and how competitions play out given how organizations behave.

Organizations Are Intendedly Rational Adaptive Systems

Most modern theories of organizations accept that organizational rationality is limited. I assume that *organizations are intendedly rational, adaptive systems.* By this I mean that organizations not only have routines for behaving in certain ways today, but that they also tend to respond to problems and opportunities in a well-intended effort to make things better. Members of organizations try to make their organizations perform at a satisfactory level. When performance falls below that level, people in organizations attempt to restore performance. Yet people in organizations have only limited information about why their organization performs as it does, and about how their actions will affect future performance. What information and know-how organizations do have is learned by inferring from experience, a process fraught with error. Consequently, although organizations are intendedly rational, the actual consequences of organizational development will fall short of what would be expected in a perfect world. In these ways, I assume that organizations develop as described by the so-called Carnegie School, which I will refer to as the adaptive systems perspective.[2]

An implication of the adaptive systems perspective is that, as long as organizations tend to keep searching until they find an improvement, we can expect that organizational learning will tend to improve performance compared to what would be the case if changes were random, or compared to remaining unchanged. Many academics studying organizations will take exception to this claim for two reasons. First, learning might not be worthwhile because adaptations come at a cost, in terms of both resources and disruptions to organizational routines. Consequently, even "correct" adaptations may turn out not to be worthwhile, if the process of getting them is too costly. Second, considerable uncertainty surrounds the process of adaptation, so the actual consequences of a change may turn out not to be what was anticipated for various reasons. Reverberations of change within an organization may be unexpected, and whether a change will ultimately match the changing conditions of the organizational environment is uncertain. Taken together, these arguments lead some to conclude that attempts at adaptation have little or no relationship to adaptive consequences.

I agree with both of these concerns, and in fact I build each into my theory. The costs of adaptation, reverberations among adaptations, and the possibility that adaptations will end up out of step with the environment are all explicit parts of the model elaborated in the chapters to follow. Holding these concerns equal, however, if organizations search until the "stopping rule" of performance improvement, then learning will tend to be adaptive. If this outcome were not the case, then empirical estimates of the Red Queen model would fail to support my theory. In this way, not only does the idea that organizational search tends, on average, to be efficacious follow from the "stopping rule" of performance improvement, it is treated as an empirical question—at least in terms of its implications for competitiveness as I model it here. This is not to say that all attempts at adaptation are efficacious, nor is it a claim that organizations will not fail and be deselected as they try to adapt.

Often organizational learning will not turn out well, given the uncertainty that surrounds the process. For example, in the early 1990s, a software startup called FITS created a revolutionary photographic imaging program.[3] The company's founder, Bruno Delean, spoke to my (extremely skeptical) MBA students of a future when people would send each other photographic images from computer to computer—an outrageous claim given that the Internet as we now know it did not yet exist. In fact, at the time, computer hardware limitations seriously constrained one's ability to manipulate digital photographic images on a computer, so much so that such tasks required the use of then-costly, high-end computer workstations. FITS' founding team of software developers came up with an elegant new approach to the job that dramatically reduced the required computing power, allowing one to use even a moderately priced Apple computer to professionally edit photographs. Although the superiority of this firm's technology was never in doubt, it was not clear at first how to turn the invention into a viable business. Over several years, management frequently changed the company as problems and opportunities arose: renaming the organization, competing in low-end off-the-shelf "shrink-wrap" software, entering into licensing deals with so-called OEMs (original equipment manufacturer), and even taking the plunge into the online world when the Internet came along. By 1999 the cumulative result of this organization's adaptations were without any clear logic; fraught within internal misalignments and a serious lack of fit between the organization and its various evolving strategies, this learning organization failed.

Of course, one can also find examples of organizations that learn and prosper. For instance, many Americans will know that Trader Joe's in 2007 is a successful specialty grocery chain that sells exotic private-labeled delicacies to an upscale clientele at a reasonable cost. Less well known is that the organization began some decades ago selling, among other things, cigarettes and ammunition. Over years of gradual changes in management and strategy, the organization incrementally altered its product mix to match the changing tastes of a shifting customer base, dropping poorly selling products and experimenting with new ones. After decades of such adaptation, one can now describe the organization as having developed routines for locating and distributing interesting foods. Each step along the way was an intendedly rational adjustment. Some succeeded, and some failed, as this organizations attempted over time to maintain or improve performance by searching for new solutions when and where necessary.

Contrasting these two examples illustrates that both successful and unsuccessful attempts at adaptation are possible, a fact with several important implications for the study of organizations. First, when thinking of organizational adaptation, beware of argument through selective examples. Of course, examples help to make abstract ideas concrete. Necessarily, one must select which examples to cite, and it is this selectivity that can lead observers to make a logical error. This approach is typical in much of the business press, and among popular writers on management. In fact, if you look back at older editions of many management books, you will see that it was necessary for the author to update the book in order to continue arguing by citing selective (successful) examples. Second, and worse yet, if such examples are allowed to take the place of systematic tests, we can find ourselves thinking that a theory about organizational adaptation has received support when, in fact, it has not. If we cite examples even-handedly, we will see that adaptive attempts by organizations often go astray, despite the best efforts of those involved. In other cases, attempts at adaptation may work out—but for reasons unknown to the participants involved at the time.

Because organizational learning may or may not lead to success, selection processes often operate to eliminate organizations that have gone too far astray. FITS was selected against in its environment, while (so far) Trader Joe's has been selected for in its market. Strangely, many writers on organizations treat the processes of selection and adaptation among organizations as alternatives. Yet if an organization ends up worse off by attempting to adapt, then selection is especially likely to eliminate this organization. Consequently, when we see among surviving organizations only examples of successful adaptations, this likely is evidence that selection has been especially important. In this way, selection operates hand-in-hand with adaptation. Searching governed by a stopping rule of improvement can be expected to work out better than random change or stasis. That said, often search will go awry, and selection processes will operate to leave us with greater apparent effectiveness in adaptation than would result from learning alone.

Thus far, I have discussed organizations as adaptive systems, but without considering that they are surrounded by other organizations. In most settings, organizations typically encounter other, competing organizations with which they must contend for resources.

Organizations Compete with Similar Organizations

I assume that *organizational environments are characterized by resource scarcity, and similar forms of organizations compete over similar resources.* Painfully obvious at first glance, this assumption leads to an ecological conception of competition[4]—an approach with several important implications. First, competition is scarcity-driven, or "zero sum," in that one organization's gain is another's loss. Competition of this sort need not be intended, nor even understood, by those who manage organizations; it takes place incidentally as organizations attempt to attract the same scarce resources. Also, such competition is especially likely among similar organizations, since similarity increases shared reliance on common resources. Finally ecological competition can occur even among organizations that enjoy cooperation, collective action, shared legitimacy, and other benefits of similarity. The point here is that, other things equal, organizations face greater difficulty securing resources when others also are attempting to secure those resources.

One useful aspect of the ecological approach to competition is that it lends itself to empirical observation. As formulated in Hannan and Freeman's theory of organizational ecology, competition is made evident when we see that organizations harm one another's viability.[5] Understanding competition as a behavior, by contrast, would require detailed observations of organizational actions. Instead, ecological models reveal competition's effects, in the form of organizations harming each other's life chances. For example, if we see that two computer manufacturers increase each other's rates of failure, we define these organizations as being in competition even though we may not have evidence of their specific competitive behaviors. By characterizing competition in this way, the ecological approach does not require strong assumptions about organizational rationality, as do more calculative theories of competition.

Ecological models of competition typically remain agnostic regarding the rationality of organizational behavior, making them theoretically compatible with adaptive systems theory. In some ways, my theory attempts to synthesize these two approaches. Similar organizations compete, but at the same time they attempt to adapt to the difficulties generated by such competition. For example, it is well known that the hard-disk-drive industry is competitive, such that similar organizations drive up each other's failure rates.[6] At the same time, however, organizations in the industry have responded to such competition by adapting in order to improve performance. Seagate, a disk-drive manufacturer, responded to competition in the 1980s by developing a global production system, including the creation of low-cost manufacturing facilities in Asia.[7] Within a very short period of time, global production systems proliferated across the industry, increasing the strength of Seagate's rivals so that this adaptation was an advantage for Seagate for only a very short period of time. More generally, this example illustrates how ecological competition and organizational learning fit together, each accelerating the other over time in what amounts to an ecology of learning organizations. And in the background of such evolution, the particular context faced by these organizations will determine the criteria on which organizations compete—what I refer to as a context's "logic of competition."

What It Takes to Win Depends on a Context's Logic of Competition

There is no one best strategy. Rather, *winning in competition requires that an organization perform better than its rivals according to the context's logic of competition*. Although one might talk about competition as a commonly occurring relationship among people, groups, or organizations, the nature of competition can vary considerably across different contexts. What an organization might do in one context that would assure victory might well be a losing approach in another context. For example, Bobs Candies managed to sustain itself in the U.S. hard-candy market for decades. Yet this organization would have been unlikely to fare well, using the same practices and systems, if it were to compete in the production and distribution of high-end chocolates where craft systems of manufacturing, boutique distribution, marketing to women, and an exclusive (and possibly non-U.S.) identity tend to fare better. So it is that different markets, even within a narrowly defined domain such as the candy industry, can have very different criteria determining success and failure. Differences in the specifics of competition are even more pronounced across entire industries, national contexts, distinct cultures, and a range of societal sectors involving diverse forms of voluntary organizations, religions, social movement organizations, and political institutions. As general as competition may seem, one of its more notable properties is *context-specificity.*

Social scientists pay much attention to the fact that how one wins or loses in a given competition can vary considerably from context to context. Research commonly notes differences in why and how actors win or lose across different labor markets, national political systems, markets for goods and services, educational systems, and cultures, for instance. Experts writing on business often refer to different "rules of the game" as competition changes over time in a market or across industries, just as experts on war lament the habit of preparing for tomorrow's battles based on the criteria relevant to the last war. In this light, an important step in contextualizing a theory of competition is to systematically describe such differences in the "rules of the game" across competitive contexts.

The rules of the game can be usefully thought of as the "logic of competition" in a given context. Specifically, I define a logic of competition as *a system of principles in a given context that determines who can compete, how they compete, on what criteria they succeed or fail, and what are the consequences of success or failure.* These principles can be formal or informal. For instance, governmental policies may require the licensing of an organization before it is allowed to compete in a given context, while in other instances restrictions on who competes arise de facto from the technologies, organizational forms, and the social networks and norms that operate in a given context. Considerable technological know-how is required to enter the market for microcircuit designs; relationships with reputable musicians are a prerequisite to competing as an agent in the music entertainment industry; the ability to organize a delivery system across a broad geography is needed to compete in many retail distribution markets. More generally, in any context one typically can identify formal and informal principles that determine who can compete and how they may do so.

As well, logics of competition include the criteria that determine success or failure in a given context. In the early years of the data storage industry, whether an organization won or lost depended in large part on whether it could produce high-capacity disk drives at relatively low cost. More recently, the criteria for winning or losing in that industry have shifted to include whether organizations are quick to develop and manufacture the next product generation. Importantly, the criteria for winning and losing can include both material practices and symbolic constructions—a useful distinction made by Friedland and Alford in their definition of institutional logics.[8] Symbolic criteria often determine winning and losing, as noted by those studying the competitive consequences of organizational identities.[9] Institutionalized identities confer legitimacy to the symbolic constructions of particular organizational forms. For instance, in some contexts value derives from being an "independent business" as opposed to a chain store, a distinction that is important to those who prefer to buy their coffee from the corner shop instead of Starbucks (even if that means drinking bad coffee). Similarly, just as one would not show up at a swanky party carrying a bottle of Gallo wine (even if it, in fact, was very good), neither would one effectively woo an attractive female with a value-pack of candy canes (even if she prefers candy canes). Such symbolic criteria operate whenever organizations are evaluated in terms of their authenticity. Anheuser-Busch is no craft brewer, despite the fact that it can brew a great craft beer.[10] So it is that symbolic, as well as material, criteria can determine winning and losing within a given context.

Logics of competition determine also the consequences of winning and losing. Contexts vary in terms of the extent of the rewards and penalties over which players compete. On the one hand, so-called winner-take-all contests reward success with an overwhelming positional advantage, as when mere prevalence reinforces the value of a computer operating system or a telecommunications standard. Losing organizations in such contexts often find it impossible to overcome their lack of position in the market, even if their products or services are attractive in other ways. On the other extreme, some contexts reward winners with only incremental gains and punish losers with modest losses. Interestingly, one often see examples of incorrect perceptions about the consequences of winning and losing in a given context. Webvan, a failed Internet grocery startup, was backed in the late 1990s by high-status private equity firms with investments that implied one of the highest valuations of any privately backed startup in history.[11] Behind this buzz was the perception that the Internet grocery market was a winner-take-all game, when in fact—now that Webvan is gone—we see a variety of organizations winning and losing incrementally in that context. More generally, an important difference among logics of competition is the magnitude of payoffs and punishments that result from winning and losing.

The consequences of competitions vary, also, in how frequently they occur over time. In a coarse-grained context, the results of competition are relatively far and few between. For example, manufacturers in large-scale aerospace projects can make or break their organization's fate for the next decade by winning or losing a contract for a military aircraft, space rocket program, or jetliner. The logic of competition in coarse-grained environments is marked by occasional, discrete "showdowns" among rivals. By comparison, in more fine-grained contexts, payoffs and punishments from competitions are relatively frequent. In the scientific instruments market, for instance, companies like Agilent sell frequently to large numbers of (often small) customers every day, effectively giving the organization a steady stream of feedback from its environment over time. Logics of competition marked by such fine granularity essentially allow organizations to adapt their strategies incrementally, as seen for instance in Intel's relatively gradual evolution among products in the semiconductor industry.[12]

Predation as an Alternative to Competition

It is possible, of course, that we could avoid competing entirely. Business executives typically react to my theory by proposing this possible solution. Organizations often strategize in an attempt to find markets where competition is less of an issue. One of the founding schools of the modern field of strategic management was built around the idea that a good strategy reduces the competition with which a firm must cope.[13] And, if we must deal with competitors, perhaps a collusive agreement of some sort would be in order, or even a merger or acquisition could do the trick. To the extent that such steps are taken, an organization can avoid competition, and the processes of Red Queen evolution will not apply.

In most industrialized economies, blatant attempts to avoid or eliminate competition are frowned upon, legally if not normatively. Consequently, when organizations do make arrangements that reduce competition, the organizations involved frame these moves as intended to enhance efficiency. Mergers, acquisitions, and other strategies that eliminate rivals may or may not be efficiency enhancing, but by definition they retard the process of Red Queen competition. In the candy-cane market, for example, Bobs Candies was acquired in 2005. This acquisition was touted as improving efficiencies all around, and that may well have been true. But it is also true that there was one less competitor in the candy market and so, if my theory is correct, that market featured less competition and consequently less development going forward.

When analyzing a context's logic of competition, therefore, an important question is whether the legal and normative context will allow organizations to eliminate rivalry. Where and when this can occur, organizations can be expected to respond by attempting to eliminate their rivals, and so essentially killing the Red Queen. Current analyses of this problem focus on the consequences of market power resting in the hands of one or only a few organizations, a topic much addressed by antitrust economics. In light of the theory of Red Queen competition, one must consider as well the developmental implications of predation. By eliminating rivals, organizations thereby eliminate the catalyst that generates capabilities in organizations as they evolve. I will develop these dynamic implications in my model.

After the fact it is possible to look back on industries and watch their competitive logics unfold. But we know that, at the time, people in organizations often are not aware of the competitive logics that are operating in context. This opens up the problem of discovery: How organizations come to know the competitive logic that is operating in any given context.

Organizations Learn a Context's Logic of Competition by Competing

The competitive logics within an industry typically are not clearly understood when organizations first enter. Rather, *organizations may not know what logics of competition are operating when they first enter a context, but they learn by experiencing competition.* For instance, Network Appliance, a company that sells file servers that speed the movement of data in computer networks, grew at an astounding rate after it was founded in 1991.[14] Yet the organization initially took time to learn its industry's competitive logic. At first the company sought to make inexpensive, simple file servers that could be sold through distributors at a low price to smaller customers. This initial strategy and organization quickly failed to meet the hopes of the founders, as they lost in competition against general-purpose computer server manufacturers. At the same time, the company's engineers discovered that once installed, their file servers were much faster at moving data than the competition, implying that the product could be useful for larger customers. In these ways, although competition initially hurt the company, dealing with competition informed the company about their industry's competitive logic. Acting on this knowledge, management shifted its strategy to aim at larger customers and built a direct-sales organization and a rationalized product development process as is appropriate for such customers. These responses to competition sent them into a period of tremendous success and rapid growth, but behind this success was an initial process of learning about competitive logic by dealing with competitors.

More generally, one can think of learning the competitive logic of the context as a sampling problem. A context's competitive logic is not known but can be discovered by drawing competitive experiences from the market. My assumption is that the size of the sample drawn by the organization depends on how varied are the competitors that it faces. Each time an organization encounters a rival, it is drawing a lesson about the context's competitive logic—either about the value of outputs or about the value of the methods of production. Ideally, an organization would have a large and unbiased sample of such experiences that informs its managers about the competitive logic of their context. This would be the case if the organization encountered many, varied competitors. But in some cases an organization may have very few competitors from which to learn. Those in an organization operating alone in a market are less likely to be pushed to question the context's competitive logic. As the only game in town, they do not know how or why they might have lost had they faced competition. Each new competitor the organization encounters, however, presents a new challenge and so offers a new lesson regarding what wins and what loses according to the context's competitive logic.

TWO

Logics of Competition

WHEN ASKING "why are some organizations more competitive than others?" no one answer will hold in all contexts. We would expect to see that a thriving steel producer, a popular restaurant, and a successful environmentalist organization all look very different from one another. In line with this intuition, considerable research shows that particular organizational features are favored when they are aligned with one another and, then, with the requirements of the organizational environment.[1] In turn, such contingency is likely to produce considerable organizational variety, reflecting the variety of organizational environments that we find as we look from context to context. The context of religious sects is very different in many ways from the context surrounding hotels, and so we are not surprised to see religions organized differently from resorts. Zooming in, we can expect to see that the context of hotels in Costa Rica is very different from the same industry in France, and again these differences are likely to result in very different organizations across these contexts. Similarly, over time in any given place one sees contextual change mirrored by changes in the characteristics of organizations that appear in that context.[2] Why some organizations are more competitive than others must depend, in large part, on the specifics of the context under study. The challenge, then, is to contextualize the theory of Red Queen competition in a systematic way.

In this effort, I distinguish among the different "logics of competition" that operate in different contexts, where a logic of competition is *a system of principles in a given context that determines who can compete, how they compete, on what criteria they succeed or fail, and what are the consequences of success or failure*. As with "institutional logics,"[3] the principles in a logic of competition may be formal or informal and may include both material practices and symbolic constructions, but operating as a system they shape the organizations we see in any context on many dimensions at once. So it is that an established candy-cane manufacturer differs from a boutique chocolatier not only because of the technical differences in how one produces and distributes candy canes versus gourmet chocolate. Organizations in these markets differ as well in terms of the scale and structures of their management systems, relationships with partner organizations, marketing channels, approaches to attracting and retaining customers,

and methods for recruiting, retaining, and directing the actions of different kinds of employees. Look at any population of organizations—say,
trade unions, churches, retail stores, or scrap metal recyclers—and one will
likely find that each kind of organization differs from the others on multiple dimensions, reflecting many differences between the logics of competition that operate across these contexts.

Explicitly considering logics of competition, and how they vary across
contexts, is important for several reasons. First, in different contexts, different logics determine what kinds of organizations win or lose in competition. In modern automobile manufacturing, scale economies have become
extremely important to winning in competition, and so scale-based models
of competition explain winning and losing well in this context.[4] And while
nowadays scale economies also are important in newspaper publishing, political newspapers in Vienna during the rise of Austrofascism, by contrast,
were especially successful competitors if they remained ideologically distinct—leading to the demise of many of the larger middle-market bourgeois newspapers in that context.[5] In another context, recently U.S. research and development consortia have competed most effectively for
organizations-as-members by maintaining a generalist strategy, so as to
serve as an adequate solution to the cooperative needs of many rather than
be the perfect solution for a few.[6] One could go on listing examples of
specific competitive logics as they have been found in one or another particular historical context. The general point is that winning and losing in
competition depends on whether organizations are well adapted to the
specific competitive logic that prevails in their contexts.

The importance of context helps to make sense of the idea, so often
discussed in business management writings, that organizations compete
well by having "distinctive competencies" or "core capabilities." Certainly
different organizations are capable of doing different things. Whether
these capabilities are valuable, however, depends importantly on the logics
of competition within which organizations find themselves. The capabilities of the brick-and-mortar retail bank, like the craft-produced watch
company, no longer provide these organizations with a competitive advantage. Yet brick-and-mortar banks did not lose their capabilities. Rather,
the logic of competition in their environment changed, rendering their
capabilities less valuable—or perhaps even counterproductive.[7] Alternatively, entrepreneurs often build organizations with novel capabilities in
the hope that a market's logic of competition will change to favor them.
Webvan, a now-dead Internet startup, promised to reduce the value of
the capabilities of traditional retail grocery stores by altering the logic of
competition in grocery retailing in the same way that online booksellers
transformed competition in that market.[8] This pitch was made especially
believable by its prestigious founding team and high-status financiers. Al-

though Webvan's capabilities turned out not to be as valuable as its backers had hoped, the problem was not that the company lacked capabilities. Rather, the problem was that the market's logic of competition did not change as rapidly as required by the company's strategy, leaving the venture misaligned with the imperatives of its environment.

A second reason for explicitly discussing logics of competition is that this effort will help to contextualize the model of Red Queen competition. I develop a general model of the Red Queen, but for the model to make sense of what we see in real organizational populations, it must allow explicitly for differences in competitive logics over time and across contexts. To some extent, one can estimate a general model of competition on data covering different industries at different times using ad hoc differences in specifications. Research in organizational ecology does this routinely by specifying a general term such as the "carrying capacity" for organizations in a particular context using variables that pertain idiosyncratically to that context.[9] In a study of early twentieth-century telephone companies in Iowa, for instance, numbers of hogs was a good measure of rural farm wealth and hence was used to help specify the carrying capacity for rural telephone companies given their dependence on the farm economy in that context.[10] One would be hard pressed to explain why heads of hogs would matter to, say, the modern computer industry, where carrying capacity would be represented by very different variables. Going further, here I discuss logics of competition in an attempt to allow explicitly for contextual differences within the structure of the Red Queen model, so that what is learned by organizations coevolving in one context in space or time has different implications for the competitiveness of organizations when they find themselves in other contexts or in other historical periods.

A third reason to analyze logics of competition is that organizations sometimes compete amidst contending logics. If competition among craft beers, for instance, hinged only on material product attributes, then large-scale brewing organizations arguably could dominate craft beers as they do the other markets in the brewing industry. Yet small, independent microbreweries have proliferated in the craft beer market because competitive advantage there depends importantly on the authenticity of the brewing organization.[11] Breweries advantaged by an authentic identity, such as the Mendocino Brewing Company, have thus fared well against better-run mass producers and so-called contract brewers with expertise in advertising and marketing beers that they do not produce.[12] So the competitiveness of microbreweries like Mendocino has resulted, foremost, from the rise of a favorable logic of competition in their market—one that favors a criterion on which they compete well. In this way, contention among alternative logics of competition can be seen as a "meta competition" that ultimately will determine which logic will prevail, and therefore which organizations will be more competitive in a given context. By explicitly analyzing logics of competition, it is possible to see when the fates of organizations depend on such meta competitions among alternative logics of competition.

Analyzing Logics of Competition

Analyzing logics of competition is challenging because so many different factors come into play in any given context. Once, pharmaceutical companies that marketed insulin for the treatment of diabetes operated large, often global manufacturing systems to acquire and purify porcine insulin. Imagine the large shipments of pig pancreases, the elaborate treatment processes and quality control mechanisms, the highly technical scientific capabilities in product design and manufacture, and ultimately the careful control of product specifications tailored to the requirements of many different national markets across the globe. On top of these procurement and manufacturing systems, now consider the disparate national healthcare markets in which such a company would need to operate—with separate organizations dealing with the idiosyncracies of so many different regulatory bodies. Finally, sales and service organizations in each market, touching physicians, patients, and pharmaceutical benefit management organizations—each of these differing dramatically as the organization moves from one national market to another. Organizations in the traditional insulin market, such as Novo Nordisk, developed ways to cope with competition amidst these various challenges.[13] To describe the logic of competition in this context, one would have to consider technologies, the design of organizations, and the varied market, social, and political forces in the organizational environment.

The debut of synthetic insulin demonstrated the complexity of this industry's logic of competition. Ultimately, fully synthetic human insulin would render obsolete the elaborate procurement and production systems that were the basis of competition for established organizations like Novo Nordisk. Yet Novo itself was among the innovators in synthetic insulin, essentially rendering outdated its own technological and organizational capabilities. Meanwhile, other changes in the organizational environment also came into play with the rise of synthetic insulin. New products and processes needed to be cleared through the regulatory bodies of various national health systems, increasing uncertainty for an organization with established market positions in many countries. And the normative environment faced by Novo Nordisk also would come into play with the introduction of synthetic insulin. Patients and physicians often were not comfortable changing from their known product to an unknown—especially one that had emerged from bioengineering technologies. To complicate these factors, legal and regulatory changes were taking place in many of the world's health-care markets at the same time, such as the movement to health maintenance organizations in the United States. Such changes made it necessary for Novo Nordisk to gain approval from pharmaceutical benefit managers, organizations that controlled whether drugs were to be covered within a given HMO or insurance plan. Obviously, when trying to understand the logic of competition in context, one cannot look only at market competition in a narrow sense. Rather, a broad range of factors come into play when one analyzes a context's logic of competition.

In order to systematically study such factors in context, I build on distinctions commonly used in organization theory and consider how logics of competition are shaped by organizational technology, organizational architecture, and the organizational environment. In any given context, any or all of these factors may change in such a way as to alter the prevailing logic of competition. Technology change makes possible production at lower costs, or the production of different products and services, which in turn alters the competitive landscape, as when innovation in wireless telephony transformed the logic of competition in the telecommunications industry. Changes in organizational architectures also can profoundly change a context's logic of competition, as occurs whenever the chain form of organization proliferates through an industry. Similarly, the organizational environment may change so as to transform a context's logic of competition. Such change may involve the so-called technical environment of production (such as changes in distribution channels or in the availability of labor), as well as normative, organizational, legal, or political changes in the "institutional environment"—as, for example, when legal regulations alter the organizations that are permitted to compete in a market.[14]

Technology, Organization, and Logics of Competition

The technologies and architectures of organizations have important effects on a context's logic of competition. The scope of markets can be transformed in a moment by a technological or organizational innovation. We now have national and international newspaper publishing organizations, for instance, where this possibility would have been unthinkable given the state of technologies and organizational architectures in the early days of that industry. The costs of production, and the possible range of products and services produced, also depend in large part on the technologies and organizational architectures available to organizations. A crucial step in contextualizing competition, then, is to understand how and when, in any given context, changes in technologies and organizational architectures have affected the context's logic of competition.

The effects of technologies and architectures on the logic of competition are most noticeable when these factors change. For instance, many who study technological change note that such changes often hinge on the development of new technologies.[15] This was the case, for instance, in the evolution of the semiconductor industry. There, early manufacturers commonly both designed and manufactured products. Doing both required capabilities in software development, microchip design, high-yield "clean room" manufacturing systems, testing, and the organizing capabilities associated with each of these functions. In that era, the industry's competitive logic rewarded organizations that could take a chip all the way from design to timely and efficient manufacture. Over time, however, technological standardization and specialization increased in the industry, so that while some organizations continued to operate manufacturing facilities, others concentrated entirely on chipset design—so-called fabless organizations. Given the considerable financial returns to successful designs, many of the industry's organizations came to be fabless—including some organizations from outside the conventional definition of the industry, such as the wireless telecommunications company Qualcomm.[16] In these ways, changes in the logic of competition may hinge on technological and organizational development.

The importance of technology and organization together in shaping an industry's logic of competition is a fundamental idea in Schumpeter's theory and continues in various research traditions.[17] Innovations may reinforce or upend a market's criteria for winning and losing, and the value of existing organizational and technological assets.[18] For instance, information technology applied to coordinating and controlling financial transactions obviously transformed the financial services industry toward the end of the twentieth century. Perhaps less widely known is that this technological revolution also has fundamentally altered the logic of competition in many other industries—such as the gaming industry, where organizations such as IGT manufacture, market, install, and coordinate networks within casinos. Who is able to compete in game manufacturing, how they compete, the criteria for winning and losing, and the consequences of that competition all have been affected by this technological development.

Although technology change is emphasized in the Schumpeterian tradition, organizational architectures sometimes are the primary force shaping logics of competition. This message was central in studies of the diffusion of the multidivisional form of organizations, a revolutionary architecture for which technologies enabling scale and scope were but a precondition.[19] Other organizational innovations similarly have dramatically affected logics of competition in many industries. Examples include the "chain" form seen in franchises such as Starbucks, "skunkworks" stimulating R&D in organizations trying to innovate, cross-functional structures combined with time-based product-development incentives in fast-changing technology markets, strong-culture organizations relying on normative control more than explicit rules, and the list goes on. The effects of such organizational innovations on logics of competition can be as profound as that of technology innovations. For instance, while competition in the early semiconductor industry was, of course, shaped by technology innovation, so was it shaped by organizational innovations that improved yields. These organizational innovations powerfully shaped the logic of competition in semiconductors, leading to the proliferation of new entrants at the expense of the established electronics firms that stayed with traditional organizational architectures.[20]

Competitive logics also hinge on the symbolic constructions associated with organizations. For instance, why does Disneyland in Anaheim, California, continue to be a popular amusement park? Teenagers will say that the rides are not sufficiently terrifying to be regarded as the best. Everyone knows that the lines are long. The setting is not lush. But anyone remotely familiar with modern American culture will tell you that these problems are outweighed by the Disney legacy, which has a value to many over and above the material effectiveness of Disney as a production process. Those in marketing call this value "brand equity," while sociologists might refer to Selznick's[21] version of "institutionalization"—where an organization per se is "imbued with value" over and above its material value. Whatever one calls it, organizations that are valued as institutions in and of themselves can take this to the bank when they compete. Just as we saw that Chrysler could not be allowed to fail, so one will routinely hear from technology salespeople that customers buy from established institutions like IBM—even when the product was not the best—because "nobody gets fired for buying IBM." Institutionalized organizations may have an advantage when competing for reasons entirely removed from their material effectiveness, demonstrating the importance of symbolic constructions to logics of competition.

Logics of competition may also depend on the institutionalization of entire forms of organization. Neo-institutional sociology has long argued that organizations are more viable when they conform to institutionalized patterns and practices.[22] Building this idea into an ecological model of organizations, Hannan and his colleagues argued and found that organizations of a given form are more viable as numbers of such organizations initially increase, reflecting legitimation of a form—with competition among similar organizations appearing only at relatively high density, defined as numbers, of organizations.[23] Ensuing tests of this model continue to demonstrate this pattern by and large.[24] More recent work finds, furthermore, that organizations are more viable if they take on the characteristics of a more institutionalized form, as measured by the rise of a given form in social discourse about organizations.[25]

Ruef's findings demonstrate the emergence of organizational identities as a process of social construction, and the important penalties faced by organizations that violate form boundaries.[26] The problem of organizational identity affects logics of competition in different, possibly opposing, ways. On the one hand, organizations are rewarded with greater legitimacy by conforming to existing form distinctions—that is, for not violating the social codes associated with particular institutionalized organizational forms.[27] In contexts where such institutionalization has occurred, formal institutional support may require that organizations look or behave in particular ways in order to compete effectively, regardless of the technical implications of such appearances.[28] Carroll's study of music recording studios, for instance, shows how these organizations took on formal structures similar to those of large entertainment firms, not for technical reasons but to satisfy institutionalized expectations of how organizations should look and behave.[29] As the institutional definitions of a particular organizational form come to be more sharply defined, organizational identities come to be associated with particular characteristics and actions, and organizations that violate these socially constructed expectations are likely to face sanctions and devaluation.[30]

Yet by penalizing deviance, institutionalized form distinctions render less effective the strategy of differentiation. We know, after all, that one response to intense competition is for organizations to move into other, less competitive domains.[31] The existence of socially constructed identities, however, constrains organizations from freely "carving out their own niche." Rather, identity implies both advantage, in the form of rewards for abiding by socially constructed expectations, as well as constraints against moving into less competitive domains. In a given domain, then, competition might end up more intense, due to high levels of density of similar organizations, precisely because organizations are advantaged by conforming to the various social codes associated with a given organizational form. In this way, by affecting who can compete, how they compete, and the sanctions or benefits associated with competing, the institutionalization of organizational forms shapes logics of competition.

In most contexts, technology and organization interact to drive the logic of competition, with the value of one contingent on the value of the other. For instance, in the U.S. window-covering industry, post–World War II expansion favored manufacturers who could standardize production and reap economies of scale to reduce manufacturing costs. Because window coverings are relatively uniform and not subject to faddish change or technological improvement (at least when compared to clothing or technology products), organizations could and did compete well by keeping large inventories to assure reliable delivery during unexpected spikes in demand. In more recent decades, however, this industry's logic of competition has shifted to favor organizations that minimize inventory costs—following the trend toward the mass retailing distribution channel featuring just-in-time logistics systems. This change favored organizations like the Newell Company (Newell-Rubbermaid as of 2007), which makes window coverings but happened to develop systems for rapid delivery and lean inventory even before the rise of the mass retailers.[32] Although window coverings have not changed that dramatically, the logic of competition in this industry has changed due to changes in both the organization and distribution technologies of retailing.

Often, the importance of organizational architecture to competition depends on the environmental context—especially on the effectiveness of markets. This idea is central to various theories of organizations, especially resource-dependence theory[33] and transaction-cost economics.[34] For instance, organizational architecture and the market environment interact to shape the logic of competition in the adventure tourism market. Some organizations offer low-budget trips of uncertain quality, given the undeveloped economies of these travel destinations. Abercrombie and Kent, by contrast, grew to be very successful in this context by providing Western tourists comfortable experiences in exotic, third-world locations.[35] Most important, Abercrombie and Kent organized in such a way as to directly control the quality of each part of the journey, rather than fully outsourcing these aspects to vendors as is more typical in the travel industry. Given the uncertainty endemic to these locations, high-end tourists place a premium on reliability, which in turn played well for Abercrombie and Kent's approach. Although such organization turns out to be much more costly, the value of reliability has given Abercrombie and Kent a competitive advantage in this particular context. More generally, this example illustrates how the competitive importance of organizational design often hinges on the challenges emanating from the organizational environment.

Logics of Competition and the Market Environment

Decades of research on organizations highlights the importance of the organizational environment to the fates of organizations. Much of what we have learned about organizational environments can help us to understand logics of competition in context. A broad range of environmental factors potentially affect logics of competition—both technical factors featured in the economic analysis of "market structure,"[36] such as market demand or the availability of inputs, as well as factors in the institutional environment such as social norms, political forces, and legal constraints. These environmental factors comprise the playing field within which logics of competition develop and function. By identifying these forces explicitly in any given context, one can consider how they shape the process of Red Queen competition over time and across places.

A primary way that the organizational environment shapes a market's logic of competition is through the preferences of customers. Market demand often is taken as "given," and qualitative shifts in market demand often fundamentally change who can compete, how they do so, the criteria for winning and losing, and the consequences of winning and losing. For instance, demographic change in the United States around the turn of the twenty-first century led to an increase in demand for comfortable, high-end entertainment venues. The so-called baby boom around the 1950s has aged sufficiently to increase demand for music entertainment venues that feature plush seating and better food. The dearth of such venues of sufficient size to hold a large crowd (but not so large as to give an "empty theater" feeling), in turn, has created an opening for new venues, and for entertainment companies to organize events in these locations.[37] Such demand shifts routinely transform industries, altering the logic of competition faced within the affected market.

The numbers, sizes, and degree of similarity among rivals are important to a context's logic of competition. This point is obvious, perhaps, and in fact many economic studies of competition limit their contextualization to these aspects of market structure. Yet the link between measures of market structure and the context's logic of competition is less straightforward than one might think. In general, analysts agree that competition becomes stronger as an organization faces increasing numbers of competitors. The precise mechanism for this increase in competition depends on what logic of competition is operating in an industry.

Economists note that competition occurs when organizations are unable to coordinate their behavior, and so must treat market prices as a given. As so-called price takers, competing firms only react to the information provided by price; they cannot work together to set prices at a higher level than would otherwise be the case. This perspective on competition puts a special premium on monopoly, since in that case an organization can set price at its profit-maximizing level. The first competitor dramatically changes this situation, of course, introducing a duopoly in which—even with coordination—profits will not be what they were. With each ensuing competitor, the competitive landscape becomes increasingly beyond the control of the participants, until at some point organizations involved are entirely constrained by market prices at the extreme of "perfect" competition. So understood, market structure determines whether the logic of competition is that of the price-setting monopolist or the price-taking perfect competitor.

Most markets are somewhere between these extreme cases, and economists often use concentration measures to depict this continuum. As a function of the number of competitors, the most dramatic impact of an additional competitor can be expected, from this perspective, from the first few rivals. These are the competitors that shift the logic of competition away from one of monopoly to one of oligopolistic coordination. The importance of the first few rivals is why many organizations engage in "second sourcing," where organizations find—or even create—a second supplier of a key input to their production process. Among other effects, this tactic uses competition as a disciplining device to keep one's suppliers from becoming too powerful. With even greater numbers of competitors, additional numbers of rivals can be expected to have less of an effect on what by then is a more competitive situation. This pattern is found, for instance, in Bresnahan and Reiss's study of competition in isolated markets.[38]

Organizational ecologists also specify competition as increasing with numbers of rivals.[39] The underlying logic of competition is subtly different from that identified by economic theory, however, because the ecological focus is on organizational founding and survival rather than pricing behavior. Ecological theory regards increasing numbers of competitors to be a crowding problem. As crowding increases, organizations increasingly find themselves struggling over the same scarce resources, making survival and new foundings difficult. For the monopolist, the situation is similar to that depicted by economic theory in its emphasis on pricing behavior; organizations in that situation are unconstrained by rival organizations. At the other extreme, again the situation is much like that depicted in economics. Organizations find themselves so intensely crowded that confronting rivals is unavoidable. Where these theories depict competition differently, however, is as one moves from monopoly to complete crowding. With the first few competitors, the environment is still not that crowded—depending of course on the size of the market (the so-called carrying capacity). A second rival might be avoided, as might a third, and so on, until at higher numbers of competitors crowding becomes especially intense. So, with a crowding imagery in mind, competition increases with numbers of rivals at an increasing rate,[40] while it increases at a decreasing rate when understood in terms of price setting versus price taking.

This contrast of interpretations illustrates how even something as apparently unambiguous as the numbers of organizations can have very different meanings depending on what logics of competition are at work. I will have more to say about market structure and competition in the chapters to follow. For now, it is enough to point out that logics of competition depend on market structure in different and interesting ways. Even greater differences between logics of competition arise due to factors in the social and political environments of organizations, given the much greater room for interpretation in these often ambiguous but important aspects of the organizational environment.

Logics of Competition and the Social and Political Environments

Logics of competition depend, also, on the social positions of organizations. In a series of studies, Podolny demonstrates the competitive importance of social status distinctions among organizations, which in turn reflect their underlying social positions as measured by the networks of deference relations among these organizations. Logics of competition among venture capital firms, wineries, investment banks, technology firms, and other forms of organizations show that, in general, competition works to the benefit of high-status organizations.[41] Podolny and his colleagues argue that the importance of social status in these various contexts hinges on its value as a signal to help resolve uncertainty, and moreover that status becomes an engine driving increasing advantage over time as it gives prestigious organizations preferential access to resources, as we see for instance in the wine industry.[42] This cumulative advantage resembles the so-called Matthew Effect that Merton identified in the sociology of science.[43] In these ways, the logic of competition in many industries depends on status orderings, which in turn reflect the social positions of organizations in their environments.

A related vein of research uses measures of social networks among organizations to describe the structure of the market environment. Burt makes the argument that social networks structure competition among organizations, although others have used similar measures to characterize the competitive context of organizations.[44] Organizations are in a position of competitive advantage, in Burt's argument, when they maintain network ties that uniquely broker the flow of information. An organization has a positional advantage, then, when it is irreplaceable in that flow of information.[45] Following this thinking, changes in the structure of social networks alter the competitive logic of a context. For instance, Barron describes the "structuring" of competition among credit unions over time and shows how ecological models of competition change over time as, presumably, network ties among organizations become more structured.[46]

Social networks also are important as a means for organizations to affect the logic of competition in their markets. Baker and Faulkner demonstrated how social networks shaped collusive behavior among organizations, providing the means through which to communicate for purposes of fixing market outcomes.[47] Similarly, Ingram and Roberts found that competition was ameliorated among hotels sharing friendship ties, since organizations so connected routinely refer business to each other, generating a collective benefit.[48] In these ways, social networks not only can be seen as a description of the market positions of organizations, but also allow organizations to directly shape the way that competition plays itself out in their context.

The value of particular social networks to an organization rises and falls in importance as logics of competition shift over time. For years, for example, so-called business incubators operated throughout the United States, specializing in assisting entrepreneurs in the process of starting a business. These organizations have competed for funding and deal flow, with a logic of competition favoring those with valuable network connections: especially connections to educational institutions, investment funds (including some to government-subsidized Small Business Investment Companies), or government-sponsored community development initiatives. The late 1990s saw the explosion of a new kind of business incubator—those that focused on fostering the creation of Internet companies.[49] Given the shift in funding toward the Internet economy, the logic of competition among incubators had shifted to favor those with the social networks and know-how required to start up an Internet business. As these new incubators attracted considerable attention, many of the traditional incubators attempted to jump on the bandwagon. The collapse of Internet startup valuations in the year 2000, however, led to the sudden disappearance of many of the Internet incubators. Ironically, many of the traditional incubators that were too slow to be on the Internet bandwagon (despite trying to do so) remained in operation, as the logic of competition among incubators reverted back to favor those with social networks that were invaluable prior to the Internet frenzy.

Competitive logics are shaped as well by institutionalized gatekeepers and evaluators in the organizational environment, as described especially in Zuckerman's research.[50] Zuckerman demonstrates that the definitions of who can legitimately compete in a given context often are shaped by institutions, as we see when financial market analysts declare certain portfolios of businesses to be legitimately combined within an organization's boundaries. Organizations violating these boundaries, Zuckerman finds, are likely to change in order to conform to the institutionalized definitions of the businesses in which such organizations may legitimately compete. In some cases, this effect holds even when managers within specific companies can argue and demonstrate an alternative logic of competition. The technology organization Varian Associates, for instance, competed in the early 1990s within semiconductor manufacturing equipment, scientific instruments, and medical diagnostic instruments.[51] These very different markets were rarely if ever combined within any given analyst's portfolios, leading many to question why this company operated in such very different markets, as Zuckerman would have predicted. My interviews with the managers at Varian yielded some persuasive reasons for the organization's scope, having to do with this company's research and development laboratory, which was uniquely capable of innovating in all three of these areas. Nonetheless, this organization finally capitulated to avoid suffering the "illegitimacy discount" of Zuckerman's theory, breaking up the company into three distinct businesses. So Varian was not able to sustain a logic of competition based on technology transfer into multiple businesses due to institutional sanctions that upheld the prevailing, taken-for-granted logics prescribing who can and cannot compete in certain markets.

More formal legal constraints shape the competitive logics of industries as well. Institutional economists have long emphasized the importance of legal context to the functioning of markets and show that who wins or loses in competition often is shaped by laws and politics.[52] Patent laws, antitrust regulation, and other such political and regulatory control powerfully shape logics of competition. For instance, competition in modern telecommunications was dramatically transformed by the antitrust settlement with the Bell System in the United States and policies designed to encourage new entries into various budding telecommunications markets. Similarly, licensing regulations determine who may compete in many professional markets. Technological regulations in the U.S. electrical power industry detail specifically how organizations may generate and transmit power, and regulations control as well the consequences of winning and losing in competition. In these ways, whether one wins or loses often comes down to whether one is permitted to do so in a given legal and political environment.

Changing logics of competition may occur, as well, for political reasons traceable to ideological sources. Regulatory change, often reflecting shifting popular sentiments, repeatedly altered the logics of competition in American commercial banking, as I explain in detail in chapter 5. Similarly, ideological change may alter logics of competition, as found among Viennese newspapers during the rise of fascism in the mid-twentieth century.[53] During the period of so-called Red Vienna (circa 1917), newspapers of the extreme Right were small and fragile and were not viewed by mainstream papers as a competitive threat. The logic of competition shifted dramatically with events such as the rise of Mussolini in Italy, the failed communist Putsch in Vienna in 1919, and the continued economic problems felt in Vienna and throughout Austria during this period. Over time, these and other forces combined to enhance the competitive strength of the political Right, whose extremist strategies went from being seen as illegitimate to eliciting greater support at the expense of the moderate political center. In general, such ideologically based political change can be seen to alter the logics of competition in many contexts.[54]

Meta-Competition among Alternative Logics

Often we see multiple logics of competition contending within the same context. For instance, a debate is raging worldwide these days over what constitutes an "ecotourism" organization for purposes of certification. A variety of questions, such as whether such an organization must be locally owned, must be audited for environmental compliance, or must include a scientific component, are in contention with various alternative certification programs taking different stands.[55] For instance, Green Globe 21 and ISO9000 each certify tourism operators according to whether they put various processes into place, without regard for the actual performance of these organizations in terms of observable environmental effects. By contrast, various other regional certifiers, such as Australia's Nature and Ecotourism Accreditation Program or Costa Rica's Certificate for Sustainable Tourism, give certifications based on the measured environmental performance of tourism operators.[56] Different organizations are able to obtain certification under each of these approaches, with the outcome-measure certifications requiring a more thorough organizational commitment and investment. The different certification approaches thus imply different logics of competition.

Contention among logics of competition can be seen as a meta-competition among logics, and which organizations come to be favored in a given context may depend in large part on which logic of competition prevails in this meta-competition. Looking again at ecotourism certification, which certification approach prevails will determine, in large part, the logic of competition faced by tourism operators in this market segment. Some organizations have adopted the processes set out by Green Globe or ISO9000, while others have focused on managing their environmental impact to receive certification from the outcome-based certifiers. Whether a particular tourism organization can compete successfully in this part of the tourism market will be decided, in large part, by this prior debate about what organizational architectures and organizational technologies will be certified as characterizing "ecotourism."

Sometimes competition among organizations takes place according to multiple logics of competitions simultaneously. For example, with the explosion of "e-commerce" over the Internet, many traditional retail organizations have attempted to compete both according to the traditional ("bricks") logic of competition in their markets, as well as through an

Internet storefront ("clicks"). In some cases, this approach has been successful—as with traditional retail grocers augmenting their business with an online grocery business, even as specialized online grocers like Webvan have sometimes failed.[57] In other cases, however, organizations attempting to flourish according to multiple logics of competition have not fared well compared to organizations specialized to one logic—as has been the case for many hundreds of failed attempts to expand from traditional into online business. One way to think of this problem is in terms of a fixed cost associated with each logic of competition. Competing on multiple logics of competition means incurring the fixed costs associated with each logic—playing strategies on multiple fronts simultaneously. Where these fixed costs are sufficiently high, the penalty for playing multiple, simultaneous logics makes this strategy not worthwhile.

Playing multiple logics also can be problematic because of interdependencies among different parts of the organization, making it necessary to incur the costs of decoupling different parts of the organization.[58] For instance, large technology firms like Agilent and IBM compete from day to day in product markets while, at the same time, they operate future-oriented research labs aimed at developing technologies that may some day become products. To use James March's terminology, such organizations attempt both to exploit what is known for today's customers and to explore for tomorrow's knowledge.[59] Competition is very different in these two arenas because one requires accountability for the efficient accomplishment of well-defined short-term objectives, while the other requires high-variance search behavior in the hope of discovering that which is not yet known. Of course, competing well in either of these contexts requires very different organizational technologies and architectures, making it necessary to design and then decouple very different formal and informal organizational practices designed for each.[60] Such decoupling may be effective in allowing an organization to operate simultaneously in different, incompatible logics of competition, but it is nonetheless costly.

Institutionally fragmented markets are another instance where multiple logics of competition appear,[61] as when gambling machine manufacturers must conform to the disparate regulatory requirements of many different legal jurisdictions across different geographic markets. Whether an organization is permitted to compete in any one of these markets depends on whether its gambling machines conform to the specific technical requirements stated in the regulations. And, if an organization is to compete across many such markets, it must manufacture machines that conform to many different regulatory specifics. In this way, institutional fragmentation can effectively lead to costly distinctions among different competitive arenas, so that organizations choosing to compete across all these contexts incur greater costs than would be the case if they were to focus on a single competition. For this reason, organizations often attempt to rule out certain logics of competition, and to influence which logics of competition come to prevail in an industry.

Sometimes organizations act directly to influence which logic of competition prevails. In the gambling machine business, for instance, it is not unusual to see manufacturers work directly with regulatory bodies to advise on the technical details of these machines. For regulators, this advice helps to create sensible regulations. For gambling machine manufacturers, offering such advice helps to ensure that their machines will be in conformity with regulations. In turn, for gambling machine manufacturers to offer such advice, they must design their organizational architecture to match the many different regulatory bodies they confront. This regulatory management function is costly, since it must be staffed with competent engineers and linked to the research and development platform and marketing or customer relations units of the organization. So while organizations may attempt to influence logics of competition in their environment, to do so can itself be a costly effort requiring a considerable organizational investment.

Perhaps the most talked-about examples of influencing an industry's logic of competition occur when entrepreneurial organizations attempt to revolutionize an industry. For instance, the well-known pillar of the investment banking community, Bill Hambrecht, in 1998 established a new investment bank in the initial public offering (IPO) underwriting business, WR Hambrecht+Co. At the outset, this organization was staffed by outsiders to the industry; as a policy, it sought to underwrite IPOs at considerably lower fees for participating underwriters than have been standard in the industry; rather than "building a book," the established practice of setting the final price going into the IPO by referring to a network of established investment banks, this company developed an on-line, Dutch-auction technology to set the price.[62] In theory, this approach would lead to a more accurate estimate of the initial market value of a company, thus allowing a new listing to enjoy its full valuation (rather than having that valuation enjoyed by those who receive the "pop" in share prices that typically occurs at the IPO). The firm also pioneered many other changes, such as an elimination of the "road show" leading up to the IPO and its replacement by Internet-accessible research. As expected, established investment banks strongly resisted Hambrecht's innovations, and to participate in some deals the company has had to compromise and accept standard practices on occasion. As of 2007, however, this company's challenge to the status quo remains—standard practice has not been transformed, but neither has WR Hambrecht failed. So there exists a contest over whether the logic of competition in IPO underwriting will change toward this new mechanism for information and access to offerings. Whether companies such as WR. Hambrecht or the more traditional investment banks succeed will depend on which logic of competition prevails in this industry.

When alternative logics of competition contend, the meta-competition between logics may be what ultimately decides the fates of the organizations involved. For instance, if Europe had allowed for CDMA-based wireless systems, then companies such as Qualcomm could have competed in those markets. Because the Europeans did not, Qualcomm is not a major player in Europe, while in the United States, Korea, and many other markets it competes well.[63] Normative and legal factors may be just as important as technology to driving such meta-competitions. For instance, the music recording and distribution business has been revolutionized by online file sharing, such that the traditional means of music distribution— selling physical CDs or other recording media—is rapidly being displaced by peer-to-peer distribution over the Internet. Because peer-to-peer file sharing does not include payment to the companies that own the music, this activity arguably is not legal, yet it continues to grow explosively. Although some legal, download-for-payment and subscription services now exist, the move to free peer-to-peer distribution continues and, left unchecked, promises to destroy the traditional logic of competition in music recording. Obviously technology is key to this disruption, but just as important are norms and laws. The difficulty of enforcing intellectual property laws in this context certainly has helped the file-sharing services to grow, and norms surrounding file sharing—especially among the young— depict the activity as a justifiable, if almost populist, blow against large, powerful music companies.[64]

Laws and regulations often decide meta-competitions, sometimes in unexpected ways. For example, in the early years of the U.S. telephone industry, as the Bell System was growing and acquiring rival "independent" telephone companies, the response of the thousands of independent telephone companies was to cooperate with one another in the face of this common threat. Legal mandates early in the twentieth century were put in place to protect the independents from Bell's predatory actions. Oddly, this change turned out to harm the independent telephone movement, in that it triggered a "competitive release" where—in the absence of the common threat—the independents began to compete with one another.[65] In this way, the legal changes meant to protect the independents from Bell also moved the industry away from a logic of collective competition toward a more individualistic logic—yet the independent movement's early successes had hinged on precisely the more collective approach to competition. Thus regulation triggered unanticipated consequences by shifting the logic of competition.

Logics of Competition as Institutional Logics

Those studying institutional logics commonly note the contention between alternative logics.[66] In some instances, contention among institutional logics has implications for logics of competition. For instance, competitions among people and among organizations often hinge on a contention between a logic of professionalism and alternative logics involving market criteria.[67] Similarly, competition among alternative forms of organization in U.S. health care has been decided by whether a particular form is favored or disfavored by emerging institutional logics.[68] In these ways, although not all institutional logics have competitive implications, many do, illustrating Powell's argument that institutional and competitive processes often blend in action.[69]

Logics of competition can be thought of as a special form of institutional logic, one that applies not only to organizing generally but to the specific questions of who competes, how they compete, on what criteria they compete, and over what outcomes they compete. So understood, many sociological studies of contention within and among institutions are, in fact, looking at contests among logics of competition. Contests between merit-based and seniority-based reward systems, the questions of whether credentials are required to participate in a profession, struggles of national trade policy, and debates over alternative systems for rewarding government contracts all are examples of institutional contests that, when settled, determine a context's logic of competition.

In sum, organizations attempt to shape the outcomes of meta-competition among logics of competition in many ways. They attempt to shape the processes of technological diffusion in their industries by patenting broadly, purchasing intellectual property in order to prevent its diffusion, or cooperating in research and development consortia to shape technology standards. They attempt to influence laws, regulations, and other political institutions that shape which logics of competition will prevail. Entrepreneurial organizations revolutionize industries by introducing novel approaches that imply a new logic of competition. In all these ways, organizations engage in meta-competitions over which logics of competition will prevail. Often the "real" competition is the meta-competition among alternative logics. Winners and losers are decided in these meta-competitions over logics, perhaps even more than in the playing out of the competition once a particular logic prevails. Meta-competition among logics thus brings to mind Boss Tweed's infamous remark: "I don't care who does the electing, so long as I get to do the nominating."

Framing Work in the Contention among Logics of Competition

As logics of competition contend in any context, organizations engage in framing work, the strategic use of symbolic representations, to reinforce favorable logics or oppose less favorable ones.[70] For instance, if buying a product is about being patriotic, then one might purchase a domestic product even if it does not stack up on the basis of cost or quality. Consequently, one sees patriotism trumpeted often in an attempt to prevent the decline of poor-performing organizations, as in the "buy British" and "made in the USA" campaigns. Swidler noted that framing work is common in "unsettled contexts" where new "strategies of action" are in formation.[71] We see other examples of such strategic behavior in attempting to shape institutional logics in the work of Friedland and Alford,[72] and in contention among social movements studied by McAdam.[73] Framing of this sort, I contend, occurs broadly among many forms of organizations involved in competition—even commercial organizations. For example, in its attempt to frame itself as the center of a new, rising market for data storage, one organization published and widely distributed a glossary of terms, each framing their products and services in a way that distanced themselves from organizations in the considerably less attractive disk-drive market. In another example, an organization that makes and sells a technical device that essentially routes digital signals and data into broadcast networks has gone to great lengths not to call itself a "router" company. Were it to be seen as a router company, this would bring it to the attention of the very competitive Cisco Systems. In these ways, organizations commonly engage in framing work to influence the logics of competition that apply to their pursuits.

The more that logics of competition contend, the more that organizations are likely to try to influence this contention by strategically framing themselves and their competition. Returning to the example of ecotourism certification, considerable framing work has surrounded the debate between outcome-based and process-based approaches. Many tourism businesses with investments in technologies and organizations in order to comply with outcome-based requirements, as well as various environmental organizations, frame process-based compliance as "greenwashing"—the cynical adoption of ecotourism as a symbolic label without substance, purely for purposes of boosting business. Meanwhile, those behind process-based certification programs such as Green Globe and ISO9000 argue that their approach is a pragmatic attempt to begin a process of change, in the hope that eventually more outcome-based compliance will be a part of these systems. As with many ideological debates, this one pits purity versus pragmatism, and in the end which of these approaches prevails will determine what logic of competition will operate in the environmental tourism market.

An important aspect of this framing work is that both sides in the battle may be factually correct in their assertions; the differences are due to the very different interpretive lenses at work. Clearly the millions of young people exchanging music over peer-to-peer networks are thieves. Yet just as clearly, to those young people, music company executives are "mafia," as said in one online chat room, conspiring to protect their "monopoly." Others regard the music companies as "dinosaurs," living out their last days in denial of a technological revolution. Someday we will look back on the current meta-competition between the old and new forms of music distribution and know which interpretation won the day, but as of 2007 the debate rages. More broadly, any industry's logic of competition can be understood to emerge from a contest among various economic, political, and social actors, in which considerable economic gains and losses hinge on the particular ways that a context's logic is framed over time.

The Logic of Predation

The ultimate meta-competition occurs when organizations acquire rivals or potential rivals, thereby directly affecting whether, with whom, and on what basis they compete. When organizations prey on other organizations, they not only eliminate potential rivals, but they may also eliminate a potential alternative to their favored logic of competition. For example, in the early years of the market for antivirus software, the McAfee antivirus company created an approach to competing in this market that threatened to completely change the context's logic of competition.[74] The company distributed its product for free, at least for home use, on computer "bulletin boards" (a pre-Internet means of communicating among computers through modems). As viruses became more common, users would use the bulletin boards to complain to McAfee about viruses that were not cleaned by the company's product—a "bottom up" source of R&D for the firm. Responding to this feedback directly from users, McAfee rapidly improved its product, often distributing updates back onto the bulletin board in time to have updated versions ready as viruses spread. When software "pirates" copied the software, McAfee responded by giving them updated versions as well, all in an effort to improve the product's reputation regardless of immediate revenues. When users began to take the product to work, however, the revenue picture changed. At the moment the software killed a virus, it announced that a license fee should be paid only if the product was being used in a business. Soon, many businesses began to discover unlicensed McAfee software on their computers, apparently brought there from home by enthusiastic employees. McAfee typically agreed to the licensing fee of two dollars per installation (that is, per desktop computer or workstation). Rapidly, this revenue stream escalated, earning the budding company about five million dollars in revenues in its first year.

Meanwhile, Symantec corporation was marketing its Norton antivirus product using a very different strategy. Originally, the antivirus market was characterized by two main channels, so called shrinkwrap sales through retail distributors to consumers and small businesses, and larger sales directly to the information technology departments of larger businesses. Norton was growing well in both of these channels but had no presence whatsoever in the mysterious world of computer bulletin boards. As McAfee grew through that alternative channel, Norton had no ready response. The problem that Symantec faced was that McAfee was creating an entirely new logic of competition in the industry—one that favored a form of organization incompatible with Symantec's existing organizational investments. In response, Symantec attempted to acquire McAfee—apparently not to reap the value of its products, but rather to eliminate the threat of this new and revolutionary logic of competition. Although this acquisition did not succeed, it does illustrate an attempt by an organization to use a strategy of predation to eliminate the rise of an alternative logic of competition.

In ecological models of organizations, predation, or "predator-prey competition," exists when some organizations increase in numbers or size at the expense of other organizations. For instance, right-wing newspapers grew through predator-prey competition against centrist, bourgeois newspapers during the rise of fascism in Vienna during the 1920s and 1930s.[75] Specifically, the growth rates of right-wing newspapers were fueled by the presence of centrist newspapers, while failure rates of centrist newspapers were increased by the presence of right-wing newspapers. In this way, the ecological definition of predation does not hinge on the particular mechanisms involved, nor even on whether predation was intended. This definition is broader, therefore, than that used among economists (and therefore in antitrust applications), where predation often is thought to imply pricing in the short run (such as below marginal cost pricing) in order to drive rivals out of the market and so result in market power in the longer run,[76] although it can also include nonprice conduct that yields long-run benefits by eliminating rivals.[77] Thus, ecological models would include in predation so-called horizontal mergers and acquisitions, those among organizations in the same industry or market (as with Symantec's attempt to acquire McAfee), while typically economists have been more precise in defining such mergers and acquisitions as a distinct means to increasing market power.[78]

Under the logic of predation, an organization eliminates its rivals—often by merger or acquisition—and so avoids market competition with these rivals. So predation resembles Simmel's idea of "conflict," in that the aim of the activity is to eliminate the rival.[79] While Simmelian competition has the quality of benefiting those being competed over,[80] Simmelian conflict allows an organization to win without generating such benefits. Fundamentally, predation differs from other logics of competition because predation is an attempt to influence who can compete, while other logics of competition take the existence of competitors as given. So the logic of predation is to shape the game that is to be played, changing the contest to be about who is to compete.

In different times and places, the logic of predation has been more or less debated as illegitimate. During the rise of the Bell System in the U.S. telephone industry during the twentieth century, for instance, populist political organizations and the Progressive party's antitrust movement attempted to restrain AT&T's purchases of independent telephone companies through state regulation and through national antitrust actions and agreements.[81] Meanwhile, many defended the rise of AT&T by framing the industry as a "natural monopoly," a term that can be found in the *New York Times* as far back as 1883, but which came into use especially during the period of antimonopoly debates in the United States in the early twentieth century.[82] By contrast, one would be hard pressed to make a "natural monopoly" argument for telephony in the twenty-first century. Like the Bell System itself, the argument for a legitimate monopoly in U.S. telecommunications is a thing of the past. As this example illustrates, the legitimacy or illegitimacy of monopolization—and so of the logic of predation—varies not only across contexts but also within a given context over time.

Where monopolization is considered illegitimate, predatory organizations risk institutional sanction and so may attempt to manage perceptions of their actions. Typically organizations attempting to dominate markets frame their actions as value-enhancing, as in AT&T's arguments aimed at keeping out the budding competitor MCI in the 1960s.[83] Alternatively, some organizations appeal for protection from competition argued to be "unfair" or "ruinous." This approach was used, for instance, in PanAm's 1940 argument that domestic competition among U.S. airlines would harm its attempt to compete with foreign carriers.[84] Such portrayals often frame the purchase of one organization by another as consistent with an efficiency rationale, at least under conditions where efficiency norms prevail. Certainly among commercial business organizations in the late twentieth century, the rhetorical accompaniment to most acquisitions included elaborate framings to demonstrate the efficiency implications of these transactions, such as quantitative estimates by investment bankers of the "synergies" that will be reaped by merging organizations. Although such synergies may result from acquiring a rival, a necessary result is the disappearance of that rival—and also the elimination of a possible alternative logic of competition.

Pursuing the logic of predation requires considerable skills. Acquiring and assimilating other organizations is not straightforward, and if done poorly it can spell the end of an organization. People, cultures, products, structures, routines, and sunk investments all become part of the acquiring organization. Failure to absorb these parts can be harmful to the acquiring organization, and in fact a cottage industry on "how to acquire" has grown in the field of strategic management.[85] The willingness of organizations to take the risks that come with predation is, itself, evidence that there is much to be gained by succeeding at this strategy. Some who study organizations have even claimed that the ability to acquire other organizations is a learned skill.[86] In any case, the acquiring of rivals—even if itself a learned skill—implies a means by which to eliminate competitors and possibly even alternative logics of competition.

Discovering Logics of Competition

Scholars, business analysts, journalists, and consultants routinely describe the imperatives operating on organizations in various contexts. Researchers in strategic management, organization theory, organizational economics, and organizational sociology, though they use different language, all study ways that organizational features meet competitive challenges—satisfying customer demands, obeying regulatory requirements, conforming to normative expectations, and the like. Two features characterize these various analyses. First, those who study organizations typically do so with considerable retrospection. As I do in this book, those who study organizations often look in hindsight at what works and what does not among organizations, and then conclude from these patterns what are the imperatives operating in the environments of those organizations. Pick up a popular business magazine, or a typical management textbook, and you will no doubt read a number of industry analyses that make claims about what is favored in a given context based on what has taken place in that context. Second, organizational analyses often disagree, even with the benefit of hindsight and even when analyzing the same data. Sociologists, for instance, continue to debate why some organizations adopt new practices or products more rapidly than others. Similar debates arise in organizational economics, as for instance in their many analyses of why we sometimes see automobile manufacturers make their own parts rather than buy them from other companies. I raise these points not to criticize these debates, but rather to emphasize that while it is clear to all of us that different organizational features do well in different contexts, there is considerable uncertainty about exactly why—even when we have the benefit of hindsight.

If, with the benefit of large samples seen in hindsight, those who study organizations face indeterminancy, then even greater uncertainty is faced by those who manage organizations. Managers, after all, are concerned more about today and tomorrow than about a long retrospective, and are more concerned with the idiosyncracies of their own organization than with general patterns. Consequently managers face the challenge of resolving uncertainty with very limited data—a problem well described by the title of a paper by James March and his colleagues, "Learning from Samples of One or Fewer."[87] A main point of that paper is that to know what environmental imperatives are important to an organization at a given point in time, those who manage organizations typically look to experience as a guide—even though such experience is necessarily limited. Entrepreneurs and their investors boldly describe "business models" that are claimed to be well suited for particular industries, based on a few observed experiences. Executives in established organizations devote considerable time, and pay for help from consultants, in an effort to identify the imperatives of their environments and ways to align their organizations with those imperatives. In short, organizations face considerable uncertainty regarding the particular imperatives that operate in their contexts, and so are challenged to discover these imperatives.

Because logics of competition are ambiguous to those managing organizations, in context one often can see participants experiment with different approaches to competition. After the fact, we can look back over the evidence of an industry's history and recount with greater clarity the various logics of competition as they have unfolded.[88] Before the fact, however, these logics are yet to be discovered. In one case study of a software organization specializing in a product that helps companies keep track of their workers, top management in this organization changed their interpretation of their industry's logic of competition repeatedly over a relatively short period of time. Initially, their idea was to be "the MRP-for-People" firm, in a bid to associate themselves with then-popular "manufacturing resource planning" software organizations. Soon this idea was adapted to be about "ERP-for-people," inserting the term "enterprise," which had become a popular way to identify software products that were important to the strategies and overall operations of an organization. With the arrival and explosion of the Internet, the organization quickly shifted again, this time to be an HR-ASP (human resources application services provider) firm using the Internet as a product delivery platform. So ambiguous are some contexts that when interviewed about them managers refer to operating in a "space" rather than a market, allowing themselves greater flexibility in adapting their own understanding and conception of their environment as time goes on.

Logics of competition are ambiguous in varying degrees, depending on the underlying uncertainty in organizational technology, organizational architecture, and organizational environment. At one extreme, competitive contexts like that of the many-labeled software firm are marked by uncertainty across all of these underlying factors. Like Musil's *Man without Qualities*, organizations of such ever-shifting identity lack both the constraints and the advantages that come with being of a sharply defined form. McKendrick and his colleagues document one such context, the market for disk arrays, in which up through the end of the twentieth century there remained considerable uncertainty about what technologies would prevail, what organizational forms would succeed, what norms would govern behavior, and whether or how laws and regulation might play a role.[89] Evidence of legitimation did not appear in ecological models of this "space." At the other extreme, some markets have become thoroughly institutionalized on one or all of these dimensions. Most organizational populations we study have come to take on such definition, which is why we know to study them in the first place. But, looked at over time, all organizational contexts see ambiguity changing in response to changes in the underlying dimensions of technology, architecture, and environment. At a point in time in any given context, then, organizations are challenged to discover the logics of competition operating around them.

Discovering Logics of Competition as a Sampling Problem

Research on organizational learning typically describes the problem of discovery using the metaphor of "search," depicting organizations as systems that are seeking useful information they lack.[90] Searching for logics of competition is a special kind of hunt, in that one discovers and shapes the competitive imperatives in one's environment by competing.[91] A lone organization, facing no rival, has an inferential problem. If things go well, this may be because they are the only game in town. If things go poorly, it is not clear what other actions might have been possible. By contrast, competition allows for inferences about the logics that determine winning and losing in a given context. When one wins while another loses, it is possible to draw an inference—if only the inference that one can "leave well enough alone." When one loses while another wins, again an inference can be made by comparison—if only that one should not stay the course compared to the other. Such learning from experience is plagued by problems of incomplete information: organizational experience is a small sample and may well be biased, so managers of organizations may be reading too much meaning into this paucity of information, a notorious problem that I discuss later.[92] Nonetheless, there is more information gained from engaging in competition than there is from operating alone. So it is that competition facilitates the process of discovering the environmental imperatives faced by organizations in a given context.

Each episode of competition can be understood, then, as a sample taken by the organization of the environment's logic of competition. Just as job seekers evaluate and reevaluate their search strategy with each interview, so with each competitive engagement do organizations obtain another sample of what works and what does not work in their competitive environment. DR Systems, for example, was in the early 1990s one of the first organizations to develop a technology for helping hospitals collect, store, retrieve, and view digitally the results of diagnostic images (such as x-rays).[93] Even at the time, there was no doubt that digital technologies constituted a dramatic improvement over film stored in paper files. What was less clear was the logic of competition in the U.S. health-care industry when it came to hospitals adopting this technology over other alternatives and the status quo. In the early period of this organization's life, each competition for business from a hospital provided information about the logic of competition in this market within health care: the characteristics that enabled an organization to be considered as a possible vendor, how a vendor could come to be considered for a possible sale, on what criteria the adoption decision would be made, and what were the consequences of winning and losing a competition. Each time this organization competed for business from a hospital, more information was gained about these questions, allowing the organization to alter its products, organization, and practices accordingly.

Seen as a sampling problem, one would ideally have large, unbiased samples of competitive experiences from which to infer. By their nature, some contexts will yield more informative samples of competitive experiences than will others. Contexts marked by relatively more frequent competitions yield a larger sample over a given period of time, while in other contexts competitions are relatively rare and so yield smaller samples. The relatively long period required from initial investment to the delivery of a large ship, for instance, gives competing shipbuilders little information over long periods of time. Similarly, defense contractors make or break a decade of business when they win or lose when competing for the production of a new military aircraft. In such contexts, competition occurs not as a constant pressure affecting organizations continuously, but rather takes place occasionally in discrete "showdowns" separated by long periods of relatively uninformative quiet. By comparison, some markets are characterized by relatively frequent feedback from competitions, such as in scientific instruments, where an organization might sell to hundreds or even thousands of customers repeatedly over relatively short time periods.[94] Organizations in such contexts sometimes explicitly collect and analyze the results of competition using statistical marketing techniques, as we see for instance among Internet companies that sell thousands or millions of items over relatively short periods of time. So it is that the ability of organizations to sample by competing is likely to vary from context to context according to the relative frequency of competitive events in a given context.

The consequences of competitions differ also in their magnitudes, and this difference may shape the quality of the sample. If losing carries with it relatively small negative consequences, then the organization lives to apply the lessons learned in the future.[95] If, however, winning and losing carry with them extreme consequences, such that to lose a competition implies the death of an organization, then the sampling process will tend to produce what Denrell calls a "success bias."[96] When penalties for losing are severe, then a losing organization gains important data but fails in the process. Consequently, those organizations that live to learn do so necessarily from a biased sample of experiences—one that omits fatally negative experiences. Denrell demonstrates that such learning produces a tendency for risky behavior among survivors, who systematically underestimate the likelihood of possible negative outcomes.

One way out of this dilemma is for organizations to learn from the failures of others. Hints of this approach to learning can be heard in conversations among business executives, who often will speak of now-dead organizations with an eye to avoid their mistakes. One wonders, however, how accurate is survivors' knowledge of the mistakes of now-dead organizations. We know that individuals tend to make inferential errors when appraising the reasons for success and failure once the results are known,[97] demonizing even the good practices of poor performers and admiring the questionable practices of winners. The Apple Newton, Webvan, the Next computer, and other such notorious failures tend to be discussed, like the Titanic, as if most anything associated with these ventures was a bad idea—despite the fact that even the Titanic had some good qualities. Nonetheless, if one is willing to assume that inferences drawn in the wake of failures are accurate, then the failure of others may benefit populations of surviving organizations.[98] Evidence of such learning appears in Ingram and Baum's study of hotel chains.[99] According to these papers, organizations learn from both sides of the competitive struggle and so gather an unbiased sample even when the implications of losing are fatal.

How Organizations Adapt to Logics of Competition

Much research and debate over the years has centered on the question of how organizations develop over time.[100] Although various research traditions have looked at this question, a common theme is that with the passage of time, organizations adjust to be more aligned both internally and with the imperatives of their environments. New organizations and newly transformed organizations may find themselves out of alignment, as initial misalignments are corrected gradually.[101] Similarly, researchers in the fields of public administration, organizational behavior, and strategic management often describe cases of organizations that develop over time in a gradual way[102]—even though this may not always be an optimal adaptive technique.[103] Although incremental change is often difficult to detect over any brief period, if you leave an organization for a prolonged period and then return, you will likely be struck by the differences that have developed—rather like returning to one's hometown after moving away. Such incremental change often accounts, over time, for the development and alignment of organizational capabilities with the organizational environment.

Going back in time, one can usually trace an organization to a point when it looked very different in terms of capabilities. Trader Joe's, a specialty retailer, is in 2007 particularly capable when it comes to acquiring odd delectables from all over the world and selling them to upscale American customers.[104] Yet in its past, Trader Joe's once sold cigarettes and ammunition to a less-than-upscale clientele. International Gaming Technologies (IGT), the maker of many of the world's gambling machines, is in 2007 particularly capable when it comes to bringing new "content"—themes from currently fashionable television shows and the like—rapidly into the experience of using a slot machine. Yet looking back, IGT was not always focused on content in gaming machines. Over time these organizations developed capabilities that once they did not have, and now they find themselves well-aligned with their competitive environments as a result. These examples illustrate what has long been regarded as a well-understood regularity in organizational development: that the capabilities of organizations gradually become more aligned with their environment as time passes.

More recently, a number of papers call into question the idea that organizations become more aligned with their environments over time, arguing instead that organizations tend to suffer a liability of aging. This literature argues that organizations tend to become obsolete and senescent with the passage of time.[105] This fact has eluded research because obsolete and senescent organizations typically fail before we have a chance to observe their decline. To detect the liability of aging, one must collect and analyze data where some compensating factor, such as organizational size, operates to keep organizations alive even after they become obsolete and senescent. As it turns out, in many contexts organizations appear to be *less* viable over time, once one controls for the survival-enhancing effects of organizational size.[106]

If organizations sample their environment by competing, as I argue, then the debate about the correct form of time-dependent adaptation may be misplaced. As it stands, the question of how organizations adapt has assumed that viability increases or decreases over time. In either case, incremental changes in an organization's viability are presumed to take place as a function of the age of the organization (or at least as a function of its tenure in a given context). Yet if organizations sample their environment by competing, then time is the incorrect metric by which to model adaptation. Rather, organizational adaptation should be modeled as a function of the competitive activity of an organization, since through such competition an organization learns about and adjusts to the logic of competition operating in its environment. This dynamic can be described as Red Queen competition.

Summary and Implications for the Model

An organization is more competitive the more that it is aligned with its context's logic of competition. Consequently, to be able to predict competitiveness, a model needs to allow for context-specific logics of competition:

Logics of competition vary over time and across contexts.
Logics of competition are specific to a given context in a given era, as a result of the different technologies, organizing architectures, and the characteristics of the context's market, social, and political environments. *A model of competition should allow for the fact that logics of competition vary across contexts at a given point in time, as well as over the history of a given context as conditions change.*

Alternative logics of competition contend for prominence in a given context.
Different combinations of technology, organization, and environment are possible in a given context, so alternative logics of competition

may contend within a given context. Organizations may be well suited to one logic of competition but ill-suited to another, so often organizations will attempt to influence the meta-competitions among contending logics in a given context. Considerable framing work may take place as organizations attempt to influence which logics prevail in their context. It can be costly and difficult for organizations to compete simultaneously according to different logics of competition. *A model of competition should allow for the costs associated with competing at once according to multiple logics.*

Organizations sometimes follow a logic of predation.

Organizations gain advantage by eliminating rivals from a given context. This strategy of predation can be thought of as a special logic of competition—one that operates to eliminate rivals directly rather than through a contest that benefits others. Of course, predation reduces the competition faced by an organization, yet this strategy may also eliminate other (possibly threatening) logics of competition from the predator's context. *A model of competition should allow for the distinct effects of predation.*

Organizations sample their context's logic of competition by competing.

Considerable uncertainty surrounds the logics of competition in any given context. We know this because analysts and scholars typically find it challenging to understand a given context's logic of competition and often cannot agree in their analyses even with a great deal of information and the benefit of hindsight. For people in organizations, this uncertainty is made worse by the need to understand today's logic of competition today, so the advantages of retrospection that we see in scholarly analyses is not possible. Instead, organizations learn about their context's logic of competition by competing.

Organizations face the problem of learning from the limited samples made available by their competitive experiences. The quality of the samples available to those who compete varies from context to context. Samples are less informative in contexts where competition is infrequent, or where the consequence of losing is so severe that organizations die while they learn. Thus whether organizations can discover the logic of competition in their context depends on the nature of competition in that context. *A model of competition should allow that organizations learn about their competition by competing, and so are faced with a sampling problem.*

With these four points in mind, next I discuss the process of Red Queen competition in detail and develop a model of the process. At first glance, the notion of Red Queen competition is straightforward: organizations learn in response to competition, making them stronger competitors and so triggering learning in their rivals. In the abstract, one can imagine such a feedback process and perhaps even a general model of such competition. The challenge, however, is to understand how such competition develops in real settings, where competitiveness depends on a context's logic of competition. This problem is the subject of the next chapter.

THREE

The Red Queen

MOST ORGANIZATIONS must compete. Commercial firms compete in product or service markets for customers, of course, as well as in capital markets, labor markets, and factor markets for the products and services that they use. But just as competitive are many noncommercial organizations. Churches compete for followers; social movement organizations vie for supporters and activists; government agencies contend for political support; voluntary organizations compete for members; trade associations and research consortia compete for organizational affiliates; universities compete for students, faculty, and donors; health-care organizations compete for patients, doctors, and institutional support. Every one of us is a member, in some way or another, of various organizations, and odds are that most organizations to which one belongs are involved in some sort of competition.

As varied as it is, competition in all cases acts as a constraint that generates scarcity in organizations. Other things equal, an organization without competition will enjoy greater access to resources and support than will an organization that must vie for such support against a rival. Collective benefits are possible, too, in the form of enhanced legitimacy or collective action among organizations with a common interest. That such mutualism takes place, however, does not diminish the fact that when and where competition occurs, the result is greater scarcity for those involved than would be the case without competition. Furthermore, competition generates scarcity even when it is indirect. Direct rivalry among two or a few organizations clearly generates zero-sum trade-offs, where one organization's gain is another's loss. Yet your organization experiences competition, too, when others secure a resource without encountering your organization head on, but in so doing increase the likelihood that others will be left vying directly with you.[1] Some have even argued that such indirect competition promises to be especially fierce, since effective collusion is unlikely among very large numbers of organizations. In any case, a theory of competition should be general enough to allow for the various kinds of contexts in which competition occurs, and the fact that despite its variety, all competition has the effect of increasing the scarcity faced by organizations.

Important also is the fact that competition acts on organizations whether the managers of organizations know it or not. Often, people in organizations are aware of competition. Top managers and their staff often identify and discuss rival organizations, and sometimes they create strategies meant to deal with these competitors. Within organizations, too, one can hear discussions about competitors, based on generally available information, managerial communications to employees, and sometimes even explicit "benchmarking" studies of the competition. Yet competition need not be identified by organizational members in order to exist. It may be difficult or even impossible to identify the source of increased competition. Rather, all that may be known is that problems are arising because of scarcity, while the less-visible fact is that this scarcity is due to an increase in competition from sources unknown to managers.

In other cases, managers may think that they know their competitive challenges, but in fact they may be incorrect. For example, archival evidence reveals that early telephone company entrepreneurs typically regarded neighboring companies to be rivals, yet systematic analyses reveal mutualism among neighbors because they so often connected their systems.[2] Competition did develop in this context, but it was between entire systems of connected organizations—community-level competition that was typically beyond the cognitive awareness of managers. In this case, competition was very important to the fates of these organizations, despite the fact that the source and form of competition were not understood by those involved. Similarly, as you read this book, organizations in which you are involved are competing. While you may be aware that your favorite airline has some rivals, you may not realize that competition is affecting your church, your favorite restaurant, and your place of employment. A theory of competition would do well to allow for the fact that organizations often compete even when this competition is not understood by their managers and other participants.

My discussion of Red Queen competition is formed around these observations about competition: The theory is meant to deal with competition generally, as it arises in various organizational contexts; the theory addresses both indirect and direct competition, since both increase the scarcity faced by organizations; and the theory applies to organizations in competition regardless of whether their managers are aware of this fact.

How Do Organizations Respond to Competition?

Theories differ fundamentally in how they portray the responses of organizations to competition. Rational models often assume that organizations are players in a game, making optimal moves and countermoves, constrained in their ability to deal with competition only by the availability of information (if at all). I do not assume that organizations behave as if they were rational actors. Members of organizations may or may not be aware of the competition their organization faces. If they do have such an understanding, it may not be correct. So I assume only that competition is known to members of an organization in terms of how it affects us in day-to-day life—as increased scarcity. The ultimate cause of an organization's difficulties may be competition, but in the ongoing operations within the organization, we can be sure only that this problem manifests as greater scarcity than would otherwise be the case.

Faced with the problem of scarcity, organizations are less likely to perform as well as members might have aspired. This situation is well described by the adaptive systems theory of organizational decision making developed by March and his colleagues.[3] This theory builds on the behavioral assumption that organizations, their subunits, and people within organizations "satisfice."[4] That is, within an organization a search for improvements occurs when performance falls below some aspiration level that defines satisfactory performance.[5] This assumption means also that people in organizations leave many areas of organizational life well enough alone and devote attention to areas that are seen as having fallen below aspiration levels—so-called problemistic search. Assuming (for now) that aspiration levels do not change, or at least are very slow to change, this search process will continue until performance increases again to meet or exceed the aspiration level, at which point the process of search ends.[6] From an adaptive systems perspective, then, competition generates in organizations a "necessity is the mother of invention" scenario, although the nature of such invention may well be quite limited and incremental.

More specifically, given that search is costly, and assuming that people in organizations pursue low-cost options first, organizations respond to competition by searching sequentially and locally.[7] Rather than "leapfrogging" to radically new solutions, as sometimes described in popular magazines, the typical response to problems in organizations is to make them right by applying the first satisfactory solution that comes along— preferably an existing one.[8] This means that rather than considering all possible options and choosing the best, people in organizations first try known routines—or at least minor adjustments to known practices—and move out to more distant options only if necessary to improve performance to a satisfactory level. If this effort is successful, such that performance improves to a satisfactory level, then the process of incremental change ends. If performance does not improve, then we can expect a wider, more "global" search for alternatives.[9] This search process is expected to continue until performance improves to a satisfactory level, or as a last resort until aspirations are lowered in the face of continued low performance, a possibility I discuss next. By these various mechanisms, then, an organization adapts to competition by changing, usually incrementally, until it reaches a new equilibrium of satisfactory performance.

One feature of this process is especially worthy of note—that organizational learning takes place without being guided by managers according to some planned development trajectory. All that is required for organizations to learn, in this theory, is that members of organizations behave according to the reasonable assumptions of satisficing, local search, and sequential search. In fact, error might well play an important role in the process. Specific aspects of a solution may be changed in implementation in unintended ways, so that what is adopted may end up quite different from what was intended.[10] Such "mutations" may even end up beneficial to organizations. Furthermore, ambiguity regarding cause-and-effect relations typically makes diagnosing the consequences of incremental adaptations difficult—so "learning" is taking place not in the sense of rigorous inference among a handful of decision makers, but rather in the sense of systemic adjustment in the direction of local improvement.[11]

Over time, the results of these search processes cumulate in organizations, making up the routines and capabilities that exist in an organization at any given point in time. In this light, we can say that organizational capabilities come from solving problems. Organizations that experience a history of dealing with certain kinds of problems, then, will be more likely to emerge having the capabilities needed to deal with these problems. Eastern European software development firms, for instance, are renowned for their expertise. This might at first seem surprising, given that the old Soviet bloc was notoriously behind in computer hardware development. In light of adaptive systems theory, however, this picture makes sense. Eastern European software developers continually were faced with the competitive challenge of making software work despite hardware constraints. Over time, this led to the development of capabilities among these organizations that would have been less likely to develop in a Western firm that never faced such constraints—capabilities that later proved worthwhile in computation-intensive specialties, such as in the manipulation of photographic images and the like.

More generally, when faced with competitive challenges, organizations respond by trying to develop capabilities that help them to overcome these challenges. In any given context, the challenges confronted by organizations as they compete reflect the logic of competition that prevails in that context. Whether realized or not, then, when organizations learn by competing, they are learning about their context's logic of competition. For instance, the Korean software firm Handysoft began in the 1990s by developing business process software for Korean firms.[12] Wanting to grow beyond their relatively small domestic market, however, this organization attempted to move into the Japanese market, but this required a very different set of relationships and software development capabilities. Competing in Japan consequently exposed Handysoft to the distinct challenges of the Japanese market. Although the adjustment was difficult and prone to error, by dealing with Japanese competition the organization ultimately developed capabilities suitable for the very different logic of competition prevailing in Japan.

Conventionally, theories taking the adaptive systems view depict organizations as reaching a new equilibrium once the search for improvement restores performance to a satisfactory level.[13] When competition is part of the process, however, equilibrium is unlikely. To the contrary, disequilibrium and continued change will be the result, as is apparent when we consider the larger ecology of learning organizations.

The Red Queen as an Ecology of Learning Organizations

"The competition" is, itself, made up of other organizations, yet we so often discuss competition as if it were an exogenous market condition. This is true within organizations, where "the competition" sometimes is taken as an abstraction. Academic treatments typically portray competition as an exogenous force—a source of "environmental uncertainty,"[14] a type of market structure,[15] or a property of social structures surrounding organizations.[16] In contrast, by considering that "the competition" comprises other organizations, one notes that these rivals, too, are adaptive systems. So when our organization searches and improves in the face of competition, these solutions become our rivals' problem, triggering the process of search in those organizations. Thus the process of adaptation does not end after our organization has restored performance, but rather continues among our rivals.

To see the implications of the fact that one's rivals also are adaptive systems, consider again the dyadic competition between organizations **j** and **k** discussed in chapter 1. Because of rivalry from **j**, organization **k** faces lower performance than would otherwise have been the case. Put differently, some of the problems faced by members of organization **k** could be traced to scarcity due to competition from **j** (whether or not **j** is recognized as the ultimate source of the problem). When these performance problems become sufficiently large, members of organization **k** will begin to search for alternatives in an effort to restore performance. Once this search improves performance at **k** to a satisfactory level, **k**'s improved performance now creates problems at organization **j**, triggering a search for improvement at that organization. Within **j**, the search for improved performance will continue until a satisfactory level of performance is restored, but this in turn will create problems for organization **k**. In this way, the adaptive system includes a sequence of causal links both within and among organizations. In an ecology of learning organizations, each organization's solution sows the seeds of a rival's next challenge.

For example, in the 1990s, the company Network Appliance grew rapidly by selling "file servers" that companies could use to improve their ability to move and store data within computer systems.[17] In a context of rapidly expanding amounts of data, the explosive availability of network technologies, and changes within organizations to better utilize large amounts of data, Network Appliance's file servers sold well and the company grew extraordinarily. EMC, another firm, also grew well during this time, building an impressive "enterprise" service organization to support its own data storage technologies. As time passed, EMC and Network Appliance increasingly competed for customers, each drawing on its own distinct advantages in this competition. Most interesting, however, is what each company has done to the other. Because of competition from Network Appliance, EMC's file-server technologies have been improved in an effort to maintain the company's position in the face of encroachment by Network Appliance. Meanwhile, competition from EMC's formidable service organization has "caused" Network Appliance to improve its own ability to deliver so-called enterprise-level service. What was a solution for one became a problem for the other, and so shaped the other's solution in this ongoing coevolution.

Figure 1.1 can help to illustrate this dynamic. Reacting to competition from j (that competition denoted by w_j), k searches and makes changes, consequently improving its viability such that β_k increases. These improvements also mean that k generates stronger competition felt by j, such that w_k increases. Reacting to this competition, j, in turn, is triggered to engage in problemistic search, which leads to improvements that restore j's viability so that ultimately β_j increases, but this further increases the competition it generates against k, so w_j increases and we are back where we started. Through this process, both rivalry and viability increase in a system of reciprocal causality: the Red Queen. These opposing outcomes, better-adapted organizations (increasing β) and more potent rivals (increasing w), will generate relative stability even as there is absolute change as long as the changes to β and w are comparable. In coining "Red Queen," the biologist Van Valen assumed these offsetting effects to be comparable, hence the reference to Lewis Carroll's character, who explains to Alice that in a fast-moving world, "it takes all the running you can do, to keep in the same place."[18] In the evolution of organizations, however, it might be that changes in β and w differ in magnitude and possibly even direction, as I discuss later.

Moving beyond the dyadic case, now consider a population of competing organizations that behave according to the adaptive systems model.

In this generalized case, a large number of coexisting rivals trigger each other's development simultaneously. Each organization is "playing the field" dynamically, so that all organizations trigger each member's improvements, that in turn feed back on the others in a collective process of coevolution. This scenario intrigued early writers on organizations,[19] who noted the complexity and uncertainty of such feedback among organizations. Through all the complexity of such back-and-forth interactions, however, two distinct and predictable dynamics can be expected. In one, we should see organizations enduring a history of competition becoming increasingly viable within a given logic of competition. At the same time, however, organizations in such a population can be expected to become increasingly powerful rivals—again within a given logic of competition. So relative to one another, organizations may see themselves as not moving, even as competition among them continuously generates change. These dynamics can be seen by estimating β_j and w_j, a task that requires separating the effects of current-time and hysteretic competition.

Specifying the Red Queen as Hysteretic Competition

Looking at the consequences of Red Queen evolution at a point in time, we would see organizations that are both viable and strong rivals; we might even be able to identify particular capabilities that give rise to these strengths in particular cases. As discussed in chapter 2, whether a capability is relevant, and whether it helps or hurts an organization, depends on the logic of competition operating in a particular context at a given time. Studying competition among modern American churches, one might note the Mormons' ability to proselytize and socialize members, while the competitive logic in the disk-drive industry would direct attention to the ability to innovate technically. To study Red Queen evolution in any context, identifying the logic of competition in a given historical and social setting opens our eyes to the specific kinds of capabilities that determine organizational success and failure. We might systematically observe and measure whether organizations in a given population had these capabilities—except that observing and measuring all those capabilities that distinguish organizations in any given context typically is not possible.

In studies of large populations of organizations, we cannot identify and observe in detail the capabilities on which success and failure hinge in each organization, because capabilities are complex, often tacit, and typically poorly understood, even by those within organizations. When one comes to know and describe in rich detail the processes and features of a particular organization, one can begin to understand in an idiosyncratic way the many and complex capabilities that make this organization able to function as it does. For instance, in Selznick's study of the Bolshevik party, he explains how that organization's "strategy of access" was carried out through various organizational means, such as by creating a distribution network around their journal that over time gave them an organizational means to influence institutions throughout Europe.[20] This organizational capability was important in helping the Bolsheviks gain an edge over other revolutionary movements, such as the Mensheviks, and was revealed by the kind of detailed case analysis for which Selznick was well known. Investigating organizational capabilities at this level of detail is not possible when studying entire populations of organizations.

We can, however, see the historical path followed by organizations over time—the path that generated these organizations' capabilities. For instance, some beer breweries in the United States survived the period of national alcohol prohibition, while others did not. It turns out that the competition generated by breweries that survived the prohibition was considerably stronger than was typical for beer breweries,[21] evidence that the prohibition acted as a "hurdle" over which breweries could pass only if they were—or became—especially competitive. More generally, if we see that some organizations have endured a history of adversity, while others have not, then we can surmise that the survivors of adversity will be more likely than the others to have some especially useful capabilities. Like the graying hair of a seasoned professional, an organization's history tells us to expect capabilities that we cannot see directly but that may make the difference.

In light of the theory of Red Queen competition, we should attend to whether or not an organization has developed through a history of having competed. To see this, we would have to broaden our perspective to allow for *competitive hysteresis*, the current-time effects of having experienced competition in the past. If we see that an organization has endured considerable competition over its history, then it is likely to have developed various capabilities aligned with the prevailing logic of competition. Consequently, such an organization can be expected to be more viable as a result of its history. Similarly, such an organization should be an especially strong rival due to its history of having competed. Thus the Red Queen process predicts competitive hysteresis, such that β_j and w_j vary as a function of the extent to which an organization has experienced competition historically. Looking across a population of organizations, their shared history of competition may have generated different capabilities in the different organizations, each dealing with the logic of competition in its own way. Yet while the specific capabilities that develop may differ, some of their consequences will manifest as the hysteretic effects of competition.

Specifically, I expect that two patterns will emerge as organizations evolve. First, organizations that have been exposed to a history of competition will prove to be more viable. For instance, the disk-drive manufacturer Seagate is among the more viable firms in its industry in recent years and can be characterized by a variety of impressive capabilities. Looking back in time, the source of these capabilities becomes clear: Year after year this company encountered fierce competition across virtually every market it entered.[22] Rapid logistics, efficient high-yield manufacturing, short product development times, and other such capabilities were developed in an effort to compete. At the same time, organizations that have been exposed to a history of competition generate stronger competition. Consequently, just as Seagate became more viable, so its rivals became stronger competitors, further accelerating the developmental process. In this way, the Red Queen can be described in terms of the hysteretic effects of competition.

Notably, these hysteretic effects of competition are very different from the effects of current-time competition; in fact hysteretic and current-time competition are oppositional. As is well known, current-time competition harms the viability of organizations. Many times over its history, industry observers voiced concern that Seagate faced "too much" competition in its markets. And at times, management attempted to move into markets where it was hoped that competition might be less fierce, though such safe niches were not long lived in that industry. Over time, however, having been through such competition turned out to enhance this organization's viability and competitiveness—the beneficial, hysteretic effects of Red Queen competition. In this way, the theory of Red Queen competition does not disagree with our established understanding that competition harms the viability of organizations. Rather, it points us to a distinction between two distinct and oppositional effects of competition: The threatening effects of current-time competition, and the viability-enhancing effects of hysteretic competition. Each of these effects needs to be separately specified to understand the full implications of organizations in competition.

Thus far, I have made the assumption that aspiration levels remain fixed, a plausible assumption given that some research suggests that aspiration levels are somewhat slow to change over time, even in response to changing performance feedback.[23] Stable aspirations work in the theory of Red Queen competition because, although the process is one of continuously self-exciting change, it also depicts stability in terms of relative performance. But a reasonable objection is that aspiration levels can and do change in organizations. If this change were to occur, then we cannot consider aspiration levels to be simply a fixed benchmark that defines the starting and stopping rules for problemistic search. It is important to consider the possibility that aspirations may change over time, therefore, and how such change is likely to affect the Red Queen process.

Escalating Aspiration Levels

Sometimes organizational members do adjust their aspirations.[24] Various studies have found that aspiration levels change over time in individuals and organizations.[25] For the purposes of Red Queen competition, an important question is whether such adjustment is likely to be upward or downward. If downward adjustment occurs readily, then organizations confronted by scarcity and unable easily to remedy the resulting performance decline will simply lower their aspirations and be content in a new equilibrium. This outcome is built into the standard neoclassical economic model of market competition, in which firms adjust to competition by immediately accepting lower prices and profits—at least above a minimum required to stay in a market. If this outcome is common when organizations are confronted with competition, then the dynamics of the Red Queen will not materialize. Instead of responding to competition by searching for new solutions and thereby accelerating the Red Queen process, organizations would just settle for less and the competitive system would equilibrate.

It is more likely, I argue, that aspirations will adjust upward if at all, for two reasons. First, empirical research on aspiration levels notes an upward bias in expectations, as compared with a model that updates future aspirations as a function of past aspirations and performance feedback.[26] Such a positive trend in aspirations would run counter to the idea that aspirations rapidly adjust downward in the face of competition. Furthermore, it is well known that incentive systems and evaluation procedures encourage improvements in performance, while stepping down performance targets is rarely regarded as an acceptable objective. At Varian Associates in the early 1990s, for instance, the exceptional performance of Varian's competitors across various markets—which included the likes of Applied Materials in semiconductor manufacturing equipment, Agilent (then Hewlett Packard) in test and measurement instruments, and General Electric in medical diagnostic equipment—pushed managers in that organization to increase aspiration levels throughout that organization. The alternative of lowering expectations to a new equilibrium of relatively poor performance would have been unthinkably counternormative, even in a company that had not performed well financially historically. More generally, I expect that organizational processes will tend to raise, rather than lower, aspirations.

A second reason to expect upward-trending aspirations is that performance typically is evaluated relative to other, similar organizations.[27] Consistent with this idea, there is considerable evidence that aspiration levels not only are linked to prior aspirations, but also are updated by social comparisons with others.[28] Although many potential "peers" may exist, the best among them are likely to become seen as the natural comparison level. Successful organizations are salient reference points in the diffusion process.[29] Furthermore, framing work goes on among managers of organizations, who draw comparisons against better-performing examples in the organizational environment. Each time an improvement occurs anywhere, this comes to represent a new definition of what is possible, ratcheting up aspirations throughout a competitive arena, as was the case in the Varian example. Furthermore, to the extent that competitive forces reward the best responses to competition and select out the worst, there will also be an upward bias in the availability of social reference points.[30]

If aspirations trend upward, the process of Red Queen evolution is further accelerated. Each successful response in the Red Queen, in turn, sets a new comparison point for aspiration adjustment among competitors. Their responses, in turn, come to redefine the possible yet again in this upward-ratcheting process. In this way, escalating aspirations may destabilize socially constructed definitions of what is thought to be achievable in a context. This outcome means that if aspiration levels adjust upward, then the prediction of the Red Queen model will be reinforced. In contrast, downward-adjusting aspirations would disable the Red Queen process, so the predictions of the theory would not be supported. A condition for the application of this theory, then, is whether aspirations adjust up or down in response to competition.

Selection and the Red Queen

Red Queen evolution may also develop purely through a selection process among organizations. Consider the extreme case where organizations differ in fitness at birth, but no individual organization's fitness varies over time; that is, no learning takes place in response to competition. Another way to think of this assumption is as an implication of Stinchcombe's idea that organizations strongly "imprint" at founding.[31] Assume that organizations are more likely to survive if they are more fit, and that competition intensifies the selection process on the basis of fitness. Assume also that competitiveness varies with an organization's fitness, so that more viable organizations generate stronger competition (an assumption I will relax later). Under these assumptions, those organizations that have been exposed to more competition historically, and yet survive, are likely to be more fit than the average organization that has not faced much competition.[32] Also, these survivors are likely to generate especially strong competition, in turn further selecting from the population, further intensifying competition, and so on. Purely through selection rather than organizational learning, we end up with a Red Queen process.

By allowing for new foundings over time, an additional impetus to increasing fitness results if new entrants must be competitive in order to "survive" the entry process.[33] Furthermore, these new entrants raise the possibility of industry-altering innovation that redefines what is possible, but here this redefinition comes about through selection rather than learning as often depicted in Schumpeterian renderings of industrial evolution. Thus far, models of organizational evolution in the Schumpeterian tradition have usually treated the source of change as exogenous to the theory, focusing instead on the fact that changes often accompany waves of new foundings that disrupt industries.[34] My argument is that such changes take place as part of a selection-driven Red Queen process, increasing and possibly transforming the competitiveness of industries, which in turn increases the strength of selection, that again increases the competitiveness of the industry in an ongoing, self-exciting process.

Support for the Red Queen hypotheses, then, might well appear in an analysis of organizational populations over long time periods, yet we would not know the extent to which these results were due to selection among organizations or to the development over time of individual organizations. To some extent, this puzzle can be dealt with in model specification, as I will explain in greater detail in chapter 4. The approach attempts to tease apart development from selection as done in the human demography literature. Vaupel et al. examine changes over time in human morbidity and mortality rates under the assumption that individuals differ in "frailty," a time-invariant, unobserved individual difference.[35] These authors show that as the members of a given cohort die, those remaining are likely to be less frail. (Specifically, frailty decreases as the cumulative hazard of a cohort increases.) Assuming that this cohort effect captures selection effects, selection and development are specified distinctly in the model.

Yet selection and development are intertwined, both empirically and theoretically. It is informative to specify models that allow for each process distinctly, but in fact the two processes work in tandem throughout the evolution of organizations. Selection and attempts to adapt are both triggered by adversity, and so both processes are likely to co-occur. Attempts at adaptation increase the chances of error, in turn increasing the selection rate. Selection through the entry and exit of organizations likely depends on the overall competitiveness of a population, which in turn depends on whether incumbent organizations have developed according to the Red Queen. Aspiration levels escalate when existing organizations change, but then such change is more likely when selection processes leave especially fit organizations as social referents. Consequently it would be misleading to overstate our ability to deal with the selection and developmental aspects of Red Queen evolution as analytically separable. In fact, one approach is to allow for both to occur together, as is the case in a "random walk" version of the Red Queen.

Random Walks and the Red Queen

It makes sense to allow that both selection and adaptation are involved in
Red Queen evolution, since competition is likely to increase both the rate
of selection and the rate at which organizations attempt to adapt. Furthermore, organizational attempts to adapt often may lead to error, escalating
the rate of selection. The search process, after all, is assumed only to be
intendedly rational, and in fact many well-intended changes turn out to be
mistakes just as sometimes errors turn out to be fortuitous.[36] In this rendering of the Red Queen, competition simply triggers reactions by organizations. If we assume that these reactions are as likely to be maladaptive
as they are adaptive, then competition triggers a random walk rather than
an adaptive trend.[37] Competition thus increases the variance in the distribution of fitnesses among organizations, rather than an increase in their
mean.[38]

   Now allow selection to operate on the results of this random walk, as
in the pure-selection model. Denrell demonstrates that selection operating on a fitness distribution with increasing variance tends to improve
average fitness, even though the changes were random, because it leaves
predominantly the fit tail of the increased variance.[39] Under this scenario,
both adaptive attempts and selection processes work together to enhance
the overall fitness of the population. Still, however, the ultimate force
driving this process is competition, which triggers both organizational
responses and stronger selection, which in turn combine to increase competitiveness, and so on in a Red Queen process driven by both adaptation
and selection.

   The interplay of selection and adaptation is interesting theoretically and
is likely to be important empirically, even as it renders inadequate attempts
to distinguish analytically between the two processes. I suspect that both
of these processes are triggered by, and further accelerate, competition
among organizations. Consequently, Red Queen evolution involves both
processes. Some managers of established organizations might be uncom-
fortable with this fact, since for them a selection-based Red Queen means
death at the hands of new entrants, even as it improves the viability and
competitiveness of their industry. Other managers, in contrast, will realize
that my theory merely acknowledges the fact that if one fails to respond
as competition intensifies, new entrants will do so instead. To scholars of
organizational evolution, my theory may seem to beg the much-trum-
peted "selection versus adaptation" debate. In my view, it is high time we
moved past a decades-old debate that has produced little. Current thinking and empirics in the field now routinely allow for the fact that both
selection and development are at work.

Consequences of Constraint in Red Queen Evolution

By competing, organizations sample their context's logic of competition, but often samples yield data that are either biased or too sparse to permit accurate inferences. Should biased or limited samples arise through the process of Red Queen competition, then organizations will learn lessons that may prove to be maladaptive. I argue that biased and limited samples are especially likely to arise from Red Queen competition because organizational evolution is constrained in three ways. First, organizations are temporally constrained, sometimes "forgetting" valuable lessons and other times retaining the lessons of the past even when environmental change renders this outcome maladaptive.[40] Second, the Red Queen describes a coevolutionary process among multiple organizations, but what is done in response to one competitor may constrain what can be done in response to another. This interdependence implies what might be thought of as a spatial constraint, affecting organizations that attempt to adapt to multiple, conflicting logics of competition simultaneously. Third, organizational learning is known to be constrained by the limitations of direct organizational experience, which often constitute biased samples of possible competitive realities.[41] The more limited these experiences, the more myopic an organization's lessons are likely to be. I build each of these forms of constraint explicitly into the theory.

Temporal Constraint: Forgetting and Remembering in Hysteretic Competition

Ideally, organizations would learn well, picking and choosing which lessons to retain and which to let go according to what would be most adaptive given the logic of competition prevailing in a given context. In reality, organizational learning is constrained in time. Lessons learned in an organization decades ago that would be valuable today may have been forgotten. Meanwhile, many habits turn out to be difficult for organizations to forget, even when times have changed and these practices are no longer valuable. So organizational learning is constrained in time in two ways— when organizations fail to remember, and when organizations fail to forget.

Regarding failing to remember, organizational memory is lost as time passes and people move on. This problem is apparent among long time employees in an organization when they see history repeat itself, while the organization around them appears to have forgotten. In the early 1990s, for instance, Hewlett Packard attempted to formally coordinate its many different parts in an effort to increase innovativeness.[42] Long-time employees noted, however, that earlier in their careers a similar attempt to create linkages across that organization failed because—it was thought—the organization's culture and informal networks were more effective at coordinating than were formal linking mechanisms. Yet memories of the earlier restructuring were largely gone by the 1990s, and lost with those memories no doubt were some valuable lessons from the earlier attempt that might have helped the next time around. In this way, organizational memory is constrained in time, with the lessons of history less available the further back in time they occurred. Consequently, organizations are more likely to remake the wheel, or to repeat past errors, as experience fades into the distant past.[43]

In terms of the Red Queen, time-constrained organizational memory implies that more recent competitive experience will be more important to current-time operations than will be distant-past experience. These arguments imply that the hysteresis due to Red Queen competition depends on the historical timing of experience:

> **Competitive Hysteresis Hypothesis: Organizations with more exposure to a recent history of competition are more viable and generate stronger competition.**

Yet organizations do not completely forget their pasts. Roles, structures, and routines established at the founding of an organization often carry far into the future.[44] More generally, organizations tend to be rewarded for reliable behavior, giving an advantage to organizations with stable routines and structures.[45] When organizations do remember, then, such memory is in the form of structures and routines, rather than the experiences that generated past lessons.[46] Consequently, the rationale for these practices is lost, and all that is remembered is the practice. Such memory loses accuracy and completeness over time. Thus practices become "objectified," understood as existing without human authorship.[47] This taken-for-granted status strips organizational activity of its basis in logic. To the extent that understanding the rationale behind a practice would help make practices mindful, organizational memory becomes increasingly applied unthinkingly as time passes—an especially dire outcome if a context's logic of competition changes.

Under changing conditions, samples taken from the distant past are unlikely to accurately reflect the current logic of competition, yet organizations typically continue to operate according to processes and routines that reflect the lessons of the past even when this behavior is maladaptive. Furthermore, past experience establishes the baseline "model" with which new information is categorized.[48] For example, the Stone Group, a Chinese technology firm, was originally established as a collective—an organizational form that conformed well to the logic of competition prevailing in China during the early years of Stone's operation.[49] As the Chinese economic system opened to a more market-oriented logic of competition, however, many of the characteristics of the collective form inhibited Stone's ability to compete –for instance, preventing the organization from instituting various financial incentive systems or from easily accessing public capital markets. What ultimately hindered Stone, then, was an architecture well aligned to the exigencies of its past. In this way, an organization that has sampled competitions largely from the distant past is likely to suffer from what March and his colleagues refer to as a "competency trap" if logics of competition change.[50]

If an organization's logic of competition changes over time, as is likely, then its habits of responding to challenges with established routines becomes increasingly dysfunctional, despite the fact that these solutions were effective in the past. Such behavior is especially likely as time goes on, because with the passage of time things are more likely to have changed. Norms to respect those who have "been there" will exacerbate this problem, since those claiming such expert authority will add weight to the repeated use of tried-and-true measures. In these ways, learning "well" ironically makes an organization at a disadvantage as its circumstances change.

The problem of the competency trap is likely to be especially severe in the case of Red Queen evolution, due to its collective nature. It is well known that organizations explicitly refer to one another to determine what actions to take under conditions of uncertainty.[51] Such social comparison might act as a corrective if organizations in similar circumstances were to make independent calculations. If, however, organizations mimic one another during the process of Red Queen evolution, then entire cohorts of coevolving rivals may collectively suffer from a competency trap. If this occurs, then social comparison processes are unlikely to solve the competency trap problem in a coevolving organizational community.

Alternatively, one might hope that selection processes will "correct" for organizations that err, improving the population as a whole by eliminating the errant organizations, as in Friedman's "as if" argument.[52] Collective coevolution into a competency trap, however, makes such corrective selection less likely, since relative fitness is key[53]—so these organizations may mutually descend unchecked into a competency trap. In that case, once selection does occur, it is against the entire organizational community. For example, Cole documents the decline of the U.S. automobile industry in modern times, during which these organizations' slow adoption of process and product innovations was mutually reinforced by social comparison.[54] So it is that selection processes will be least useful as a corrective mechanism in precisely those contexts where social comparison processes reinforce the maladaptive outcomes of the Red Queen.

The problem of the competency trap in Red Queen evolution is especially a concern because one can argue that it might arise through selection as well as learning. Organizations selected under one set of environmental conditions would have competencies that are particularly poorly suited if the environment changes. A large population of technology organizations, born during the late 1990s, was designed around capital-intensive, rapid-growth strategies. The restriction in the availability of capital in the United States during and after the year 2000 caught these organizations by surprise and left many of them poorly adapted for this new environment. In this way, the Red Queen operating in one period can intensify selection pressures, reinforcing characteristics that will prove to be maladaptive if environmental conditions change. Consequently, the predicted hysteretic effect can be expected to reverse as an organization's competitive history becomes outdated.

Competency-Trap Hypothesis: Organizations with more exposure to competition in the distant past are less viable and generate weaker competition.

Notably, this decline in viability and competitiveness hinges entirely on environmental misalignment. Even "costless" learning backfires under this circumstance. Yet adapting to rivals surely is not costless. An even more sobering picture is painted if one allows for such costs as well.

Spatial Constraint: The Costs of Adaptation

The process of responding to competition by searching and implementing changes in an organizations is costly. These costs include what it takes to develop and implement new products, services, and routines, as well as the costs involved in the process of change per se.[55] Among technology organizations such as Applied Materials, Seagate, and Varian, for instance, establishing a common platform for developing products has helped to reduce the costs of change, making these organizations more profitable as a consequence.[56] I argue that the costs of adaptation increase as a function of the number of distinct rivals faced by an organization over time. In the Red Queen process, each rival organization represents an adaptive challenge, and each such challenge requires costly adaptations if it is to be met. The more rivals an organization encounters, the more coevolutionary "games" involve the organization. In the early telephone industry, for instance, the large successful companies were particularly challenged by the many thousands of small, nonstandard companies that proliferated throughout rural areas.[57] In such cases, the costs of adaptation increase as a function of the number of rivals to which an organization must adapt.

By this argument, spreading a given amount of competitive experience over only one or two rivals will be less costly than spreading the same amount of competitive experience over hundreds of rivals.

A second form of cost appears when adaptations made to deal with one rival constrain the adaptations that can be made for the others. Again looking at the example of relying on a common product development platform across technology product markets, organizations that tailor these platforms in order to win any particular competition pay the price of not being able to perform as well in other competitions. In short, one cannot be all things to all people, so complex organizations often find themselves paying a cost when they attempt to adapt simultaneously in conflicting directions. Thus adaptation to any one challenge carries some opportunity costs as well, in terms of what cannot then be done to adapt to another.

One way to think of these opportunity costs is in terms of whether an organization's coevolutionary relationships are not independent. With an assumption of independence across relationships, an organization can freely coevolve with each of its rivals, without the coevolutionary changes made for one rival constraining those made for another. In most organizational systems, however, various activities are interdependent, so that changes in one part or aspect of an organization typically interact with changes made in another.[58] These interdependencies lead to a "complexity catastrophe" when multiple adaptations take place simultaneously.[59] An example of this problem in organizational life is seen in Padgett and Ansell's study of the rise of the Medici.[60] Managing multiple, conflicting social relationships required a compromised "robust strategy," since one could not be all things to all people without some interference across relationships. In the same way, the problem of nonindependent adaptations magnifies the costs of dealing simultaneously with multiple competitors. When facing multiple rivals, what one does to adapt to one rival interferes with what is done to deal with another at a rate that increases as a square of the number of such constraints.[61]

More generally, this thinking raises the question of whether the benefits of coevolution are sufficient to offset its costs. Two organizations with a similar amount of competitive experience might differ considerably in the costs they incurred along the way, with one gaining this experience over a few competitive relationships and the other spreading this experience over many. For instance, if an organization has competed for ten years against one rival, while another has competed for one year against each of ten distinct rivals, the first economizes on costs much more than the second. The benefits of the Red Queen are more likely to outweigh its costs when a given amount of historical experience is amortized over fewer rivals. In biology, this problem is sometimes referred to as the "rare enemy" problem, wherein it is assumed that evolutionary adaptations are made only when they are worth the costs.[62] Although such an assumption may be defensible in biology, it implies a strongly functionalist prediction in a model of organizational evolution.

Instead, it is possible that organizations might attempt to respond to a wide variety of competitive threats even when a cost-benefit calculation might suggest that they should not. After all, I have assumed only that adaptations emerge from day-to-day processes wherein organizational members do their best to deal with challenges. Consequently, it is possible for an organization to be too responsive—so responsive that it incurs more costs to adapting than it enjoys benefits. With this possibility in mind, my model of the Red Queen allows for the costs of adaptation to be estimated as a function of the number of distinct rivals faced over time by an organization.

> **Costly Adaptation Hypothesis: For a given amount of historical competition, an organization's viability falls with the number of distinct historical rivals it has faced.**

An alternative approach to this line of reasoning is to allow the costs of adaptation to increase with the number of distinct logics of competition encountered by an organization. That is, if an organization adapts to many rivals, all of whom are pursuing the same logic of competition, then this adaptation should be less costly than would be the case if an organization were to adapt to a population of rivals each pursuing a distinct logic of competition. Operationally, modeling the costs of adaptation in terms of logics of competition is less attractive, given how difficult it is to identify distinct logics of competition. In large data-collection projects, it is likely that the best one could do would be to indirectly infer logics of competition based on general strategic differences, as is done, for instance, in work on strategic groups.[63] However, most analyses allow competition to vary with the number of rivals, and in that spirit here I model the costs of adapting to rivals as a function of the number of rivals that an organization encounters historically.

One odd implication of the Costly Adaptation Hypothesis is that organizations are best off if they gain all of their experience from one source. When it comes to paying the costs involved in learning from multiple sources, this may be true. Yet we know that learning gained from a limited sample is fraught with the possibility of bias. More generally, the theory thus far has assumed that information gained from competitive experience is unbiased—at least if it is recent enough to pertain to one's current competitive logic. Rather than depend on this claim by assumption, my preference is to systematically build the likelihood of biased learning into the theory.

Constrained Sampling: Myopic Learning in Red Queen Evolution

For learning to be adaptive, an organization's accumulating lessons need to represent well the prevailing logic of competition. But, as March and his students elaborate, organizational experience often is too limited or restricted in range to provide organizations with unbiased lessons.[64] Despite the best intentions of managers, the limited range of information available through organizational experience typically constitutes myopic lessons, where a myopic understanding is one that reflects information from only a restricted portion of the full range of possibilities.[65] Although such myopia can appear in exceptional situations, such as restricted sampling after unusually negative feedback,[66] myopia can result as well from the general tendency of organizations to respond according to immediate performance feedback from their environments.[67] Given that learning in Red Queen evolution is experiential, myopic learning might plague organizations as they develop through this process.

Myopic learning would arise if an organization were to experience a relatively narrow range of competitions, leaving it with a limited and biased understanding of the context's logic of competition.[68] For example, this problem arises in the market for computer software "tools," software products that are used, in turn, by software developers to make software systems, components, and products. In order to win in competition, software tool manufacturers often are asked to tailor their products and support organizations to the needs of a specific customer.[69] Taken too far, such tailoring develops the organization myopically, leaving the organization and its products poorly adapted to the rest of the market. By the early 2000s, companies like WindRiver and Borland had grown in this market, ironically, by refraining from being too well adapted to any one customer. More generally, the myopia problem appears whenever an organization's competitive experiences are focused too narrowly on a small range of all possible competitions. When this bias arises, an organization becomes poorly adapted to other possible competitions even as it learns.

To assess whether an organization's competitive experience generates myopia, it helps to consider first what an unbiased sample of experiences would look like. Ideally, an organization would experience competitive threats in a pattern that samples without bias from the full distribution of possible challenges that might arise in the organization's environment. Myopic sampling, in this context, would be samples taken from a restricted portion of that total possible distribution. In the Red Queen, the "sample of challenges" is the set of competitors encountered by an organization over time. The more that these competitors come from a restricted range of all possible competitors, even those competitors that might but have never (yet) come about, the more that Red Queen competition will generate myopic learning. By comparison, organizations facing the widest possible variety of competitors will draw less biased inferences from this experience, a conclusion intuitively similar to the idea that organizational variety is evolutionarily adaptive.[70] The challenge, then, is to develop a way to systematically identify a varied set of competitors.

There exist several different approaches to identifying variation among competitors. The most typical is to distinguish among organizations according to characteristics that correspond to their strategies, as in Carroll and Swaminathan's analysis of strategic groups in the brewing industry.[71] This approach works well for studying a single industry but does not lend itself to identifying variety in a similar way across very different contexts as in this study. Another is to look at organizations in terms of performance outcomes, an approach used sometimes in the strategic management literature. This approach, however, defines types of organizations by the outcomes that ultimately I wish to study, so it is not useful for creating an explanatory model. Rather than specifying particular characteristics or outcomes in each setting studied, I would prefer to consider a more general approach to identifying differences in variability across the histories of various organizations—even those in very different contexts.

Generally, one can distinguish among organizations according to the dispersion of their competitive histories. So conceived, each organization's history at any given point in time can be regarded as a distribution of competitive experience. By looking at the amount of historical competition experienced by an organization, one is comparing the first moments of the experience distributions of different organizations: controlling for the ages of organizations, those with a higher mean competitive experience would thus be regarded as more experienced than those with a lower mean competitive experience. Regarding dispersion, then, it is straightforward to think as well of the second moment of the experience distribution—the variance in competitive experience. Given two organizations of equal age, each having experienced the same amount of competition historically on average, one might have a more dispersed competitive history than the other. For instance, one organization might have experienced most of its competition within only a few years, while another organization might have experienced a more broadly spread history of competition. By distinguishing among organizations according to the dispersion of their competitive experience distributions, a more general comparison is possible.

Two fundamentally different aspects of dispersion can be captured by looking at the variability of organizations' competitive experience distributions—dispersion over market conditions and dispersion over competing organizations. Looking at dispersion over market conditions, one characterizes an organization's competitive experience over time in terms of how evenly or unevenly dispersed were the density of competitors faced by the organization. Even if two organizations have experienced the same amount of competition over their histories, they may differ in terms of the historical dispersion of that competition. For instance, an organization might have been continuously exposed to moderate amounts of competition all its life, while another might have endured a short but severely competitive period. The first of these organizations would have been exposed to a much broader range of competitive circumstances than the second. In terms of myopia, this means that the first organization will have been able to "sample" from a broader range of competitive circumstances—defined in terms of market conditions—than the second organization, even though both organizations faced the same overall amount of historical competition. The second organization, then, is likely to have been exposed to a more myopic sample than the first.

By contrast, another approach to measuring dispersion focuses on differences among particular competitors, rather than on differences in the degree of market competition. To do this, I build on Stinchcombe's observation that organizations founded under similar historical times are relatively similar in various ways, reflecting the similar social and economic conditions that existed when they were "imprinted" at birth.[72] With this idea in mind, I assume that organizations are more similar the closer is their founding date. Banks born during the Depression, for instance, should appear to be relatively similar to one another compared to a cohort of banks born after the deregulations of the late twentieth century. This demographic approach to identifying variety suffers from the fact that it does not measure the specific dimensions on which organizations vary. On the other hand, birth cohorts are identifiable in population-level data on organizations and so can be built into the model of Red Queen evolution. Most importantly, by considering the dispersion of founding cohorts among an organization's historical rivals, variability among competitors is identified as distinct from variability among the degree of competition.

Specifically, this approach allows an organization facing rivals all from a single cohort to have a much more focused competitive exposure than does an organization facing rivals across a variety of cohorts. For instance, take two organizations, each of which has survived a history of competition against one hundred rivals over a century. For one organization, however, all one hundred rivals appeared in the same year, while for the other, each rival appeared in a different year over the century. The second organization has the good fortune of having "sampled" from the greatest possible dispersion across competitive cohorts, while the first organization sampled only from a single cohort. In terms of myopia, one would expect the first organization to have a much more limited range of information, and so to have learned more biased lessons over its history of competition. Over time, an organization might be confronted with a very new, highly concentrated challenge from a wave of new foundings—the so-called waves of creative destruction described by Schumpeter and commonly referred to in studies of industrial evolution.[73] Organizations experiencing most of their competition from such a wave would have a more myopic understanding of the possible range of competitive threats than would an organization that has experienced the same amount of historical competition spread over many, more dispersed, cohorts.

So I propose to measure dispersion in two different ways, reflecting two fundamentally different theoretical claims about how an organization's competitive experience samples from the range of possible lessons. In one approach, dispersion over market conditions is the relevant sampling criterion. Consequently, this approach depicts an organization's experience as a sample that is more or less dispersed in terms of market conditions, with some organizations concentrating their experience into a few high-density years while others spread it over many. In the other approach, dispersion over the features of an organization's rivals is the important dimension from which experience samples. So understood, an organization's experience is more or less dispersed according to the variety of cohorts from which its competitors are drawn. Measured either through dispersion of density or dispersion among competitors' cohorts, these arguments imply:

Myopic Learning Hypothesis: The greater the dispersion of historical exposure to competition, the more viable the organization.

Given two organizations that have been exposed to the same amount of historical competition, the one with more dispersed exposure would have a less biased sample of experiences from which to infer about the context's competitive logic. In many cases, however, those organizations with more dispersed competitors will also have had greater costs associated with adaptation. As I argued earlier, an organization incurs a cost to adapting, and that cost will increase with the number of distinct rivals faced by the organization. In earlier papers, my colleagues and I argued that high variance among an organization's rivals would be harmful to an organization's viability because of these costs.[74] That argument conflates the cost and dispersion effects of an organization's competitive experience. So it is perhaps not surprising that the earlier empirical investigations on variability in competitive experience yielded mixed results. More appropriately, in this book I will attempt to disentangle the cost of adaptation from effects of the dispersion of experience.

Killing the Red Queen through Predation

Organizations do not always respond to competition by competing. Rather, sometimes organizations are able to avoid competing, or to acquire or merge with their rivals. As discussed in chapter 2, the strategy of predation can be seen as its own logic of competition—where organizations succeed by eliminating rivals and thereby shift the competitive landscape in their favor. Thus mergers and acquisitions intended to eliminate rivalry can be understood as a strategy to gain advantage without having to engage in Red Queen competition—essentially a way to kill the Red Queen.

As discussed in chapter 2, in most contexts it is illegitimate for managers of organizations to state that their intention is to merge with or acquire a rival in order to eliminate competition. One virtually never reads a press release saying something along the lines of: "Tired of competing relentlessly, and preferring instead to enjoy a more secure place in the market regardless of how well we manage, we and our rivals have decided to settle on terms for a merger." Instead, mergers and acquisitions are accompanied by a rhetoric of efficiency, claiming scale economies or other value-creating benefits that will result from combining the organizations. Sometimes, managers of organizations might, in fact, merge with or acquire competitors in order to reap scale economies, or to create "synergies"—capabilities, market position, organizational assets, human resources, or other valuable assets created by combining complementary features of organizations. But in many cases the merger or acquisition, though accompanied by such efficiency rhetoric, will be a way to end competition—as documented by antitrust economists.[75] For my purposes, the question is how to build the logic of predation into the model of Red Queen competition.

My approach is to allow for the fact that, when circumstances permit, organizations will attempt to eliminate their rivals through merger and acquisition. If effective in pursuing this strategy, organizations remove themselves from the dynamics of Red Queen competition. The importance of this choice can be understood in terms of three distinct kinds of consequences that are likely to result—each of which has a bearing on Red Queen competition. First, organizations that merge with or acquire rivals in order to eliminate competition of course reap the benefit of an improved market position. Reduced current-time competition makes organizations more viable, the so-called positional advantage that is a primary objective of strategic management,[76] although by gaining such an advantage organizations eliminate the Red Queen as a source of learning. A second kind of consequence of merger and acquisition are the "compositional" results of combining organizations, in that the resulting organization now comprises structures, people, routines, capabilities, and the like from both of the parent organizations. And, thirdly, organizations that merge or acquire in order to reduce competition will also face consequences in terms of their ability to learn—what I refer to here as "learning process" effects. Each of these kinds of effects have implications for organizations that opt for a strategy of predation.

Compositional Consequences of Predation

Merging with another organization will change an organization's composition, its people, size, structures, routines, technologies, and capabilities. When mergers and acquisitions improve scale economies or create synergies, these compositional effects will translate into greater viability for the resulting organization.[77] But compositional effects can be neutral or value harming, too. Many a tale is told of mergers and acquisitions gone awry, as in the business press's criticism of the Daimler-Chrysler merger or the mega-mergers among Japanese banks.[78] If the acquiring organization adds nothing to what is acquired, and assuming that the value of the acquired assets is fully reflected in the purchase price of the acquisition, then there is no net gain in value to an organization for having made the acquisition. And if the two organizations are poorly matched, the compositional effects of combining the organizations may even harm the resulting organization's viability.

Such viability-reducing mergers should be uncommon, happening only in error, unless organizations are merged for reasons other than improving the composition of the organization. Motivated only by the desire to increase scale economies or create synergies, we can expect mergers and acquisitions to be value-enhancing (on average). Mergers and acquisitions meant to reduce competition, however, can improve an organization's viability simply by isolating it from competition—a gain from predation that will enhance an organization's life chances even without compositional advantages such as synergies and scale economies. Mergers and acquisitions that reduce competition, then, are likely to include value-enhancing matches as well as value-neutral and value-reducing matches, since the gains from reducing competition will sometimes make even "bad" mergers worthwhile.

In a model of organizational viability, the harmful compositional effects of predatory mergers and acquisitions could be isolated if the benefits of predation—increased scale and reduced competition—are controlled separately. Such a model would essentially distinguish among large organizations that face little competition, comparing those that developed these advantages organically with those that achieved them by preying on rivals.

Presumably, those that achieved these advantages by following a logic of predation will include "bad" mergers, with compositional disadvantages, making the resulting organizations less viable once one controls for scale and reduced competition.

Predation and the Learning Process

By acquiring their competitors, organizations also affect the process of learning—which in turn affects what organizations learn. Often one reads in the business press of organizations that shift to an "acquisition strategy" in an attempt to deal with competition, typically featuring high-profile organizations that attempt to acquire major rivals.[79] In such cases, the strategy of acquiring competitors often raises the concern that competition will be lessened, or that the acquiring organization will "lose focus" in terms of its own business strategy. Here I raise a different issue: that by following a logic of predation, an organization changes the way it learns from competition. I have argued that organizations, faced with competition, cope by improving their products or services in order to maintain a satisfactory level of performance. Presumably, managers in such organizations might wish they could avoid competition, but typically they have no choice but to try to cope. In some situations, however, where merging with or acquiring rivals is an option, competition might trigger a very different process. Instead of stimulating attempts at improving products and services, competition may trigger in such organizations attempts at eliminating competition. Should organizations opt for this response, competition would trigger learning—but of a very different form from that presumed in the theory of Red Queen evolution.

With use, the option of dealing with competitors by acquisition becomes all the more likely the next time an organization faces competition. The process of acquiring rivals is itself a set of routines established and elaborated within organizations. Identifying the competitive threat, setting in motion the various legal and financial steps necessary to acquire or merge, and then completing the acquisition and assimilating the acquired organization constitute routines that must be developed initially and can be institutionalized with use. In this sense, organizations "learn" to acquire other organizations by doing.[80] Consequently, the more that an organization responds to competition by acquisition, the more that the organization's process of learning from competition will center on acquisition. By comparison, an organization that rarely or never has responded to competition by acquisition will have at its disposal only the option of improving when confronted by a rival. Thus, organizations with a history of acquiring competitors are less likely than other organizations to have developed routines for improving in the face of competition.

Taking these various arguments together, I conclude that acquiring one's rivals carries harmful compositional and process effects, although this strategy also has clear benefits in terms of lessened competition and increased scale. So in models that control for the advantages of lessened competition and increased scale, I expect:

Costly Predation Hypothesis: Controlling for the current-time position of an organization, an organization's viability falls with the number of distinct historical rivals it has acquired.

Argument Summary

Competition generates scarcity in organizations, triggering attempts to restore performance to satisfactory levels—even if the ultimate cause of scarcity is unknown. Over time, this response to competition builds capabilities in an organization. Assuming that an organization's competitive experience is an unbiased sample of the prevailing logic of competition, then its responses to competition, in turn, make it a stronger competitor against its rivals. These rivals, then, are confronted by stronger competition, eliciting in them attempts to restore their performance, and these responses in turn make them stronger competitors, again triggering a search for improvements in their rivals. In this ongoing, self-exciting process of Red Queen competition, learning and competition each accelerate the other, so that relative to their rivals organizations appear to be unchanged even as they are learning in absolute terms. Over time, the Red Queen gives rise to competitive hysteresis, where an organization that has survived a history of competition is more viable and generates stronger competition. This outcome is accelerated if the aspirations of organizations mutually escalate through a social construction process. As well as through learning, selection processes play a role in Red Queen competition, deselecting errant solutions, assuming that the rate of selection is intensified by competition.

Three forms of constraint call into question the assumption that an organization's competitive experience is an unbiased sample of the prevailing logic of competition. Due to these constraints, learning through Red Queen evolution may lead to dysfunctional consequences. First, the abilities of organizations to selectively remember and forget are constrained, yet over time a context's logic of competition is likely to change. Consequently, distant-past competitive experience may lead organizations into a competency trap, so that only an organization's more recent competitive experience is likely to enhance its viability and competitiveness. A second constraint occurs at a given point in time, in that adapting to any particular rival is costly, and organizations are constrained in their ability to coevolve simultaneously with the different requirements of different rivals. Consequently, it is costly for an organization to spread its competitive experience over many historical rivals. Third, sampling constraints may lead to myopic learning among organizations that experience competition within only a narrow range of possible contexts.

In some cases, organizations will respond to competition not by improving, but rather by preying on their rivals. When successful, organizations following the logic of predation gain advantages in terms of scale and reduced competition. By opting to acquire their rivals, however, such organizations face possible mismatches in the composition of the combined organizations. Furthermore, predatory organizations learn to respond to competition by acquiring their rivals, rather than by improving. Once the advantages of scale and reduced competition are controlled, these organizational effects of predation are likely to viability harming.

The next chapter specifies the arguments of this chapter in the form of an empirical model. My strategy is to systematically build each of the arguments into a part of a model that can be estimated in terms of observable organizational outcomes—and to do so in a way that my predictions are falsifiable.

FOUR

Empirically Modeling the Red Queen

TO STUDY THE RED QUEEN EMPIRICALLY, it is useful to formulate an estimable and falsifiable model of the process. The goal is to represent the ideas of this theory in terms that can be operationalized across a variety of organizational populations, albeit with adjustments to take into consideration the distinct logics of competition that operate in different contexts during different historical eras. To this end, I will initially model the theory in terms of the abstract concept organizational "viability," where an organization is more viable when its life chances are greater. Operationally, viability manifests in various observable outcomes, and my empirical tests will feature the most commonly analyzed manifestations: organizational founding and organizational failure. Presumably, the creation of an organization is evidence of its viability, and organizational failure is evidence of a lack of viability.

Three general kinds of factors determine the viability of an organization: features of the organization, its ecological relationships—competitive or mutualistic—with other organizations, and the characteristics of its broader environment. The Red Queen operates through the first two of these. Most models of organizational viability look at current-time aspects of each of these forces, such as an organization's (current) strategy, the (current) strategies of its rivals, or the (current) social or economic context of an organization. Support for the theory of Red Queen competition would require that exposure to *historical* competition affects viability, over and above such current-time effects. In particular, if $v_j(t)$ is the viability of organization j at a given time t, then the model to be estimated is of the form

$$v_j(t) = v_j(t)^* exp[H_j],$$

where $v_j(t)^*$ is the baseline viability of organization j given its current-time characteristics, those of its rivals, and those of its broader environmental context. Over and above these current-time effects, H_j represents the competitive hysteresis effects implied by Red Queen theory. To specify this model, it is necessary to translate the Red Queen predictions into operationalizations of H_j. This, in turn, requires that "competitiveness" be specified as a property of organizations, rather than of markets.

Modeling "Competitiveness" as a Property of Organizations

It is one thing to talk about Red Queen competition, and another to formulate an empirically testable model of the process. One of the biggest challenges in this regard is that most models of competition describe it as a property of the organizational environment—perhaps following well-established economic models that feature "competitive markets." So conceived, "strong competition" occurs in a market where organizations cannot differentiate or collude to avoid struggling over resources. Such competition depends on structural characteristics of the environment, such as whether there are distinct market segments, or "niches," into which organizations might sort. In this way, most models of competition do not lend themselves readily to an analysis of the Red Queen, since this theory describes competitiveness not as a property of the environment, but as an organizational property, varying from organization to organization according to their different histories.

One way to solve this analytic problem is to distinguish between *whether* organizations compete and *how strongly* they affect one another—given that they are competing.[1] Models that characterize competitiveness as a property of the organizational environment usually refer to the extent to which organizations compete, not to how strongly they affect one another given that they are competing. For instance, both "niche overlap" in organizational ecology and "structural equivalence" in network models of economic sociology are measures of the degree of competition, and each increases in magnitude as organizations increase in their probability of vying for the same resources. Yet holding constant the degree of overlap among organizations (whether they compete), some rivals are to be feared more than others. This second aspect of competitiveness, which I will refer to as *competitive intensity*, needs to be distinguished from whether firms compete in order to treat competitiveness as varying from organization to organization.

To investigate the Red Queen empirically, I distinguish these two aspects of competition in an ecological model. In the ecological approach, empirical evidence of competition is found when model estimates yield a negative value for the so-called competition coefficient, α_k, representing the effect that organization k has on its rival's viability.[2] α_k might also be positive, in which case organization k enhances another organization's viability—so-called "mutualism."[3] Hannan's well-established legitimacy-competition model finds mutualism among organizations when the number of organizations is relatively low, evidence of increasing legitimacy as organizations of a given form proliferate—with competition appearing at higher levels of density as the environment becomes more crowded.[4]

Although studies ordinarily estimate α_k, one can think of this term as composed of two terms, each representing one of the two distinct aspects of competition: $\alpha_k = \mathbf{w}_k\mathbf{p}_{jk}$, where $\mathbf{w}_k$ is the competitive intensity of rival $\mathbf{k}$ (as in figure 1.1), and $\mathbf{p}_k$ is the probability that organization $\mathbf{k}$ competes with another organization in the population. Most theorizing about competition focuses on $\mathbf{p}_k$ and allows this probability to vary according to the overlap between the resource bases of organizations[5] or their similarity in form or size.[6] An organization's competitive intensity, $\mathbf{w}_k$, is not explicitly considered in most models, so the competitive intensity of rivals at a given level of overlap is implicitly assumed to be homogeneous. A purely density-dependent model of competition results if $\mathbf{w}$ is assumed to be the same for all rivals. Under this assumption, the competition generated by a given organization $\mathbf{k}$ is $\alpha_k = \mathbf{w}\mathbf{p}_k$, and the competitive intensity term $\mathbf{w}$ does not vary from rival to rival but acts simply as a coefficient of proportionality. If the competitive effects of all of $\mathbf{j}$'s rivals are independent, then we can represent the aggregate competition generated by these rivals against $\mathbf{j}$ as $\Sigma_k\alpha_k = \alpha\mathbf{N}$, where $\alpha = \mathbf{w}\mathbf{p}$, and α and $\mathbf{p}$ are the averages of the specific α_k and $\mathbf{p}_k$. In a density-dependent model, then, differences in the observed strength of competition are attributed to differences in the probability or extent of competitive interactions ($\mathbf{p}_k$), rather than in differences in how formidable a rival is ($\mathbf{w}_k$) given that competition occurs.

In the few cases where researchers have endeavored to estimate $\mathbf{w}_k$, most discussions of competition suggest a history-independent model, where $\mathbf{w}_k$ is understood in terms of characteristics or positioning of a rival at a given point in time irrespective of its history. For instance, Barnett and Amburgey estimated a model of "mass dependence," in which $\mathbf{w}_k$ is modeled as a function of the sizes of one's rivals, under the idea that scale carries economic and political advantages that make firms more formidable rivals.[7] Although Barnett and Amburgey did not find evidence that larger organizations generate stronger competition, neither did they control for the likelihood of competing ($\mathbf{p}_k$). This turns out to be an important omission, given the increasing evidence that competition is "size-localized," which implies that organizations of different sizes have a lower likelihood of competing.[8] In this light, Carroll and Swaminathan looked again at the scale competition question.[9] In models that controlled for $\mathbf{p}_k$, they found greater competitive intensity ($\mathbf{w}_k$) generated by relatively larger rivals. As in this example, when research does consider why some organizations are potent rivals, the typical approach is to conceive of competitiveness as history-independent. To model the Red Queen, one should explicitly allow for differences in the competitive intensities of rivals ($\mathbf{w}_k$), varying according to each organization's history of exposure to competition, consistent with the theory.

The Red Queen Model

According to my theory, unless there has been a change in the prevailing logic of competition, w_k should be greater for organizations that have survived more competition. That is, these organizations should have a stronger competitive effect on their rivals. Meanwhile, organizations that have survived more competition historically also should be more viable, implying a greater value for the term β in figure 1.1 due to an organization's historical exposure to competition. In sum, then, the basic prediction of the Red Queen theory is that β and w will be greater for organizations that have been exposed to competition in the past, so long as competitive conditions have remained largely unchanged. The task now is to specify the competitive intensity model in order to allow for the estimation of these parameters.

Start with a given organization j that has been competing against a rival k. Let h_{jk} represent the effect of this history of competition on j's viability at a given point in time. The current-time competitive effect of k on j is to be specified distinctly from the hysteretic effect h_{jk}:

$$h_{jk} = a + b\tau_{jk},$$

where τ_{jk} is the duration of the competitive relationship between j and k historically, b is a coefficient showing the effect of this historical competition on j's current-time viability, and the parameter a is the effect of the fixed cost associated with j adapting to rivalry from k. Note that this specification is based on an assumption of stationarity in the context's competitive logic, so that what was learned in the past remains relevant and that past adaptations remain appropriate. Later I relax this assumption.

Now consider that j may compete with a population of organizations. Under the assumption that j's competitive relationships are independent, and letting k denote any rival from the population, the total effect of j's historical competition over the population can be specified as an additive aggregation across all of j's dyadic competitive relationships:

$$H_j = \Sigma_k h_{jk} = aK_j + bT_j$$

where K_j is the number of distinct rival organizations faced historically by j, a is the average effect of the fixed cost incurred by organization j in attempting to adapt to each of these rivals, and $T_j = \Sigma_k \tau_{jk}$ is the number of organization-years of rivalry faced by j historically. Another way to think of T_j is as the cumulative annual density faced historically by organization j. H_j decomposes j's historical competition, distinguishing the distinct effects of the breadth and depth of competitive experience. That is, for a given T_j, a low K_j implies fewer, longer competitive relationships.

Meanwhile, a high K_j implies that j's experience has been spread over more historical rivals.

So specified, competitive hysteresis can now be included in the baseline model of organizational viability:

$$v_j(t) = v_j(t)^* \exp[aK_j + bT_j].$$

The Costly Adaptation Hypothesis finds support if estimates of this model reveal $a < 0$, such that there are costs associated with adapting historically to different rivals. Meanwhile, the Competitive Hysteresis Hypothesis is supported if estimates show $b > 0$, where j's current-time viability improves due to its exposure to historical competition—holding constant the costs of adaptation.

Next, consider the possibility that competitive logics do not remain stationary over time, but that more recent lessons are more appropriate for current-time competitive conditions than are lessons learned in the distant past. In this case, we need to relax the model's stationarity assumption and instead discount competitive experience in any given year according to when it occurred. Specifically, I use the discount rate $1/\sqrt{\delta}$, where δ is the absolute value of a given historical year's distance from the current year. Imposing this discount on each organization-year of historical competitive experience (before summing), I create in each year for each organization j the recent historical experience term T_{Rj}. The total competitive experience of organization j then can be disaggregated into its recent and distant-past competitive experience terms: $T_{Dj} = T_j - T_{Rj}$. Now the model allows for separate effects for recent and distant-past competitive experience:

$$v_j(t) = v_j(t)^* \exp[aK_j + b_D T_{Dj} + b_R T_{Rj}].$$

The more the context's competitive logic changes over time, the more recent must competitive experience be if it is to improve organization j's current viability. In that case, estimates of the model will reveal $b_R > 0$ and $b_R > b_D$. A more extreme form of nonstationarity appears if changes in the competitive logic render established capabilities harmful, as in the Competency-Trap Hypothesis, wherein organizations dysfunctionally apply yesterday's solutions to tomorrow's (different) problems.[10] In this situation, distant-past competitive experience will be harmful to an organization's current-time viability, and estimates will show $b_D < 0$.

The model also must allow for the strength of competition to vary among rivals, as implied by Red Queen theory. Specifically the strength of competition generated by each rival should vary according to the rival's history of having competed. Let the strength of competition generated by k against any given rival vary as a linear function of its history of having competed, T_k, so that $w_k = \varsigma + \gamma T_k$. Now it is possible to denote the competition generated by k against any of its rivals as $\alpha_k = \varsigma p_k + \gamma p_k T_k$, where ς

is **k**'s history-independent competitive effect and γ is the effect of **k**'s historical exposure to competition on its current-time competitive strength. Assuming that the competitive strategies of **j**'s rivals are independent, then the total competition generated against **j** by these rivals can be aggregated additively:

$$\Sigma_k \alpha_k = \eta N + c\Sigma_k T_k,$$

where **N** is the density of the organizational population, $\eta = \varsigma p$, $c = \gamma p$, and as before **p** is the average of the rival-specific probabilities p_k. By design, my studies identify organizations according to whether or not they compete in the same context, so it is possible to assume that **p** approaches 1. If **p** = 1, then it is irrelevant to the model. If **p** < 1, but if it can be assumed not to vary systematically with the variables in the competition equation (**N** and T_k), then it acts as a coefficient of proportionality.

Including $\Sigma_k \alpha_k$ in the viability model results in:

$$v_j(t) = v_j(t)^* \exp[aK_j + b_D T_{Dj} + b_R T_{Rj} + \eta N + c\Sigma_k T_k].$$

If, as Red Queen theory implies, the strength of a rival's competition intensifies as it experiences historical competition, then estimates of the model will reveal **c** < 0. Note that under the null hypothesis, where **c** = 0, competition is density dependent. In that case, competition depends only on the number of competitors **N** and so is homogeneous across rivals, varying only according to the probability that **j** encounters a given rival.

Modeling a Pure-Selection Process

As explained in chapter 3, it is possible that the Red Queen could come about purely through selection processes. Without any variation over time in fitness within the lives of individual organizations, if competition enhances the strength of selection among organizations, then those that survive a history of competition will be more viable. These survivors consequently will generate stronger competition, in turn intensifying selection, and so on. If the Red Queen model finds support, therefore, it is possible that such results come about by selection alone, and that learning by individual organizations played no significant role. Historical competition effects, in this case, merely act as a proxy for unobserved, enduring differences in fitness among organizations. If these differences were entirely responsible for evidence of Red Queen competition, then modeling such differences directly would eliminate the effects of historical competition. For this reason, I attempt to estimate the effects of enduring, time-invariant differences in fitness among organizations.

The approach draws on the formal analysis by Vaupel et al. of how unobserved differences in fitness vary with selection.[11] They demonstrate that the average "frailty" of a cohort of survivors at any given time is a function of the cumulative hazard of that cohort up to that point in time. In their formulation, average frailty is falling as failures occur, not because any individual's frailty is declining, but because the composition of the population is changing. Although the Vaupel et al. model does not consider the idea that competition might accelerate the selection process, it nicely represents the pure-selection alternative, in which an organization survives not because it learns, but because it was strong to begin with. (Other models in organizational research have parameterized heterogeneity in fitness as a function of organizational age.)[12] In the Vaupel et al. model, average frailty in a given cohort varies with the cumulative hazard of failure over the life of the cohort, a strictly increasing function, but one that may (but need not) change as a proportionate function of cohort age. Specifications of the Red Queen model should therefore include the cumulative hazard of failure for each organization's cohort. If including this selectivity effect were to eliminate the effects of historical competition, then we could conclude that evidence of the Red Queen was due strictly to the operation of unobserved, time-invariant differences in fitness. Consequently, I will estimate the model

$$v_j(t) = v_j(t)^* \exp[aK_j + b_D T_{Dj} + b_R T_{Rj} + \eta N + c\Sigma_k T_k + sZ],$$

where Z is the cumulative hazard as of the end of the prior year, calculated using the so-called Nelson-Aalen estimator.[13]

Modeling Myopia

According to the Myopic Learning Hypothesis, bias results when an organization's competitive experience is restricted to a relatively small range compared to the full range of competitive experiences that might have been possible. To test this hypothesis, it is necessary to measure the degree of dispersion of an organization's competitive experience over its history. Other things equal, the more dispersed an organization's competitive experience, the less myopic the lessons it will have learned. Broader dispersion in competitive experience thus is predicted to make an organization more viable.

As I argued in chapter 3, this dispersion can be conceived in terms of variance among competitive conditions, with some organizations concentrating their experience into a relatively few high-competition years while others spread their experience more broadly over more years. Such an approach is appropriate if the space being sampled by an organization's experiences comprises different market conditions across various years. Alternatively, if the space being sampled is the array of possible kinds of rivals one might encounter, then dispersion is appropriately measured in terms of variance among cohorts of rivals. By this conception, one organization's rivals might all have come from a single wave of foundings, while another organization's rivals might be spread across many different cohorts.

The catch is measuring dispersion of either form so as to keep other things held equal. Many possible dispersion measures exist, but often these measures vary not only with dispersion but also according to other features of the experience distribution. Most notably, measuring dispersion in terms of the variance in the experience distribution, as my colleagues and I did in some earlier papers, does measure dispersion—but this measure also increases as a function of the number of historical competitors.[14] If the costs of adaptation increase with the number of competitors as I have predicted, then a measure of the variance over the experience distribution unfortunately conflates these costs with dispersion. Alternatively, one could measure dispersion using Theil's index, but this measure increases in magnitude with the number of observations (in my data, the number of years) in a distribution. Clearly, I want to use a measure of dispersion that is sensitive neither to the number of competitors nor to the organization's age.

The most widely used such measure is the Gini index. Formally, this measure is defined as:

$$G = 1 - \Sigma_i \, (Y_{i+1} + Y_i)(X_{i+1} - X_i),$$

where, after ranking the i years of an organization's competitive history from least to most competitive, each Y refers to the cumulative percent of total historical competition faced by the organization up to year i, and each X refers to year i's cumulative percentage in that ranking. Intuitively, a Gini approaching 1 indicates that an organization's competitive experience is as unequally dispersed as possible—concentrated into a single year. Alternatively, an organization that has experienced a completely smooth distribution of historical competition—the same number of competitors in every year—will have a Gini of 0. Of course, most organizations' histories are described somewhere in between. Also, for any particular organization, its Gini can and likely will vary over time. If a sudden surge of new competitors enters the market, or if a large number exit without being replaced, then an organization's competitive experience distribution will become more unequal—meaning that its Gini will increase.

Similarly, the Gini will also be used to measure the dispersion of cohorts of rivals over an organization's experience distribution. In this approach, the i years in an organization's competitive history are ranked from the least to the most in terms of the number of rivals entering in that year's cohort. A history featuring all rivals entering in a single cohort implies the least-dispersed distribution of rivals, indicated by a Gini of 1. By contrast, if an organization's history features broadly dispersed cohorts of rivals with the same number entering in every year, then this wide sampling evenly from every possible cohort would yield a Gini of 0.

Note that this approach works well in the computer industry data, but in the banking data, markets are measured too finely to result in meaningful differences in cohort size. Instead, with entries measured at the level of each locale in Illinois, most years have no entries, and when organizations do enter, they typically do so individually. For such fine-grained data, the cohort-dispersion Gini needs to be computed in terms of the interarrival times of rival foundings. In this approach, a roughly equal distribution of cohorts is evidenced by equal spacing among the entry times of rivals, yielding a Gini of 0. Meanwhile, the least dispersed distribution of cohorts would result if all rivals were founded in the same year (yielding long waiting times before and after a set of 0 interarrival times). In this way, the dispersion of rival cohorts over an organization's history can be calculated in terms of interarrival times, or in terms of event counts, whichever is more appropriate for the data at hand.

In terms of the Red Queen model, including either form of dispersion Gini for each organization implies the specification,

$$v_j(t) = v_j(t)^* \exp[aK_j + b_D T_{Dj} + b_R T_{Rj} + \eta N + c\Sigma_k T_k + sZ + dG_j],$$

where for each organization the measure of G is allowed to vary over time. If the Myopic Learning Hypothesis is correct, then organizations with greater dispersion in their competitive experience will be more viable, such that $d < 0$.

Using the term "viability" keeps the discussion at a general level, but to test the model empirically requires that viability be specified operationally. To do this, I follow the demographic approach typical in organizational ecology research.[15] In this approach, an organization's viability is manifest in terms of its ability to exist. Specifically, higher rates of organizational founding and lower rates of organizational failure are seen as evidence of viability. By estimating models of these processes, then, I can specify the Red Queen model operationally.

Modeling the Implications of Predation

As discussed in chapters 2 and 3, often organizations respond to competition by attempting to eliminate their competitors. In light of the Red Queen, organizations following a logic of predation may enjoy reduced current-time competition, but this positional advantage is likely to come at a cost. I have argued that the compositional consequences of mergers and acquisitions, as well as the consequences for the process of learning, will be harmful to organizational viability. The goal here is to build the Costly Predation Hypothesis explicitly into the model.

In terms of viability, two different modeling approaches are appropriate, depending on whether organizational founding or failure is being studied. For failure models, the organization is the unit of analysis, so the viability of a given organization j can be expressed:

$$v_j(t) = v_j(t)^* \exp[aK_j + b_D T_{Dj} + b_R T_{Rj} + \eta N + c\Sigma_k T_k + sZ_F + dG_j].$$

Note that in this specification the cumulative hazard of failure, Z_F, is included in order to allow for a pure-selection process. However, the Costly Predation Hypothesis opens up another possibility. Organization j may have outsurvived its rivals not only through their failure, but instead because they were acquired by a rival—either by organization j or by another of j's rivals. The theoretical implications of preying on rivals, compared to outsurviving them with respect to failure, can be investigated by including not only Z_F, but also the cumulative hazard of organization j having acquired its rivals, Z_A. According to the costly predation hypothesis, organizations that have acquired their rivals at a higher rate over time—those with a higher value for Z_A—will be predicted to be less viable as a result. Of course, organizations with a higher value for Z_A might also enjoy an isolated market position, but this beneficial positional advantage is controlled elsewhere in the model. As well, it is possible to include the cumulative hazard that an organization's rivals were acquired by other rivals. This form of disappearance would also imply that the population was reduced in size by a process other than failure, but by not involving organization j directly. In fact, if j's rivals are pursuing a logic of predation, then j's viability might well be improved by the fact that its rivals are following the (costly) predation strategy.

In founding models, the unit of analysis is the context rather than the organization. Consequently, the degree of predatory acquisition activity in a given context must be modeled to see whether this reduces the viability of the surviving, incumbent organizations consistent with the Costly Predation Hypothesis. That is, if predation makes the survivors less viable, then entry by new foundings should be more likely than would be the case if incumbent organizations were strong competitors. As in the failure models, in the founding process I operationalize the degree of predation in terms of the cumulative hazard of acquisition. Already, the founding model contains the cumulative hazard of failure, Z_F, in order to allow for a pure-selection process where higher rates of organizational failure leave the population with more viable organizations. In light of the Costly Predation Hypothesis, the cumulative hazard should be specified distinctly for failures, $\mathbf{Z}_F$, and for acquisitions, $\mathbf{Z}_A$. The pure-selection process then would result in $s_F < 0$, where s_F is the coefficient of $\mathbf{Z}_F$, meaning that founding rates are lower in environments with organizations that have survived a rigorous selection process. By contrast, the Costly Predation Hypothesis would imply $s_A > 0$, where s_A is the coefficient of $\mathbf{Z}_A$, meaning that founding rates are higher in contexts where incumbents have been weakened by acquiring their rivals.

Modeling Organizational Founding

I estimate two different kinds of organizational founding models, each corresponding to one of the different data structures to be analyzed. For the Illinois bank data, the unit of analysis is the locale, with foundings taking place across many local banking markets. This extremely fine-grained data structure makes it very unlikely that two foundings occur in the same place at the same time. In fact, simultaneous events occur only rarely in these data (see the appendix). Consequently, the founding rate is best understood in terms of the waiting time (or interarrival time) between organizational founding events in any given locale. A community with only a few foundings over the twentieth century has a low founding rate, and this low rate is well represented by its low average waiting time between events. Pooling the waiting times of the various Illinois communities, it is possible to estimate piecewise exponential founding models of the form:

$$\lambda(\tau) = \lambda(\tau)^* \exp[\beta_\lambda' \mathbf{W}],$$

in which λ refers to the instantaneous transition rate, or hazard rate, of organizational founding. τ is the waiting time between founding events in a given locale, which is allowed to vary across selected time intervals, but is assumed to be constant within interval. This is an especially flexible functional form for duration dependence, an important quality for a founding model given that very little research measures founding events at a sufficiently fine-grained level to permit the estimation of founding rates using waiting time data. The environmental and competitive conditions in each locale that are likely to affect the rate of organizational founding are then included in $\mathbf{W}$. Also, the trade-off between organizational founding and growth is explicitly modeled, with recent growth by organizations included as a variable in $\mathbf{W}$. To the extent that growth by incumbents retards the founding of new organizations, this variable will have a negative effect on the rate of organizational founding.

Using this model, the competitive effects implied by the theory of Red Queen competition can be estimated. Specifically, I estimate the model:

$$\lambda(\tau) = \lambda(\tau)* \ \exp[\beta_\lambda'W + c_\lambda\Sigma_kT_k \ | \ s_\lambda Z].$$

According to the theory, estimates of these parameters should reveal c_λ < 0, such that environments with competitively experienced incumbent organizations will have lower founding rates. Also, if s_λ < 0, then environments marked by a greater rate of historical selection also will have lower founding rates. In this way, the intensified competition predicted by the Red Queen theory is modeled as an increase in barriers to entry in a given market.

In the computer industry data collected for this study, markets are delineated by general product area: mainframe computers, midrange computers, and microcomputers. Data on waiting times between founding events are not available. Rather, counts of numbers of foundings per year per market are the only information on foundings. With such data, it is possible to estimate the founding rate using as an operational dependent variable the observed count of the number of foundings per market per year. I specify these counts as a negative binomial process—similar to a Poisson process but less constrained, in that the dispersion of the process can be greater or less than the mean. Although this approach does allow tests of the Red Queen hypotheses, it requires an assumption of a constant founding rate with respect to duration.

Modeling Organizational Survival

Ecological models of organizations often focus on differences among organizations in their likelihood of surviving. More viable organizations, by definition, will be more likely to survive than less viable organizations, and when organizations compete this often is evidenced by the fact that they increase one another's chances of failure. Similarly, the competitive hysteresis effects predicted by Red Queen theory can also be tested in models of organizational survival. I include the predicted effects of the theory within a piecewise exponential model of the organizational failure rate, a model with sufficient flexibility to have become typical in demographic studies of organizations:[16]

$$r_j(t) = r_j(t)*\exp[a_rK_j + b_{rD}T_{Dj} + b_{rR}T_{Rj} + \eta_rN + c_r\Sigma_kT_k + s_rZ + d_rG_j],$$

where $r_j(t)$ is the instantaneous rate of failure of organization j, allowed to vary with t, the market tenure of organization j, across several time periods.

$r_j(t)*$ refers to the baseline rate for organization j at any given time, estimated as a function of variables reflecting differences in organizational factors, environmental conditions, and current-time competition. These various effects increase or decrease the carrying capacity for a given kind of organization in a given market. The competitive hysteresis effects, then, should hold over and above these other effects. Specifically, the Competitive Hysteresis Hypothesis predicts that organizations with more exposure to a recent history of competition are more viable. This implies $b_{rR} < 0$ and $b_{rR} < b_{rD}$, where an organization's failure rate is lower the more that it has experienced recent history of competition. Similarly, this hypothesis predicts that organizations with more exposure to a recent history of competition generate stronger competition. In the failure model, this hypothesis would be supported if $c_r > 0$, where rivals with more (recent) competitive experience generate stronger competition. By contrast, if organizations are less viable when they have faced a larger number of distinct historical rivals—the Costly Adaptation Hypothesis—then in the failure rate model one would expect $a_r > 0$. Finally, the Myopic Learning Hypothesis is evidenced in the failure model by $d_r > 0$, where organizations that have been exposed to a broader range of competition over time are more viable.

As stated, these models are meant to be of a general enough form that they could be estimated on any organizational population. Of course, in practice each context is marked by idiosyncratic factors that must be considered when estimating such models. Here, I have collected datasets that are particularly well suited to identifying different aspects of the Red Queen process. To properly specify the various models for each organizational population, it is necessary to review some of the context-specific factors that shape competition, especially the different competitive logics operating in each organizational population, and how they change over time.

The rich and varied histories of computing and commercial banking differ in so many important ways that no one familiar with these industries would draw a parallel between them. It is for precisely this reason that I look to both of these contexts to estimate the Red Queen models. Despite the different logics of competition at work in these different contexts, I expect to see in both the general processes characteristic of Red Queen evolution. Of course, the specifications of models will differ from context to context, since the contextual factors important to banking differ from those important to computing. Also, the sample designs differ in their degree of specificity, with especially fine-grained delineation of commercial banking markets enabling me to identify local monopolists there, while my measures of computing markets are somewhat more coarse. Similarly, mergers and acquisitions have been more common in commercial banking, making it possible to trace the consequences of such meta-competition in that context. But aside from these differences, I am able to estimate the models across both contexts.

Comparisons to Other Ecological Models of Organizations

Because the Red Queen model builds upon the thinking, research, and modeling approach of organizational ecology, it is worth considering how and why this model differs from existing ecological models of organizations. Among the many different ecological models of organizations in the literature, three general kinds potentially relate to Red Queen theory: the density-dependent model of legitimation and competition, models of founding conditions, and models of vicarious or imitative learning among organizations.

The most widely known ecological model is that of density-dependent legitimation and competition.[17] Since it was developed by Hannan and his colleagues, this model has found support in a wide variety of organizational populations. The main arguments in the theory of density dependence are that the competition among and legitimacy of organizations increase as such organizations grow in number (density). When there are few organizations of a particular form, the form is less legitimate than when the density of such organizations is greater. Specifically, the theory predicts that increases in density increase the legitimacy of such organizations at a decreasing rate. At higher levels of density, further increases cause competition to intensify at an increasing rate as organizations crowd the niche. The net effect of these two patterns is a nonmonotonic relationship between the density of organizations and their viability. Increases in density increase the viability of such organizations at low density levels due to strong legitimacy effects, while at high levels of density, further increases in density reduce the viability of such organizations because of strong increases in competition.

The most direct connection between density dependence theory and Red Queen theory is in their approaches to modeling competition. The Red Queen model allows the competitive intensity generated by organizations to vary according to the historical experiences of these organizations; in particular, their historical exposure to competition. If, instead, we constrain the model so that organizations do not differ in their competitive intensity, then the Red Queen model reduces to a model of density dependence. When it comes to competition, then, the Red Queen model is an elaboration of the density-dependent model: The competitive significance of organizations' historical exposure to competition is modeled over and above the "baseline" model of density-dependent competition. So competition through market crowding may well occur, as in density dependence theory, but Red Queen theory suggests that this is only part of the story.

Regarding the early period of market formation, Red Queen theory and density dependence theory direct our attention to very different processes.

Density dependence theory emphasizes the importance of increasing legitimation early on, as organizations initially increase in numbers. Red Queen theory does not contradict this prediction; indeed, one can estimate the Red Queen model while including the nonmonotonic density specification suggested by the legitimation argument. (In fact, the models reported in this book either include nonmonotonic density specifications or were found to be robust to such specifications.) Where Red Queen theory differs from the legitimation argument is in its conception of the early period of industry development. Red Queen theory argues that competition is important early in an industry's history, because through such competition organizations discover logics of competition. As this early discovery takes place, increasing legitimation may well also be taking place with increases in density. So the two theories are complementary in their conceptions of the early development of markets, with Red Queen theory highlighting the role that competition plays even early in an industry's emergence.

Red Queen theory also is related to models of founding conditions. Arguably the most well-established model of founding conditions is density delay, which predicts that density at the time an organization is founded has a permanent, negative effect on an organization's viability.[18] The idea behind this prediction is that organizations born in a crowded environment are damaged, permanently, by the ordeal of trying to get off the ground under conditions of resource scarcity.[19] To some extent, this idea is consistent with a premise of Red Queen theory: Scarcity creates problems for organizations. Where the theory differs is in the implications of scarcity for ongoing organizational viability. In density delay, the problems due to scarcity "imprint" the organization as marginal, while in Red Queen theory scarcity intensifies both adaptation and selection so that the survivors of scarcity are better off.

In this light, Swaminathan's "trial by fire" model of founding conditions shows how these opposing theories might be reconciled.[20] The trial by fire model argues that scarcity due to high density-at-founding intensifies selection pressures. This leads initially to higher failure rates for organizations founded under such conditions, but this initial effect attenuates as weak organizations are deselected over time until ultimately the long-term survivors of the "trial" are more viable. Swaminathan's model places the logic of the Red Queen in the context of founding conditions and shows that the problem of scarcity at founding can be understood as having both the failure-increasing implications highlighted by density delay and the survival-enhancing implications of Red Queen theory. In the models estimated in this book, density-at-founding is included in all failure models along with the historical competition effects of Red Queen theory.

Other ecological models depict organizations as learning from the experiences of other organizations.[21] Red Queen theory differs from such models in two fundamental ways. First, the underlying processes operating in the Red Queen are adaptation and selection, each of which is triggered by competition. By contrast, most other models describe a collective learning process, in which organizations either imitate one another or learn vicariously from each other's performance. Red Queen theory would not deny that vicarious learning and imitation occur in organizational life, but these processes are distinct from the ongoing processes of adaptation and selection that are driven by competition among organizations. A second, unique aspect of the Red Queen model is its reciprocal nature, where competition enhances viability, which in turn intensifies competition. Presumably, other ecological models of organizational learning could also build in the reciprocal causality that is a central feature of the Red Queen model.

FIVE

Red Queen Competition among Commercial Banks

AT THE DAWN of the twentieth century, many in the United States were ambivalent toward banks, as summed up by U.S. Treasury Secretary Lyman J. Gage in an address to a gathering of New York bankers:

> The consolidation of capital, and the centralization of industries, excite new and serious inquiry as to the consequences and effects they may carry in their train. . . . Two dangers are apparent. One is that through prejudice and ignorance we may block the path of natural progress. The other is that the force and power involved in these great organizations may be utilized for oppression and robbery.[1]

Behind Gage's concern were two vividly contrasting facts about banks. First, economic life in the industrializing United States required access to capital—typically through banks. Consequently, banks proliferated in the United States during the nineteenth century, so that by the time the National Bank Act of 1864 established a national currency, thousands of banks had been formed.[2] Meanwhile, well known by the end of the nineteenth century was the image of the banker as a "Robber Baron"—a member of the economic elite who prospers even through panics, depressions, and wars.[3] As the twentieth century began, the organization of U.S. banking took shape in light of the material fact of banks as central to economic life, and the social fact of banks and bankers viewed as elite exploiters worthy of suspicion. Banking regulation in the United States was formed amidst the tension between these two facts, and in turn the regulatory environment of banking shaped the logics of competition the emerged among U.S. banks in the twentieth century.

The Institutional Context of Twentieth-Century U.S. Commercial Banking

Many Americans have long feared that banks—and especially big banks—are too powerful. Antibank sentiments surfaced in the early American debates over whether to have a centralized national bank and have been seen as partly responsible for the decentralized structure that ultimately emerged in the U.S. Federal Reserve system.[4] Early legal restrictions on

U.S. banks reflected these antibank sentiments. The 1864 National Bank Act was interpreted by many at the time as prohibiting branching by national banks,[5] and even stronger antibank controls were instituted in some states, such as the complete prohibition on bank branching in the Illinois State Constitution of 1870. One sees evidence of antibanking sentiments in the American populist movement—in particular in the Bryant candidacy at the turn of the twentieth century. Similarly, the Progressive political movement loudly questioned the legitimacy of banks. For instance, the Wilson administration's antitrust campaign included banking reform as part of antitrust reform, and regarded banks as among the most notorious of anticompetitive trusts.[6] Opposition to powerful banking interests came from within the banking industry as well, with rural and regional banks throughout the United States favoring regulatory controls to contain so-called money center banks—especially from New York.[7]

By contrast, it has also been understood for some time that banks are necessary to modern life, and that a well-run banking system is fundamental to economic prosperity.[8] Looking back to the mid-nineteenth-century, most local capital markets in the United States were plagued by inefficiencies when compared to what we would regard as typical in the twenty-first century. Most American states maintained during the nineteenth century very difficult requirements for the chartering of new banks, which retarded the spread of alternative banking institutions early on.[9] To the extent that banking spread in those states, then, it was through the expansion of older, more traditional organizations, many of which lacked modern expertise in managing banking transactions.[10] Meanwhile, other states passed so-called free-bank laws, dramatically easing the entry requirements for banks during the antebellum period.[11] Given that the United States lacked a single currency at the time, these banks generated a proliferation of different currency issues, with the obvious inefficiencies that this implies. The 1864 National Bank Act (and its 1865 amendment) provided strong incentives for banks to apply for national charters. This law, combined with the end of the Civil War, led to a proliferation of new and rechartered national banks. Together, these factors led to a newer, more modern commercial banking movement by the turn of the century.[12]

Meanwhile, the central importance of banks and capital throughout the United States by the twentieth century also aligned the interests of most people with those of the banks, whether they liked it or not. When most organizations fail, those served by the organization are inconvenienced to some extent as they must find other organizations to fulfill their needs. By contrast, when banks failed in the United States early in the twentieth century and before, their customers often would lose all their financial assets. The importance of this fact is magnified by the self-fulfilling nature of confidence in banks. Banks do not keep all deposits on hand in liquid (cash) form, of course, but rather lend most of their assets and keep some assets on reserve in other banks. This approach allows capital markets to function but works under the assumption that not all depositors will demand to withdraw their funds at once. Yet because a depositor will lose if his or her bank fails, the perception that a bank might fail creates an incentive to withdraw one's funds, in turn increasing the likelihood of failure, and so further increasing the incentive to withdraw funds—the notorious bank-panic problem. Prior to deposit insurance, which was not instituted in the United States until the 1930s, bank panics were relatively common, making salient the nation's economic dependence on banks.

The need for banks, combined with widespread mistrust of banks, led to policies and regulations that at the same time restricted and fortified banks. A complex mesh of banking regulations in the United States during the twentieth century pushed in these opposing directions. In Illinois, suspicion of large banks was widespread, leading to that state's prohibition on branch banking for most of the twentieth century. My statistical analysis focuses on Illinois, since the prevalence of single-establishment ("unit") banks there enables me to analyze that state's hundreds of locales as distinct banking markets. Consequently, I pay special attention to Illinois as I review the most important of these regulatory restrictions and fortifications in order to identify how they shaped the logics of competition available to twentieth-century banks in the United States.

Institutional Restrictions on U.S. Banks

Since the National Bank Act of 1864, U.S. national regulations have been subservient to state regulations when it comes to banks. This approach effectively allowed different states to have different degrees of stringency or leniency in their treatment of banks. For instance, while Illinois completely prohibited bank branching in any form until very recently, California has long encouraged the growth of large branch systems. Similarly, in another compromise, since 1864 banks could be chartered as either national or as state banks—the so-called dual banking system of banks answering to both state and national regulatory agencies.[13] Charter availability and reserve requirements often have differed from state to state and between national and state bank regulators, so the dual banking system effectively has allowed varying degrees of stringency in what is required to start a bank in different states.

The failure of banks to make payments during the bank panics of 1873, 1893, and 1907 raised suspicions that bankers first tended to their own interests.[14] These concerns were intensified by the fact that larger banks were aided during these crises by New York bankers such as J. P. Morgan, giving evidence to suspicions of a bankers' conspiracy centering around New York money center banking interests.[15] Consequently, populist and Progressive politicians and activists, as well as many bankers outside of New York, called for a monetary control and reserve system independent of the New York bankers.[16] In particular, bankers from the Midwest, West, and South pushed for the establishment of regional bank clearinghouses to ensure the viability of banks without relying on the money center bankers. The American Bankers Association, organized in 1876, played an important role in the push toward banking reform on a regional basis.[17]

Ultimately, both banking and political interests were involved in the drive for a Federal Reserve System, culminating in the Federal Reserve Act of 1913. This debate was marked by a tension between banker control and political control of the board overseeing the Federal Reserve.[18] As one would expect, bankers—especially money center bankers—insisted on banker representation and control of the system. Political control of the Fed won out in the end, however, given the suspicions aroused by money center bankers among populists, political support for such a policy (including from President Wilson), and the view of many rural bankers that government control would be preferable to control by Wall Street.[19] In fact, the ultimate lobbying efforts in favor of the Federal Reserve Act purposely excluded money center bankers so as to avoid the appearance that the act favored banking interests.[20]

Antibanking sentiments sounded loudly, as well, in the debate over branch banking throughout the United States over the late nineteenth and twentieth centuries. During this time, the structure of the banking industry was shaped differently in the different states. The modern branching movement did not appear until after 1900, with several thousand branch systems developing from 1900 to 1930.[21] Meanwhile, the first bank holding companies were formed during the 1920s.[22] A few states even passed laws explicitly permitting statewide branch banking. Most notably, California's branching law of 1909 became a model for pro-branching interests nationwide.[23] Then and now, many interpret the ascendance of branch systems as evidence of efficiency in action, since such systems can achieve scale economies and spread professional management systems to small locales. Others, however, saw the spread of branch systems as evidence of institutional power plays by banking interests.

In particular, various political forces and considerable public opinion opposed the branching movement of the early twentieth century. This reaction became especially strong during the 1920s, partly because of very high failure rates among rural unit banks.[24] In response, Congress passed the 1927 McFadden Act.[25] The law prohibited interstate branching and allowed intrastate branching by national banks only within one city, and only when explicitly permitted by state law.[26] (These restrictions were al-

ready begun under a 1922 ruling by the Comptroller.[27]) In reaction to
the McFadden Act, a number of states then passed branching prohibitions
of their own. These prohibitions were established especially outside of the
American South, where a tradition derived from the Scottish branch-
banking system is thought by some to have made the region less suspicious
of branch banks than were the North and West.[28]

The banking crisis of the 1930s fed mistrust of banks and bankers, with
growth by surviving banks seen by many as evidence of undue power
among large banks. Congressional testimony featured stories of bankers
prospering at the expense of small-town businesses and ordinary citizens.[29]
Such sentiments are reflected in provisions of the Glass-Steagall Act of
1933 restricting the range of businesses in which banks could operate—
in particular restrictions on their operations in the brokerage industry.
Following this act, Regulation Q then further regulated banks by putting
into place interest rate ceilings on deposits.[30] In some states, the antibank
reaction triggered by the banking crisis also led to the strengthening of
antibranching laws.

Often, prominent local bankers were among the staunchest opponents
of branch banking. Such opposition could be extremely effective because
within a small town, the prominence of the local banker—often in funding important improvements or as a pillar of the community—stands in
contrast to the more general image of the banker as a self-interested seeker
of gains.[31] Not surprisingly, self-histories sponsored by unit banks routinely portray their founders as local advocates of the public good—often
in contrast to the money centers of New York and Chicago. Public discourse over banks and bank regulation mirrored this framing, often depicting local bankers as strong, but working for the betterment of the
local economy, as "men who command the confidence of the communities
in which they are located."[32] By contrast, the big-city bankers were more
likely to be discussed in terms of power and wealth, or as having little
regard for the common person. This framing helped to fuel the antibranching movement, especially in areas with strong populist sentiments
such as Illinois.

In this light, it is notable that antibranching regulations, though meant
to restrain banks from becoming powerful, often had the effect of helping
local bankers to consolidate power. In particular, states with strong antibranching laws turned out to have many one-bank towns, effectively lessening competition and so allowing the local banker to enjoy monopoly
control over local banking services. Of the 73,298 location-years in the
Illinois banking market from 1900 through 1990, 50,568—or over 70
percent—were years when a single bank monopolized the local market.
So although antibranching regulations were effective in keeping large,
multibranch banks out of Illinois and some other parts of the United

States, they also led to de facto monopolies in many towns where consumers and businesses had but one banker to whom they could turn for banking services.

Taken together, the various institutional restrictions on U.S. banks led to a clear definition of what constituted a commercial bank, and a precise delineation of where and how such banks could compete. To be a bank, one needed to obtain a charter, which in turn required that one satisfy a set of explicit requirements in terms of staffing, organization, and financial backing. When operating as a bank, organizations were restricted explicitly and unambiguously. Operations were to be confined geographically according to state law. In terms of products, banks could not innovate but remained restricted to offering savings accounts, demand (checking) accounts, certain forms of loans and credit, and transaction services such as check cashing and foreign exchange. Even prices were set by regulation, at least for attracting depositors, in that competing on interest rates offered on accounts was not possible (although interest rates on loans were not set by regulators, with the exception of a very high "usury" ceiling). Consequently, when banks operated in the same locations, they were unable to differentiate their products and most prices. Rather, colocated banks competed over customers on the basis of service, perceived security, reputation, and interest rates on loans. Institutional restrictions on banking thus created a context for banks to contend for customers directly, without ambiguity over what constituted a banking product, and with little ability to differentiate.

Institutional Fortifications of U.S. Banks

Even as regulations restricted banks to clearly defined geographic and product markets, so did they fortify banks in an effort to avert bank failures. The passage of the National Bank Act of 1864 opened the way for the chartering of national banks with a stipulated amount of capital and government-backed reserves and established a single national currency and the Comptroller of the currency.[33] The capital stock and reserve requirements for nationally chartered banks were meant to reduce the chances of bank failure.[34] These requirements also made it more difficult to found a national bank than was the case for founding a typical state-chartered bank. Consequently, when new national banks were founded, they were thought to be less likely to fail given that they fulfilled the more stringent capital and reserve requirements of the National Bank Act.

Yet the system created by the National Bank Act had neither a central bank nor any mechanism to prevent bank panics from escalating, as evidenced by the postbellum bank panics. During these panics, banks suspended payments to depositors and to one another, as bank reserves proved inadequate once panic-driven withdrawals escalated. These events led many to voice concern over the effectiveness of the banking system, monetary regulation, and the continued proliferation of small state-chartered banks in some areas.[35] In an attempt to answer these concerns, over several years federal policymakers created what would ultimately become the Federal Reserve Act of 1913.[36] The act was a compromise between pro- and antibanking interests. On the one hand, it established a Federal Reserve Board overseen by political appointees (as opposed to bankers). On the other hand, banks were fortified by the establishment of the Fed's flexible system of national monetary control, and by increased access to liquid assets made possible by the system of regional Federal Reserve Banks.

Despite the establishment of the Federal Reserve, however, bank panics and bank failures continued to be a problem nationally in the United States. These events fueled an ongoing debate nationally about the culpability of banks and bankers, and what could be done to reduce bank failures. Although bankers were depicted in a negative light during the testimony leading up to the Banking Acts of 1933 and 1935, in the end these acts included federal deposit insurance, which drastically reduced the likelihood of bank panics.[37] Deposit insurance also reinforced banks in a way that allowed all banks—not just large, well-capitalized banks—to offer security to their depositors. In this way, the regulatory changes of the 1930s dramatically fortified small banks in the United States—an especially important development in places such as Illinois, where small unit banks were numerous.

The banking crisis of the early 1930s also rekindled the debate over bank branching, giving greater force in some areas to the argument for larger, multibranch banks. It was widely thought that the banking crash especially affected unit banks, and that individual branches of larger systems were less susceptible to failure.[38] In response to these concerns, the Glass-Steagall Act of 1933 permitted national banks to branch on an equal footing with state banks according to each state's laws.[39] By reducing both the bank founding rate and bank failure rates, the Banking Acts of 1933 and 1935 stabilized the number of banks in the United States. These acts also restricted the entry of new banks, a change meant to limit the proliferation of unit banks encouraged by the earlier free-banking laws of the nineteenth century.[40] Many state regulators also reacted by permitting branching, in some cases reversing prohibitions that had been passed only six years earlier.

Finally, the regulatory environment of commercial banking increasingly managed the process of bank failure in the United States in the twentieth century. Regulators tracked bank performance in order to intervene when banks failed. With the onset of Federal deposit insurance in the 1930s, regulatory involvement in the process of bank failure was typical. Reviewing my data documenting all bank failures in Illinois over most of the twentieth century, I note that increasingly over the period failures were "managed" by regulators so as to move at least some of the assets and liabilities of the failing bank into another (typically rival) bank. In this way, regulators actively assisted the consolidation of banks and even initiated mergers and acquisitions in many cases in order to avert an outright bank liquidation. Unlike most other industries in the United States, banking has been regulated in such a way as to favor the continuing survival of incumbent organizations—even if this has meant combining organizations and lessening competition.

In the same way, the issuing of charters at both the national and state levels shielded incumbent banks from competition as much as possible in order to prevent bank failures. To obtain a charter, a potential banker needed to do several things.[41] First, capital needed to be raised and a board of directors assembled. The board's composition would be scrutinized by banking regulators, whose concern was making sure that the new bank would remain solvent. Second, the founders would prepare a charter application, detailing exactly where the bank would operate and including pro forma statements showing projected financial returns for the new bank. Importantly, this charter application needed to show why it was that the new bank would not harm the solvency of existing banks in the locale. For instance, one could point to a growing population or local economic climate as evidence that the locale could handle another bank. In this sense, the charter application has served, historically, as a check to make sure that new bank entry did not create too much competition.

Logics of Competition among U.S. Banks

The combination of institutional restrictions and fortifications of banks in the United States would appear, on balance, to set the stage for moderate levels of bank competition. On the one hand, colocated banks were restricted to offering identical products and prices (on savings accounts), making strong competition likely. On the other hand, regulators managed bank entry and exit in order to prevent especially strong competition. The ideas in chapter 2, however, lead to a very different prediction. Thinking in terms of logics of competition, the combination of institutional restrictions and fortifications invited banks to compete according to either of two distinct logics. The clear definitions of banking markets left banks to compete over customers based on how well they operated as banks, essentially competition according to a logic of *fiduciary effectiveness*. Alternatively, the institutional fortifications safeguarding banks and encouraging mergers and acquisitions invited banks to follow a logic of institutional power featuring *predation,* where banks acquired rivals in order to enjoy a protected market position. As discussed in chapter 2, these alternative logics have profoundly different implications for Red Queen evolution.

When banks competed for customers, they could do so only based on their effectiveness as a fiduciary institution. Unable to engage in product differentiation, innovation, or price competition, banks in the same location found themselves attempting to attract customers based on their ability to provide banking services, their ability to effectively organize and manage banking transactions on the operations side, and their ability to rationally balance risk and returns on the lending side. In short, banks could compete for customers according to a logic of fiduciary effectiveness. Organizations with the capabilities required for fiduciary effectiveness would be especially viable[42] and would likely generate stronger competition. By contrast, banks that fell short on fiduciary effectiveness relative to their competitors would be less viable and would be weaker competitors.

Meanwhile, the institutional fortification of commercial banks also made possible competition among banks according to a very different logic—one of predation. Some banks actively pursued a policy of acquiring rival banks in the same locale, sometimes in response to distress among rivals when times were tough, but in other cases paying top dollar for competitors. In either case, the result of merger and acquisition activity among competing banks often was to reduce or eliminate competition altogether—the form of ecological competition known as predation discussed in chapter 2. Banks that competed well in terms of predation would, of course, be under less pressure to compete in terms of fiduciary effectiveness. In the extreme, an effective strategy of predation would give a bank monopoly power in its markets.

In light of Red Queen evolution, a bank's strategy to follow one or both of these logics of competition would be very important to its development. Winners and losers in competition over fiduciary effectiveness were decided by the market—by business and retail customers as they chose among rival banks. So banks that competed according to a logic of fiduciary effectiveness would develop over time through Red Queen evolution, becoming more viable and stronger as competitors, as the theory predicts. By contrast, those banks that prevailed through a logic of predation might "win," in the sense that they would survive as others did not. However, winning through a logic of predation would not involve comparing banks according to their ability to satisfy customers and so would not trigger the processes of Red Queen evolution. Next I discuss each of these logics of competition in more detail and elaborate their implications for the Red Queen model.

Bank Competition through Fiduciary Effectiveness

Because commercial banking was tightly regulated over most of the twentieth century, banks in the same geographic market found themselves in direct competition for customers. When business and consumer depositors and borrowers chose to give their business to one bank, less business was available for other banks in the same local banking market. In this sense, banks stood in zero-sum relation to one another even though products, most prices, and bank entry and exit were regulated. Consequently, banks were less viable when they faced larger numbers of competitors in a given market.[43] This meant that banks facing more rivals were more likely to fail,[44] and also that there was a trade-off between the growth of incumbent banks and the foundings of new banks. That is, the more that new banks were founded, the slower the growth rate of existing banks, and similarly the higher the growth rates of incumbent banks, the lower the founding rates of new banks.[45] The specific processes involved in this competition varied depending on the particular product market in question.

The twentieth-century business of commercial banking in the United States included products and services offered to consumer and business customers.[46] Historically, banking regulations in the United States limited these products and services to the market for transaction processing, savings, and credit. A fourth market, risk management (such as insurance), has more recently been opened up to banks, but for most of the twentieth century it was off-limits to commercial banks. Transaction processing services included check cashing and processing wire transfers and other sorts of monetary flows. Checking accounts have been the primary product offering in payment processing, and grew over the twentieth century to be a dominant means of making financial transactions. In the regulated era, checking accounts did not pay interest. Consequently, for those carrying large checking account balances, this product essentially was "sold" at a very high price (equal to the opportunity cost of that amount of capital). Over and above this cost, banks also were permitted by regulators to charge fees associated with checking accounts.

Savings accounts, paying a relatively low, regulated interest rate, were another staple product during the regulated era. Unable to differentiate on the basis of interest rates, commercial banks could do so instead by cultivating a reputation for safety. Often, local commercial banks would create impressive physical facilities to give customers a sense that the bank was a safe place to keep money. Banks in Illinois, in particular, were known for impressive and sometimes opulent structures, since each bank could have only one physical location. Large, visible bank vaults and dramatic stone facades were typical in these establishments. It is possible that large banks, and those with high-profile affiliations and customers, also were more likely to benefit from a reputation for safety and security.

The credit market, including both consumer and business loans, was also tightly regulated in terms of the products offered. For instance, unsecured lines of credit, such as credit cards, are a more recent development. Secured business loans and agricultural loans also were important aspects of the commercial banking business. In the credit market, local commercial banks could compete on rates and often attempted to provide better customer service, in the form of relatively rapid lending decisions, forbearance from demanding payment for "preferred" customers, and loan approvals despite apparent hardship (again for preferred customers).[47] To provide such service, a bank needed to know which customers were better risks than their circumstances might otherwise have suggested. Lending committees and bank boards were often used as conduits for information about customers through the social networks of board and committee members.[48]

An important aspect of competition under regulation was the ability to identify, attract, and retain "better" customers. Banks that could attract lower-risk borrowers were at a considerable advantage in terms of loan losses and, ultimately, profitability. Similarly, customers who kept larger balances in their accounts were considerably more valuable because they essentially paid a higher "price" for banking services, given their higher opportunity costs—a benefit enjoyed by banks since they could then lend out those deposits to borrowers. Competition among commercial banks thus was a contest to gain access to better customers on both the credit and account sides of the business, and to retain these customers by providing service in a way that favored better customers.

One way to identify and attract such customers was through the social networks of the local banker and the bank's board of directors, typically made up of luminaries from the local community.[49] Such networks allowed banks to identify and "acquire" high-value customers but also helped banks to make more informed lending decisions in many cases. Tacit knowledge about customers in a locale was available to a banker or a bank's board member who had a relationship with a customer. Alternatively, a banker might have a relationship with someone who, in turn, had a relationship with a potential customer.[50] In any case, banks and bankers that cultivated social networks of this sort would be advantaged when it came to having information about customers.[51] For example, in 1911 the First National Bank of Coal City was founded in Coal City, Illinois, by a group that included a mine superintendent, two farmers, a merchant, and a lawyer.[52] Collectively, this founding team had a network of relationships in each of Coal City's important industries, which in turn improved its access to information from those diverse sectors. Banks that built such a position within the local community would have access to information enabling them, presumably, to make better lending decisions.

Various organizational capabilities also improved a bank's ability to attract and retain more valuable customers. With products and most prices equal, customer service was a primary means to outcompete rival banks. This service typically included allowing for the suspension of standard operating procedures in the processing of transactions—as when for a valued customer no "hold" would be placed on a large check being deposited. Furthermore, preferential treatment by one's banker was a valued privilege in its own right—valuable both for the material advantage of gaining access to capital and for the social status implications of such treatment. Favorable treatment from the local banker was a form of payment, in terms of both financial and social exchange, made to especially valuable customers. Banks with greater capabilities in the area of selective customer service thus had a distinct advantage in competition under regulation.

Banks also varied in terms of the cost effectiveness of their managerial and organizational capabilities, with some doing a better job than others at reducing transaction and organizing costs at a given level of service.[53] Much of the operations side of a commercial bank concentrated on reducing transaction costs, improving organizational efficiencies, enhancing services, and creating and maintaining bureaucratic accountability—with any gains in such areas providing the bank with greater financial returns and more effective operations. Meanwhile, on the lending side of the bank, organizational effectiveness meant improving and rationalizing lending decisions, with the goal being to reduce loan losses while improving service to the "right" customers. In the twenty-first century, such practices are organized according to formulaic rules among very large banks using codified information. Local bankers in small, unit banks in the twentieth century typically relied much more on techniques developed tacitly through trial-and-error learning.[54]

Overall, competing within a logic of fiduciary effectiveness, banks engaged in Red Queen evolution would drive each other's adaptations, pushing one another to improve in terms of lending practices, customer service, organizational efficiency, and position in the community. As they competed over time, these banks might not seem to improve much relative to one another, but compared to banks facing little or no competition the differences should be apparent. These differences likely were embodied, at any given time, as better business practices or organizational attributes that would be difficult to measure systematically over a large number of organizations. According to my theory, however, these differences can be modeled by estimating the viability of organizations as a function of the degree to which they have been exposed to competition historically.

Bank Competition through Predation

Even as competition was driven by the logic of fiduciary effectiveness among twentieth-century banks, regulatory policies friendly to mergers and acquisitions, and cautious about new bank entry, allowed also for an alternative logic—that of predation. As discussed in chapter 2, this logic potentially operates in any organizational population but it is especially likely among banks given the importance of the control of capital, and of capitalists' interests in assuring returns to capital.[55] Especially in settings where a local bank has market power, local capital markets are not likely to be as efficient. In particular, banks could exercise their control of capital in two ways. First, they of course could exercise direct control of capital, and so wield power directly by granting and denying access to capital, and setting the terms for such access. Second, banks and bankers could wield indirect control by influencing others, who in turn affect outcomes in ways that benefit the bank.

Gaining and retaining power is a central concern in such a competition, so strategic actions by banks under this logic would aim at coopting or somehow eliminating threats to their dominance. Of the tools available to banks for such dominance, acquisition is likely among the most effective. By acquiring competitors, or by engaging in efforts to harm competitors and then acquiring them when they go into default, a bank could dominate or even monopolize its local market. In many cases, especially among high-profile mergers and acquisitions, banking and antitrust authorities both have scrutinized bank mergers and acquisitions for their antitrust implications.[56] Yet, over the period 1900–1993, 318 (nearly 11 percent) of Illinois commercial banks, excluding Chicago-based banks, had over their history acquired at least one rival bank, and some had acquired as many as seven. When one considers the legal prohibitions on branching over nearly that entire period in Illinois, and the relatively small size of most Illinois locales, this much merger and acquisition activity is substantial with respect to lessening the numbers of rivals faced in any given locale. Of course, these acquisitions may have been reasonable under a logic of fiduciary effectiveness, increasing scale economies and the like. Nonetheless, mergers and acquisitions are a way to eliminate one's competition.

Faced with the rising power of branch-bank systems and urban bankers, rural bankers—typically running unit banks—spent considerable time and effort trying to influence state and national regulatory policies in order to protect themselves. In particular, local bankers cultivated political networks within their states in an effort to maintain antibranching laws.[57] These actions typically were framed in populist terminology.[58] For instance, it is common to see references in historical documents to "country banks" and "country bankers," a mix of national and state banks united by their common rural locations and by their lack of ties to Federal Reserve banks.[59] One country banker, testifying before a Senate committee, conveyed a resolution from a meeting of country bankers that illustrates their identity claim: "Country banks, as distinguished from the banks in the fiscal centers, represent in number about 75 per cent of all the banks in the United States. They bear the burden of national prosperity in proportion to their numbers—legislation hostile to the welfare of American citizens, whether farmers, wage earners, or business men."[60] In this way, rural bankers saw themselves in opposition to expanding urban banking interests and emphasized their precarious position in debates over regulatory reform.

Contending Logics of Competition and Red Queen Competition among Illinois Banks

So U.S. commercial banking has seen, over the twentieth century, contending logics of competition. Notably, these logics mirror the twin images of banks and bankers that set the stage for bank regulation at the start of the twentieth century. Consistent with the importance of banking to capitalist development, U.S. banks often competed according to a competitive logic of fiduciary effectiveness. Within this logic, banks succeeded when they could offer better service, organize more effectively, better rationalize risk and return in lending decisions, and better respond to competition from other banks engaging in such adaptations. Meanwhile, many viewed these same institutions as members of an elite, wielding the power that comes with the control of capital. Consistent with this image, bank competition also could be described at times as abiding by a logic of institutional power, with banks growing through predation and sustaining their advantage by foreclosing markets to entry. That both of these logics can be seen to have operated in banking is not evidence of a factual disagreement among experts. Rather, these have been alternative logics playing out in parallel, each vying for prominence both in how competition is structured and regulated, and in how the winners and losers in competition are understood.

In the context of Illinois banking, these two logics serve as alternative criteria deciding winners and losers, and therefore as alternative lenses for understanding competition. As explained in chapter 2, multiple logics often arise when understanding competition in context. When alternative logics of competition come into contention, one's conclusions about competition depend not only on the facts at hand, but also and importantly on the logic employed to make sense of the facts. For example, I have explained that bank regulation put a premium on attracting and retaining wealthier customers and left banks to compete over those customers by offering them better customer service and preferred treatment in lending. Yet making sense of these different levels of service depends on which logic of competition one employs. Following the logic of fiduciary effectiveness, it is noteworthy that wealthier customers were paying more for the same banking products by virtue of keeping larger account balances without compensation. This difference explains why wealthier customers consistently were treated to better customer service.

These same actions have often been interpreted as evidence of a very different logic of competition—that of the unscrupulous robber baron arrogantly pursuing institutional power. Within the same establishment, two different customers would typically receive very different treatment, reflecting differences in their economic and social standing in the community. In light of the populist mistrust for bankers, such differences starkly reinforced the idea that wealth and status were given preferential treatment in the bank, and that the local banker was "bought" by the monied interests of the community. The view of the institutional power perspective, then, was reinforced by behaviors that—in fact—made sense just as well from a fiduciary effectiveness perspective. Ironically, it was the fixed pricing and product regulations meant to prevent bankers from unscrupulous behavior that led to much more visible, status-laden service discrimination.

So it is that, in any particular case, one can often reasonably view competition as making sense according to either or both of these logics. This holds for apparent predatory behavior among banks as well. For instance, by the 1990s the Petefish, Skiles, & Co. Bank of Virginia, Illinois, was the only commercial bank in town. Looking back through history, one sees that this bank once had rivals but acquired these rivals over time. Looking at this fact from the perspective of fiduciary effectiveness, one would note, for instance, that Petefish's takeover of the Farmer's National Bank of Virginia in 1918 increased Petefish's scale, likely resulting in a more efficient bank. Furthermore, Petefish's takeover of Centennial National Bank of Virginia in 1930 was during the great American banking crisis, as was their takeover of the liquidating People's Bank of Virginia in 1936. Arguably, such takeovers reflect Petefish's ability to survive market competition better than these failing rivals. By comparison, the institutional power perspective would note the fact that, in the wake of these three locally important acquisitions, Petefish, Skiles, & Co. was left as the only commercial bank in town—a monopolist. In this way, both logics can be used to interpret the same facts; the logic of fiduciary effectiveness seeing mergers and acquisitions as a means to efficient outcomes, and the logic of institutional power seeing them as evidence of organizations destroying one another in an attempt to dominate their local markets.

As explained in chapter 3, these two logics of competition have very different implications in light of Red Queen evolution. Because many banks competed within the logic of fiduciary effectiveness, the parameters of the Red Queen model should show that colocated banks improved each other's viability and made each other stronger competitors. By contrast, the logic of predation would show banks benefiting from current-time market power as they acquire their rivals. Over time, however, banks should suffer the more that they rely on predation to eliminate rivals—an effect that is likely to appear only after the current-time benefits of market power are controlled. In this way, both the competitive hysteresis hypothesis and the costly predation hypothesis pertain to twentieth-century commercial banks.

Specifying the Red Queen Model for Illinois Banks

To specify the Red Queen model for Illinois banks, the first step is to delineate the appropriate geographic unit of analysis. A main reason for studying Illinois commercial banking is that state's regulatory history over the twentieth century, which makes it possible to treat the 1,182 locales of Illinois as distinct markets. (See the appendix for more detail.) Illinois severely restricted branching over most of the twentieth century. The other American states permitted branching in various degrees and sometimes prohibited branching but still allowed "nonbranch branches" or bank holding companies as ways around these laws. The Illinois laws, by comparison, unambiguously defended the single-establishment unit bank until some restrictions were dropped in 1988, and unrestricted intrastate branching was not allowed until after 1993 (the last year of my data). This made it possible for me to measure each bank's geographic market for most of the century in terms of a single locale. Furthermore, the human ecology of Illinois, with its one massive metropolis and many hundreds of disparate communities, enabled me to treat the various locations as independent markets. Specifically, referring to bankers' directories from over the century, I defined each market as a banking market if bankers did so. This approach resulted in a fine-grained definition of the state's many banking markets, including both incorporated and unincorporated places, all of which stood out as distinct banking markets in the opinion of those who tracked the industry over the years. Figures 5.1 through 5.4 describe these banks over time.

As explained in chapter 4, the founding and failure models are allowed to be duration dependent, and they also require that I specify the effects of broad environmental conditions as well as the effects of the banking population at any given point in time. For the failure models, I also must specify the effects of organizational characteristics. (For a detailed explanation of the measurement and coding of all variables, see the appendix.) As for environmental effects, I allow the viability of banks to depend on the size, and change in size, of the human population in a given locale. Also, the degree of urbanization of the human population is measured. The

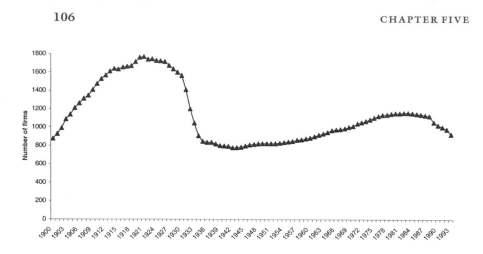

Figure 5.1. Commercial banks in Illinois (excluding Chicago).

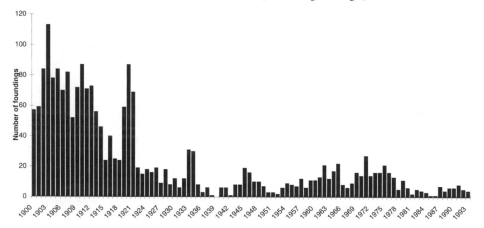

Figure 5.2. Bank foundings in Illinois (excluding Chicago).

broader organizational context in a given bank's environment is measured in terms of the density of manufacturing establishments, retail establishments, wholesale establishments, and farms in a bank's county. Wealth and income are included, too, in terms of the (indexed) wage per worker in a bank's county, and the average farm value in a bank's county. Finally, the age of each banking market is included in all models, measured in years starting with the date of founding of the first bank in a given locale.

Ecological effects among banks are measured in terms of the density of banks in a given locale, as well as an indicator variable in the founding models for whether a given banking market has any competition. This approach allows for a distinct difference in competition with the entry of the first rival in a given locale, important in light of the many years of

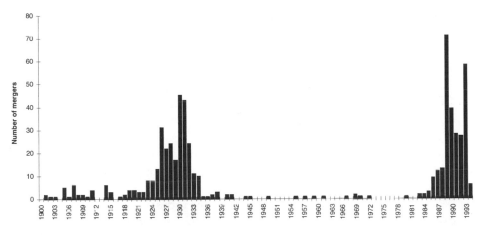

Figure 5.3. Bank mergers in Illinois (excluding Chicago).

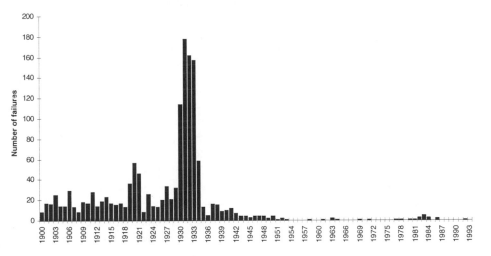

Figure 5.4. Bank failures in Illinois (excluding Chicago).

local-monopoly banking observed in these data. (In the failure models, monopolization is measured at the organization level, in terms of the more general measure of a bank's local asset share.) Further, the models include the natural logarithm of "nonlocal" density—the number of banks in other locales. This formulation follows earlier work, in which the legitimating effects of organizations of a given form increase as a logarithmic function of nonlocal density.[61] The density of banks at the time of an organization's birth is included in the failure models, following the theory of "density delay," which predicts that organizations founded in dense contexts suffer lower viability throughout their lives.[62] The population mass of the local banking market, measured in terms of the aggregate bank assets in a given locale, is specified in the natural logarithm to allow greater effects with the initial growth of the banking market. This measure allows for competition to vary with the sizes of banks in a given locale.[63] Finally, the one-year lagged numbers of bank failures, foundings, and acquisitions are included, in case there are distinct effects of such population dynamics on failure and founding rates—again following the existing literature in organizational ecology.

The failure models control for size-dependence by including the natural logarithm of each bank's assets in a given year, although this variable is measured in (roughly) five-year panels so it was necessary to interpolate linearly to obtain values for intervening years (as described in the appendix). Piecewise duration periods were established for both founding and failure models, delineated as fined-grained as possible given the observed frequency of events. At the organization level, that meant one- or two-year intervals for very young organizations, five-year intervals for intermediate ages, and ten-year intervals and greater for especially old organizations. For the founding models, it was possible to specify one-year intervals throughout.

A large number of calendar periods were specified for both the founding and failure models, in an attempt to capture some of the effects of the many normative, legal, and market changes occurring in the commercial banking market over the twentieth century. Each of the first two decades was given its own effect. An effect for the 1920s was created up to but not including 1929, so that the panic and upheaval of 1929–1932 could have its own distinct effect. Much of the remaining Depression era was given a period effect, beginning in 1933 with the beginning of the Glass-Steagall era of regulation and ending in 1939. A distinct effect was created for the period 1940–1945. Decade-by-decade effects were included for the second half of the century.

The hypotheses were tested in terms of both founding and failure by including in the models the hysteretic effects described in chapter 4. This approach required that "recent" and "distant-past" historical competition be distinguished. I established this distinction by discounting a given year's rivalry by $1/\sqrt{\delta}$, where δ is the time from the present to a given year in the past, before entering that year's rivalry into an organization's recent competitive experience score. Distant-past rivalry was then defined as the difference between total (organization-years of) historical rivalry and recent-past historical rivalry. The square root form was used to attenuate the speed of discounting, but in general the results turn out not to be sensitive to the particular function of δ used in the discount rate.

Estimates of the Bank Founding Models

The collection and structure of the data used for the bank founding analysis are described in the appendix. These data include a history for each of the 1,182 locales in Illinois where a bank existed at any time from 1900 to 1993, excluding Chicago. As described in chapter 4, this fine-grained geographic detail permits the analysis of founding rates in terms of the interarrival times of founding events within each locale. So the analyzable data are in the form of pooled event-history data covering 72,515 local market-years. Over these histories, 1,360 bank founding events are analyzed—excluding from analysis the first founding event in each locale as explained in the appendix. Table 5.1 describes this dataset.

Estimates of various specifications of the founding rate models for Illinois banks are shown in table 5.2. Seven models are shown in order to investigate the robustness of the results across different specifications. Model $\lambda_B 1$ is a baseline model, including all control variables and duration effects, as well as the effects of current-time competition.[64] Model $\lambda_B 2$ then includes the sum of organization-years of rivalry faced historically by incumbent banks alive in a given year ($\Sigma_k T_k$ in chapter 4). To test the Competitive Hysteresis Hypothesis and the Competency-Trap Hypothesis, Model $\lambda_B 3$ disaggregates $\Sigma_k T_k$ into two terms, one for recent competitive experience and another for distant-past competitive experience as described above. Models $\lambda_B 4$, $\lambda_B 5$, and $\lambda_B 6$ include, separately and together, average Gini coefficients measuring the degree of inequality of the historical competition faced (on average) by incumbents alive in a given year. As explained in chapter 4, these terms measure the inequality of the density of competitors over time and the inequality of the sizes of rival founding cohorts over time, thus allowing for two different approaches to testing the Myopic Learning Hypothesis. Finally, Model $\lambda_B 7$ is a re-estimate of the full model, $\lambda_B 6$, to investigate the robustness of this model to a specification that includes the effect of the aggregate ages of incumbents. This specification can reveal whether competitive intensity increases with age, regardless of an organization's competitive experience[65]—although an earlier investigation of these data did not reveal such an age effect.[66] All models include the cumulative hazard of bank takeover, as of a given year in a given locale, in order to test the Costly Predation Hypothesis.

Competition—Current Time and Hysteretic Effects

Among commercial banks in Illinois, Red Queen competition turns out to generate a significant barrier to entry. In the full model, $\lambda_B 6$, the coefficient of $\Sigma_k T_k$ is estimated to equal −0.0061 (when estimated for recent

TABLE 5.1
Description of the Founding Data for Commercial Banks in Illinois, 1900–1993

Independent Variable	Min	Max	Mean	Std Dev
Cumulative hazard of bank failure in locale	0	3.16	0.49	0.61
Cumulative hazard of bank takeover in locale	0	1.5	0.08	0.21
Natural log of bank assets in locale	9.69	21.23	15.75	1.65
1-year change in log of bank assets in locale	−4.16	3.73	0.03	0.15
Nonmonopolized local banking market	0	1	0.99	0.02
Number of banks in locale	0	14	1.44	0.91
Log of the number of banks in other Illinois locales	6.63	7.45	7.02	0.26
Σ past organization-years of rivalry faced by incumbents	0	3,557	49	168
Σ recent-past org-years of rivalry faced by incumbents	0	1,223	13	46
Σ distant-past org-years of rivalry faced by incumbents	0	2,671	35	124
Inequality of past rivalry faced by incumbents (average gini)	0	0.98	0.18	0.26
Inequality of past rival cohorts faced by incumbents (average gini)	0	0.65	0.08	0.13
Age of local market	0	148	51	31
Population in locale/1,000	0.016	139	4.37	10.39
1-year change in population in locale/1,000	−1.11	5.32	0.05	0.20
Proportion of population urban in county	0	1.008	0.43	0.28
Number of manufacturing ests. in county/1,000	0.001	19.99	0.84	2.81
Number of farms in county/1,000	0.161	5.82	2.11	1.08
Number of retail ests. in county/1,000	0.013	55.69	3.21	10.17
Number of wholesale ests. in county/1,000	0	11.27	0.71	2.38
Indexed average value of farms in county/1,000	0.006	4.36	0.24	0.29
Indexed wage per worker in county	0	0.42	0.01	0.01
Lagged number of bank foundings in locale	0	3	0.02	0.17
Lagged number of bank failures in locale	0	3	0.01	0.12
Lagged number of bank takeovers in locale	0	3	0.006	0.08

historical competitive experience). At the mean observed value of this variable (13.44), this implies a multiplier of the founding rate of 0.92—meaning an 8 percent reduction in the founding rate on average due to recent competitive experience by incumbents. Thus these models demonstrate support for the Competitive Hysteresis Hypothesis in founding rates among Illinois banks.

Although exposure to recent competition increased barriers to entry among incumbent banks, this effect reverses entirely when competition was in the more distant past. This evidence in support of the Competency-

TABLE 5.2
Founding Rate of Commercial Banks in Illinois, 1900–1993

				Models			
Independent Variable	(λ_B1)	(λ_B2)	(λ_B3)	(λ_B4)	(λ_B5)	(λ_B6)	(λ_B7)
Cumulative hazard of bank failure in locale	0.0828 (0.0706)	0.0761 (0.0708)	−0.0559 (0.0716)	0.0096 (0.0716)	0.0246 (0.0714)	−0.0107 (0.0719)	−0.0239 (0.0832)
Cumulative hazard of bank takeover in locale	0.0842 (0.1766)	0.0741 (0.1785)	0.0801 (0.1770)	0.1732 (0.1755)	0.3806** (0.1720)	0.4158** (0.1724)	0.4054** (0.1755)
Natural log of bank assets in locale	1.014** (0.0356)	1.032** (0.0361)	1.040** (0.0362)	1.076** (0.0347)	1.083** (0.0348)	1.107** (0.0339)	1.108** (0.0340)
1-year change in log of bank assets in locale	−0.7707** (0.1878)	−0.7633** (0.1885)	−0.7456** (0.1882)	−0.8000** (0.1929)	−0.8326** (0.1808)	−0.8686** (0.1874)	−0.8703** (0.1876)
Nonmonopolized local banking market	−2.921** (0.2499)	−2.869** (0.2504)	−2.817** (0.2519)	−2.808** (0.2515)	−3.029** (0.2527)	−3.008** (0.2528)	−3.021** (0.2559)
Number of banks in locale	−0.5099** (0.0393)	−0.5724** (0.0460)	−0.6436** (0.0597)	−0.5236** (0.0609)	−0.2184** (0.0647)	−0.1548** (0.0668)	−0.1454** (0.0729)
Log of the number of banks in other Illinois locales	−0.5582** (0.2787)	−0.5619** (0.2787)	−0.5546** (0.2786)	−0.5568** (0.2786)	−0.5591** (0.2808)	−0.5420* (0.2805)	−0.5392* (0.2806)
Σ past organization-years of rivalry faced by incumbents		0.0005** (0.0002)					
Σ recent-past org-years of rivalry faced by incumbents			0.0036** (0.0016)	0.0013 (0.0018)	−0.0047** (0.0018)	−0.0061** (0.0019)	−0.0062** (0.0019)
Σ distant-past org-years of rivalry faced by incumbents			−0.0005 (0.0006)	−0.0003 (0.0006)	0.0018** (0.0006)	0.0018** (0.0006)	0.0019** (0.0007)
Inequality of past rivalry faced by incumbents (average gini)				−3.131** (0.2577)		−2.456** (0.2590)	−2.463** (0.2596)
Inequality of past rival cohorts faced by incumbents (average gini)					−6.086** (0.4420)	−5.280** (0.4575)	−5.241** (0.4734)

TABLE 5.2 (*cont.*)
Founding Rate of Commercial Banks in Illinois, 1900–1993

Independent Variable	Models						
	(λ_B1)	(λ_B2)	(λ_B3)	(λ_B4)	(λ_B5)	(λ_B6)	(λ_B7)
Σ ages of incumbents							-0.0006
							(0.0020)
Age of local market	-0.0209**	-0.0207**	-0.0196**	-0.0138**	-0.0161**	-0.0123**	-0.0117**
	(0.0022)	(0.0022)	(0.0023)	(0.0024)	(0.0024)	(0.0024)	(0.0030)
Population in locale/1,000	0.0245**	0.0198**	0.0219**	0.0197**	0.0220**	0.0198**	0.0197**
	(0.0026)	(0.0032)	(0.0034)	(0.0033)	(0.0034)	(0.0034)	(0.0034)
1-year change in pop. in locale/1,000	0.2958**	0.3311**	0.2940**	0.2984**	0.2072**	0.2195**	0.2184**
	(0.0734)	(0.0756)	(0.0781)	(0.0771)	(0.0806)	(0.0798)	(0.0798)
Proportion of the pop. urban in county	-0.6578**	-0.6683**	-0.6938**	-0.7832**	-0.6242**	-0.7014**	-0.6988**
	(0.1622)	(0.1617)	(0.1617)	(0.1639)	(0.1678)	(0.1690)	(0.1691)
Number of manufacturing ests. in county/1,000	-0.0472	-0.0505	-0.0477	-0.0471	-0.0700*	-0.0651	-0.0660
	(0.0421)	(0.0418)	(0.0418)	(0.0419)	(0.0424)	(0.0423)	(0.0424)
Number of farms in county/1,000	0.0853**	0.0859**	0.0871**	0.0832**	0.0865**	0.0814**	0.0814**
	(0.0346)	(0.0346)	(0.0346)	(0.0347)	(0.0349)	(0.0349)	(0.0349)
Number of retail ests. in county/1,000	0.0154	0.0166*	0.0166*	0.0178*	0.0179*	0.0180*	0.0181*
	(0.0100)	(0.0100)	(0.0100)	(0.0101)	(0.0102)	(0.0102)	(0.0102)
Number of wholesale ests. in county/1,000	-0.0679*	-0.0603	-0.0639*	-0.0525	-0.0316	-0.0241	-0.0235
	(0.0374)	(0.0374)	(0.0374)	(0.0373)	(0.0375)	(0.0374)	(0.0375)
Indexed average value of farms in county/1,000	0.2328**	0.2502**	0.2495**	0.3356**	0.2884**	0.3454**	0.3449**
	(0.0955)	(0.0960)	(0.0961)	(0.0956)	(0.0969)	(0.0962)	(0.0962)
Indexed wage per worker in county	-6.433	-5.890	-5.546	-8.457	-14.16	-16.26	-16.30
	(9.702)	(9.305)	(8.945)	(9.606)	(12.46)	(12.54)	(12.54)

TABLE 5.2 (cont.)
Founding Rate of Commercial Banks in Illinois, 1900–1993

Independent Variable	Models						
	(λ_B1)	(λ_B2)	(λ_B3)	(λ_B4)	(λ_B5)	(λ_B6)	(λ_B7)
Lagged number of bank foundings in locale	-3.263** (0.2139)	-3.291** (0.2133)	-3.287** (0.2134)	-3.160** (0.2142)	-3.510** (0.2155)	-3.382** (0.2163)	-3.375** (0.2176)
Lagged number of bank failures in locale	0.3465** (0.1209)	0.3115** (0.1209)	0.2813** (0.1216)	0.3311** (0.1214)	0.4968** (0.1207)	0.5076** (0.1209)	0.5053** (0.1210)
Lagged number of bank takeovers in locale	0.2756 (0.1884)	0.2247 (0.1881)	0.2012 (0.1878)	0.2376 (0.1873)	0.4310** (0.1814)	0.4231** (0.1825)	0.4212** (0.1826)
Calendar period							
1910–19	-0.3746** (0.1275)	-0.3736** (0.1275)	-0.3737** (0.1276)	-0.3764** (0.1279)	-0.3902** (0.1275)	-0.4016** (0.1278)	-0.4029** (0.1279)
1920–28	-0.7605** (0.1560)	-0.7626** (0.1560)	-0.7601** (0.1558)	-0.7648** (0.1562)	-0.7976** (0.1571)	-0.8092** (0.1573)	-0.8102** (0.1573)
1929–32	-2.051** (0.1953)	-2.064** (0.1954)	-2.079** (0.1957)	-2.044** (0.1955)	-2.013** (0.1947)	-2.008** (0.1949)	-2.008** (0.1949)
1933–39	-2.474** (0.1772)	-2.511** (0.1779)	-2.544** (0.1792)	-2.418** (0.1769)	-2.413** (0.1794)	-2.348** (0.1779)	-2.351** (0.1782)
1940–45	-4.667** (0.3549)	-4.708** (0.3549)	-4.722** (0.3548)	-4.587** (0.3542)	-4.624** (0.3565)	-4.558** (0.3563)	-4.563** (0.3567)
1946–59	-3.884** (0.2140)	-3.943** (0.2145)	-3.944** (0.2136)	-3.864** (0.2136)	-3.895** (0.2203)	-3.869** (0.2203)	-3.872** (0.2205)
1960–69	-2.984** (0.2106)	-3.039** (0.2100)	-3.061** (0.2087)	-3.111** (0.2109)	-3.106** (0.2272)	-3.162** (0.2274)	-3.163** (0.2275)
1970–79	-3.167** (0.2309)	-3.234** (0.2305)	-3.267** (0.2289)	-3.453** (0.2346)	-3.347** (0.2532)	-3.508** (0.2550)	-3.509** (0.2551)
1980–93	-4.094** (0.2414)	-4.159** (0.2417)	-4.198** (0.2409)	-4.330** (0.2426)	-4.304** (0.2578)	-4.425** (0.2573)	-4.426** (0.2573)

TABLE 5.2 (*cont.*)
Founding Rate of Commercial Banks in Illinois, 1900–1993

Independent Variable	Models						
	$(\lambda_B 1)$	$(\lambda_B 2)$	$(\lambda_B 3)$	$(\lambda_B 4)$	$(\lambda_B 5)$	$(\lambda_B 6)$	$(\lambda_B 7)$
Duration							
0–1 year	−6.578**	−6.720**	−6.838**	−7.666**	−7.760**	−8.442**	−8.483**
	(2.046)	(2.047)	(2.045)	(2.030)	(2.049)	(2.045)	(2.049)
1–2 years	−10.33**	−10.51**	−10.64**	−11.12**	−11.19**	−11.65**	−11.68**
	(2.047)	(2.049)	(2.048)	(2.040)	(2.048)	(2.043)	(2.046)
2–3 years	−10.23**	−10.42**	−10.55**	−11.00**	−11.14**	−11.57**	−11.60**
	(2.046)	(2.049)	(2.048)	(2.040)	(2.050)	(2.045)	(2.047)
3–4 years	−10.12**	−10.31**	−10.45**	−10.90**	−11.05**	−11.47**	−11.51**
	(2.048)	(2.050)	(2.050)	(2.042)	(2.052)	(2.047)	(2.049)
4–5 years	−10.23**	−10.42**	−10.56**	−10.99**	−11.17**	−11.58**	−11.61**
	(2.050)	(2.053)	(2.052)	(2.044)	(2.055)	(2.050)	(2.052)
5–6 years	−9.979**	−10.18**	−10.32**	−10.76**	−10.99**	−11.39**	−11.42**
	(2.048)	(2.050)	(2.049)	(2.041)	(2.052)	(2.047)	(2.049)
6–7 years	−10.02**	−10.23**	−10.38**	−10.81**	−11.07**	−11.46**	−11.49**
	(2.043)	(2.046)	(2.045)	(2.037)	(2.049)	(2.043)	(2.045)
7–8 years	−9.875**	−10.09**	−10.24**	−10.67**	−10.95**	−11.33**	−11.36**
	(2.039)	(2.042)	(2.042)	(2.033)	(2.045)	(2.039)	(2.041)
8–9 years	−9.839**	−10.05**	−10.20**	−10.63**	−10.94**	−11.32**	−11.35**
	(2.039)	(2.042)	(2.042)	(2.033)	(2.046)	(2.039)	(2.041)
9–10 years	−9.719**	−9.931**	−10.08**	−10.53**	−10.86**	−11.24**	−11.27**
	(2.036)	(2.040)	(2.039)	(2.031)	(2.042)	(2.037)	(2.039)
11–12 years	−10.12**	−10.33**	−10.48**	−10.95**	−11.26**	−11.66**	−11.69**
	(2.039)	(2.041)	(2.041)	(2.032)	(2.045)	(2.039)	(2.041)

TABLE 5.2 (*cont.*)
Founding Rate of Commercial Banks in Illinois, 1900–1993

	Models						
Independent Variable	($\lambda_B 1$)	($\lambda_B 2$)	($\lambda_B 3$)	($\lambda_B 4$)	($\lambda_B 5$)	($\lambda_B 6$)	($\lambda_B 7$)
12–13 years	−9.950**	−10.16**	−10.31**	−10.79**	−11.09**	−11.49**	−11.52**
	(2.038)	(2.041)	(2.041)	(2.031)	(2.044)	(2.038)	(2.040)
13–14 years	−9.794**	−10.01**	−10.16**	−10.65**	−10.96**	−11.36**	−11.39**
	(2.042)	(2.045)	(2.045)	(2.036)	(2.048)	(2.042)	(2.044)
14–15 years	−10.07**	−10.28**	−10.44**	−10.94**	−11.25**	−11.66**	−11.69**
	(2.047)	(2.049)	(2.049)	(2.040)	(2.053)	(2.047)	(2.048)
15–16 years	−9.789**	−10.01**	−10.16**	−10.67**	−10.97**	−11.40**	−11.42**
	(2.047)	(2.050)	(2.049)	(2.041)	(2.054)	(2.048)	(2.050)
16+ years	−9.747**	−9.980**	−10.14**	−10.72**	−10.91**	−11.39**	−11.42**
	(2.038)	(2.040)	(2.040)	(2.032)	(2.044)	(2.039)	(2.040)
Log likelihood	−2257.05	−2253.82	−2252.08	−2147.52	−2124.11	−2064.79	−2064.74
(df)	(45)	(46)	(47)	(48)	(48)	(49)	(50)

Note: Data include 1,360 foundings in any of 1,182 local markets over 72,515 market-years. Other variables are included, as shown below.

* p < .10
** p < .05. Standard errors are in parentheses.

Trap Hypothesis is unambiguous, estimated at 0.0018 in model $\lambda_B 6$. At the average observed level of distant-past historical competition among incumbents in the data (35.83), this estimate implies a multiplier of about 1.07. Thus, founding rates were 7 percent higher among Illinois commercial banks due to incumbent banks' *outdated* competitive experience. Although the Red Queen operated in these data to increase barriers to entry at first, over time the lessons learned by these banks appear to have led to a competency trap, inviting new entrants into contexts where incumbents had outdated competitive experience.

Aside from these historical competition effects, barriers to entry among banks were higher, as well, in local markets with more current-time competition. The biggest marginal effect on current-time competition is seen in the comparison of monopolized and nonmonopolized markets. According to the estimates from model $\lambda_B 6$, founding rates in nonmonopolized markets were 95 percent lower than those in monopolized markets. (The nonmonopoly coefficient -3.008 implies a multiplier of $\exp[-3.008]$, which is approximately equal to 0.05, meaning that nonmonopolized market founding rates were 0.05 of the founding rates in monopolized markets.) Additional increases in the density of competition also decreased the founding rate, although the change is an order of magnitude lower for the addition of competitors after the first rival.

Density in other locales also decreased the founding rate, implying some degree of cross-market competition that I did not predict. Most ecological models find that nonlocal density corresponds to increases in the founding rate, possibly reflecting increased legitimacy of an organizational form with increases in numbers. The countervailing effect of competition with increasing numbers in more distant markets is less apparent in most studies that are able to identify this distinction.[67] All in all, current-time competition was a strong contributor to entry barriers in the Illinois commercial banking markets.

The Myopic Learning and Costly Predation Hypotheses

Unexpectedly, the effects of inequality in organizations' historical experience decreased bank founding rates in Illinois. Drawing on organizational learning theory—and in particular on concerns about myopic learning from the work of March and his colleagues—I expected to see higher barriers to entry in contexts where organizations had more equal historical exposure to competition. In contexts where exposure to competition had been concentrated into only a few years—or a few cohorts of rivals—learning would be more myopic among incumbents and so barriers to entry would be lower. I found the opposite pattern, however. Models $\lambda_B 4$ through $\lambda_B 6$ show strong negative effects for the gini coefficients indicating inequality in historical experience—both for the past rivalry faced by incumbents and the past cohorts of rivals faced by incumbents—and including these terms dramatically improves the fit of these models.[68]

Why would founding rates be higher in contexts marked by more equal spreading over time of historical competition? One possible explanation might be that contexts with equal spreading of competition have a higher carrying capacity for banks, but that my other control variables did not fully capture this higher carrying capacity. Such contexts would be generally more inviting, leading to higher entry rates over time and also to ongoing (and so more evenly spread) entries. By the same thinking, contexts that experience foundings only in infrequent waves might do so because they are less attractive as banking markets. In any case, I do not find evidence to support the Myopic Learning Hypothesis affecting incumbent's susceptibility to new entries among Illinois banks. Rather, I find strong evidence that founding rates are lower in contexts marked by unequal distributions, over time, of organizations and founding cohorts.

Thus far the models have focused on competitive hysteresis, important to the extent that banks competed according to a logic of fiduciary effectiveness. But, as discussed above, often banks have attempted to shape whether, or at least with whom, they compete. In these instances, banks could sometimes eliminate rivals through merger and acquisition. Furthermore, if mergers and acquisitions for the purpose of eliminating competition are targeted at precisely those rivals that would have caused the organization the most problems in competition in the market—and so would have stimulated the most development in a Red Queen—then such predation would lead organizations to develop less than would otherwise have been the case. These arguments are the essence of the Costly Predation Hypothesis.

To investigate this hypothesis among Illinois banks, the founding models in table 5.2 include as a covariate the Nelson-Aalen estimate of the cumulative hazard of bank disappearance in a given locale over time, distinguishing between disappearance due to failure and disappearance due to merger and acquisition. Recall from chapter 4 that increases in the cumulative hazard with respect to failure can be expected to correspond to decreasing frailty among survivors. This "pure selection" process implies increasing competitiveness among incumbent survivors—that is, lower founding rates—as the cumulative hazard with respect to failure increases. The Costly Predation Hypothesis, by contrast, shifts our focus to the cumulative hazard of merger and acquisition and predicts that locales with more of a history of merger and acquisition will have higher founding rates. The estimates in model $\lambda_B 6$ support this prediction. Meanwhile, the cumulative hazard of failure in a locale does not have a significant effect in any of these founding model specifications.

The Importance of Historical Timing

Comparing across the founding models, estimates of the historical competition effects are biased unless the timing of historical experience is distinguished. Because recent and distant-past historical experience have opposite effects, failure to distinguish timing apparently leads to the suppression of their effects. Most notably, models that omit measures of the dispersion of organizations and foundings over history show *higher* founding rates in locales with greater recent competitive experience. This pattern, then, is completely reversed once measures of dispersion are included in the model. The fact that suppression effects operate when models do not include historical timing raises a caution. One should be sure to specify the historical timing and dispersion of competitive experience when estimating these models.

This pattern of results should make one cautious also when interpreting the theory of Red Queen competition. Many scholars think of this model of competition as being about "what does not kill you makes you stronger." In fact, the competency trap findings suggest otherwise: In the long run, most banks' experience becomes outdated. Having learned from this (outdated) experience, organizations will have become outdated due to their involvement in Red Queen competition. Of course, it is possible that new competition will generate a strong enough recency effect to offset this competency trap, but in the long run this experience, too, will become outdated. In short, among organizations the Red Queen is not about an endless drive to improvement, but rather is about organizational learning—for better and (in changing conditions) for worse.

Other Founding Model Effects

Table 5.2 also shows three distinct effects of time on the bank founding rate, duration (since the last founding), market age, and calendar periods. Comparing the piecewise duration effects reveals an initial decline in the founding rate after one year with a relatively constant rate thereafter. Given that most founding models are estimated on count data—as I do in the analysis of computer manufacturer foundings in chapter 6, for instance—these findings are some of the few estimates available of duration dependence in organizational foundings rates. Count models typically require that one assumes a constant rate with respect to duration. That assumption turns out to be reasonable according to my findings here, given the mostly constant rate at least after the first year. Market age was consistently and significantly negative in all models. Table 5.2 also includes various calendar period effects, all large and significantly negative compared to the high founding rate observed in the comparison period 1900–1909. The substantial differences from period to period illustrate the importance of including the different historical eras when modeling bank founding rates.

Failures and foundings, each lagged one year, significantly affect the founding rate, although lagged takeovers do not. The effect of failures on foundings is positive and significant, consistent with studies claiming that a "renewal process" operates in population dynamics—where organizational failures release resources that are recombined in new foundings thereafter.[69] Lagged foundings are negatively related to the founding rate, suggesting a negative first-order autoregressive process in foundings. This process would be consistent with a queuing process wherein a "stock" of nascent foundings is available over any given (multiyear) period, so that a surge of foundings in one year depletes the stock of nascent founding available in the following year.

The sizes of banks in a locale affected founding rates in contradictory ways. On the one hand, the level of bank assets in a locale increased the bank founding rate. Given that numbers of banks is separately controlled in the model, this finding implies positive "mass dependence," in that founding rates were higher where banks were larger.[70] This finding could reflect, however, an effect of market size on foundings, with larger markets inviting bank foundings, other things being equal. On the other hand, the growth of incumbent banks decreased the founding rate, consistent with the idea that growth and founding are competing processes.[71] Thus, it appears that organizing capacity in banking could grow through either the expansion of existing organizations or the creation of new ones.

Exogenous factors affected bank founding rates in two distinct ways. More bank foundings occurred in locations with more people or more retail establishments—each an indicator of the size of the consumer and business retail banking markets, respectively. Meanwhile, the other exogenous variables affected the bank founding rate in a manner consistent with the idea that urbanization led to fewer but larger banks compared to rural areas: Urbanization depressed founding rates, while numbers and the value of farms increased founding rates. In this way, the identity distinction drawn among bankers between city and country banks appears to be mirrored by distinct urban and rural banking niches.

Estimates of the Bank Failure Models

The construction of the bank failure analysis dataset is described in the appendix. These data include the life histories of the 2,970 banks that operated at any time in Illinois from 1900 to 1993 (not including Chicago), 1,444 of which failed at some point over that period. The life of each organization was divided into yearly segments, so that the independent variables could be updated over time. Banks entered the data in the year of their birth, or as of 1900 for banks founded prior to that year. Banks then left the data upon failure, or when they were merged or acquired, although only outright failures are treated as such for purposes of the event being analyzed. Banks that continued through 1993 were treated as right censored. This procedure resulted in 108,209 organization-years of data, as described in table 5.3.

The estimates of various specifications of bank failure models are shown in table 5.4. Each model extends over all five parts of the table. In all, there are seven (7) models shown, each estimated on the same data but varying slightly in specification. The model specifications differ only in their treatment of the various effects implied by the theory of Red Queen competition, as reported in the first part of the table. A variety of models are shown in order to check for robustness as the various hypotheses are tested. Models r_B1 and r_B2 include competitive experience and rivals' competitive experience, to test the Competitive Hysteresis Hypothesis. Model r_B2 is the same as model r_B1, except that it excludes the number of distinct rivals faced by the organization over its history, in order to test the Costly Adaptation Hypothesis. Models r_B3 through r_B6 then separate the various competitive experience effects according to the recency of experience, allowing for tests of the Competency-Trap Hypothesis. Model r_B7 includes the gini coefficients measuring the inequality of an organization's historical exposure to competition, relevant to the Myopic Learning Hypothesis. Finally, all models include the cumulative hazard of bank failure in the locale over the bank's history to date and the bank's cumulative hazard of acquiring its rivals, to test the Costly Predation Hypothesis.

Competition—Current Time and Hysteretic Effects

First, across all the failure models, I find a consistent negative effect of an organization's competitive experience on its failure rate. A bank that experienced more competition over its history was less likely to fail. Meanwhile, the models also show across all specifications that a bank's rivals generated stronger competition if those rivals endured more competitive experience. These findings support the Competitive Hysteresis Hypothesis.

The models show that banks with more exposure to historical competition were more likely to survive, and meanwhile their rivals generated stronger competition if they had been exposed to more competition over their histories. These dual effects suggest that among these commercial banks both viability and competitiveness increased over time according to the Red Queen. Specifically, the estimates of model r_B2 imply that each

TABLE 5.3
Description of the Failure Data for Commercial Banks in Illinois, 1900–1993

Independent Variable	Min	Max	Mean	Std Dev
Cumulative hazard of failure in locale over organization's history	0	2.06	0.13	0.27
Cumulative hazard of acquisition of rivals in locale by organization over its history	0	2	0.05	0.21
Cumulative hazard of acquisition of rivals in locale by other local rivals over organization's history	0	1.83	0.03	0.13
Σ past rivalry faced by organization	0	841	33.23	63.58
Σ recent-past rivalry faced by organization	0	148	9.06	14.88
Σ distant-past rivalry faced by organization	0	700	24.16	49.64
Σ past rival organizations faced by organization	0	26	1.68	2.53
Inequality of past rivalry faced by organization (gini)	0	0.9889	0.18	0.27
Inequality of past cohorts faced by organization (gini)	0	0.7483	0.1192	0.17
Σ past rivalry faced by organization's competitors	0	3,509	96.38	302.14
Σ recent-past rivalry faced by organization's competitors	0	1,194	28.13	87.67
Σ distant-past rivalry faced by organization's competitors	0	2,581	68.24	216.99
Number of banks in locale at organization's birth	0	13	0.76	1.30
Log of the number of rival bank in other Illinois locales	6.63	7.45	7.05	0.26
Number of rival banks in locale	0	13	1.021	1.58
Bank's share of local market	0.0010	1	0.6840	0.33
Lagged number of bank foundings in locale	0	3	0.0421	0.21
Lagged number of bank failures in locale	0	3	0.0174	0.14
Lagged number of bank takeovers in locale	0	3	0.01	0.11
Age of local market	0	148	54.15	32.62
Population in locale/1,000	0.016	139.42	8.62	17.87
1-year change in population in locale/1,000	−1.41	34.76	0.1081	0.37
Proportion of the population urban in county	0	1.0088	0.46	0.28
Number of manufacturing establishments in county/1,000	0.001	19.99	0.93	2.93
Number of farms in county/1,000	0.161	5.827	2.13	1.10
Number of retail establishments in county/1,000	0.013	55.696	3.48	10.52
Number of wholesale establishments in county/1,000	0	11.278	0.7922	2.49
Indexed average value of farms in county/1,000	0.0063	4.3673	0.2493	0.30
Indexed wage per worker in county	0	0.3715	0.0118	0.0095

TABLE 5.4
Models of the Failure Rates of Commercial Banks in Illinois, 1900–1993

Independent Variable	Models						
	(r_B1)	(r_B2)	(r_B3)	(r_B4)	(r_B5)	(r_B6)	(r_B7)
Cumulative hazard of failure in locale over organization's history	0.3432** (0.1748)	0.2625* (0.1389)	0.2297* (0.1390)	0.2696* (0.1388)	0.2504* (0.1378)	0.2589* (0.1396)	0.4141** (0.1510)
Cumulative hazard of acquisition of rivals in locale by organization over its history	0.5679** (0.1390)	0.5288** (0.1291)	0.5276** (0.1294)	0.5286** (0.1290)	0.5207** (0.1290)	0.5282** (0.1292)	0.6487** (0.1372)
Cumulative hazard of acquisition of rivals in locale by other local rivals over organization's history	−0.1589 (0.3212)	−0.2215 (0.3115)	−0.2917 (0.3136)	−0.2077 (0.3109)	−0.1937 (0.3060)	−0.2408 (0.3135)	−0.0956 (0.3118)
Σ past rivalry faced by organization	−0.0030* (0.0017)	−0.0038** (0.0013)			−0.0032** (0.0012)	−0.0039** (0.0013)	−0.0044** (0.0014)
Σ recent-past rivalry faced by organization			−0.0127** (0.0053)				
Σ distant-past rivalry faced by organization				−0.0052** (0.0017)			
Σ past rival organizations faced by organization	−0.0426 (0.0565)						
Inequality of past rivalry faced by organization (gini)							−0.2908** (0.1473)
Inequality of past cohorts faced by organization (gini)							−0.2956 (0.2525)
Σ past rivalry faced by organization's competitors	0.0020** (0.0003)	0.0021** (0.0002)	0.0020** (0.0002)	0.0021** (0.0002)			0.0020** (0.0002)
Σ recent-past rivalry faced by organization's competitors					0.0104** (0.0009)		
Σ distant-past rivalry faced by organization's competitors						0.0024** (0.0003)	

TABLE 5.4 (cont.)
Models of the Failure Rates of Commercial Banks in Illinois, 1900–1993

Independent Variable		Models					
	(r_B1)	(r_B2)	(r_B3)	(r_B4)	(r_B5)	(r_B6)	(r_B7)
Number of banks in locale at organization's birth	0.0356 (0.0483)	0.0215 (0.0380)	0.0190 (0.0383)	0.0050 (0.0382)	0.0129 (0.0361)	0.0104 (0.0391)	-0.0221 (0.0394)
Log of the number of rival bank in other Illinois locales	-0.7072** (0.2860)	-0.6309** (0.2867)	-0.7110** (0.2860)	-0.7116** (0.2859)	-0.7094** (0.2864)	-0.7115** (0.2858)	-0.7007** (0.2860)
Number of rival banks in locale	-0.5935** (0.0723)	-1.335** (0.0935)	-0.5992** (0.0656)	-0.6299** (0.0627)	-0.8712** (0.0744)	-0.5450** (0.0593)	-0.5802** (0.0651)
Bank's share of local market	-3.191** (0.2701)	-3.406** (0.2689)	-3.192** (0.2693)	-3.211** (0.2694)	-3.328** (0.2699)	-3.161** (0.2691)	-3.169** (0.2703)
Lagged number of bank foundings in locale	0.0560 (0.2004)	0.3974** (0.2008)	0.0778 (0.1962)	0.0981 (0.1951)	0.2036 (0.1970)	0.0555 (0.1947)	0.0252 (0.1967)
Lagged number of bank failures in locale	0.4241** (0.1070)	0.1585 (0.1209)	0.4489** (0.1077)	0.4085** (0.1067)	0.3885** (0.1073)	0.4276** (0.1065)	0.4311** (0.1073)
Lagged number of bank takeovers in locale	0.2103 (0.1445)	-0.0307 (0.1487)	0.2468* (0.1438)	0.2038 (0.1441)	0.1408 (0.1425)	0.2402* (0.1447)	0.2177 (0.1444)
Age of local market	-0.0236** (0.0027)	-0.0199** (0.0026)	-0.0233** (0.0027)	-0.0230** (0.0026)	-0.0228** (0.0026)	-0.0231** (0.0027)	-0.0236** (0.0027)
Population in locale/1,000	0.0044 (0.0049)	0.0074* (0.0046)	0.0025 (0.0045)	0.0028 (0.0044)	-0.0003 (0.0045)	0.0046 (0.0044)	0.0040 (0.0044)
1-year change in population in locale/1,000	0.1351 (0.0881)	0.1457* (0.0752)	0.1474* (0.0836)	0.1377 (0.0866)	0.0895 (0.1018)	0.1511* (0.0808)	0.1381 (0.0864)
Proportion of the population urban in county	-0.2422* (0.1352)	-0.2448* (0.1342)	-0.2381* (0.1349)	-0.2342* (0.1348)	-0.2415* (0.1350)	-0.2332* (0.1347)	-0.2278* (0.1347)
Number of manufacturing establishments in county/1,000	0.0261 (0.0483)	0.0441 (0.0493)	0.0266 (0.0481)	0.0301 (0.0480)	0.0343 (0.0480)	0.0280 (0.0481)	0.0288 (0.0479)

TABLE 5.4 (*cont.*)
Models of the Failure Rates of Commercial Banks in Illinois, 1900–1993

Independent Variable	Models						
	(r_B1)	(r_B2)	(r_B3)	(r_B4)	(r_B5)	(r_B6)	(r_B7)
Number of farms in county/1,000	0.0419	0.0450	0.0403	0.0406	0.0410	0.0407	0.0416
	(0.0327)	(0.0328)	(0.0327)	(0.0327)	(0.0327)	(0.0327)	(0.0327)
Number of retail establishments in county/1,000	0.0014	−0.0041	0.0009	0.0003	0.0009	0.0002	0.0008
	(0.0133)	(0.0134)	(0.0132)	(0.0132)	(0.0132)	(0.0132)	(0.0132)
Number of wholesale establishments in county/1,000	−0.0097	−0.0118	−0.0063	−0.0089	−0.0114	−0.0097	−0.0121
	(0.0772)	(0.0783)	(0.0772)	(0.0772)	(0.0772)	(0.0772)	(0.0772)
Indexed average value of farms in county/1,000	0.6339**	0.5985**	0.6335**	0.6235**	0.6181**	0.6274**	0.6365**
	(0.2825)	(0.2878)	(0.2828)	(0.2834)	(0.2861)	(0.2819)	(0.2826)
Indexed wage per worker in county	10.84**	10.91**	10.82**	10.85**	10.71**	10.88**	10.73**
	(3.798)	(3.827)	(3.779)	(3.804)	(3.757)	(3.809)	(3.775)
Log of bank's assets	−0.4686**	−0.4367**	−0.4696**	−0.4646**	−0.4423**	−0.4742**	−0.4696**
	(0.0390)	(0.0388)	(0.0388)	(0.0389)	(0.0393)	(0.0386)	(0.0388)
Duration							
0–1 year	6.980**	6.164**	7.034**	7.017**	6.800**	7.084**	6.944**
	(2.091)	(2.102)	(2.091)	(2.090)	(2.095)	(2.089)	(2.091)
1–2 years	8.892**	7.895**	8.890**	8.852**	8.583**	8.947**	8.849**
	(2.050)	(2.060)	(2.050)	(2.049)	(2.054)	(2.048)	(2.048)
2–3 years	9.112**	8.343**	9.143**	9.108**	8.933**	9.169**	9.046**
	(2.040)	(2.050)	(2.040)	(2.040)	(2.044)	(2.038)	(2.040)
3–5 years	9.454**	8.666**	9.491**	9.446**	9.265**	9.515**	9.397**
	(2.037)	(2.046)	(2.038)	(2.037)	(2.042)	(2.036)	(2.037)
5–10 years	9.753**	8.901**	9.797**	9.740**	9.539**	9.820**	9.703**
	(2.033)	(2.042)	(2.034)	(2.033)	(2.038)	(2.032)	(2.033)
10–15 years	9.822**	8.942**	9.871**	9.809**	9.610**	9.890**	9.791**
	(2.031)	(2.040)	(2.031)	(2.031)	(2.036)	(2.030)	(2.031)

TABLE 5.4 (*cont.*)
Models of the Failure Rates of Commercial Banks in Illinois, 1900–1993

				Models			
Independent Variable	(r_B1)	(r_B2)	(r_B3)	(r_B4)	(r_B5)	(r_B6)	(r_B7)
15–20 years	9.820**	8.914**	9.868**	9.806**	9.604**	9.887**	9.804**
	(2.035)	(2.043)	(2.035)	(2.035)	(2.039)	(2.033)	(2.035)
20–25 years	9.959**	9.034**	10.00**	9.943**	9.743**	10.02**	9.956**
	(2.034)	(2.043)	(2.034)	(2.034)	(2.038)	(2.033)	(2.034)
25–30 years	10.19**	9.270**	10.23**	10.18**	9.973**	10.26**	10.20**
	(2.032)	(2.041)	(2.032)	(2.032)	(2.037)	(2.031)	(2.032)
30–40 years	10.18**	9.252**	10.22**	10.16**	9.956**	10.24**	10.20**
	(2.033)	(2.042)	(2.033)	(2.033)	(2.037)	(2.032)	(2.033)
40+ years	10.46**	9.513**	10.47**	10.43**	10.22**	10.51**	10.50**
	(2.035)	(2.043)	(2.036)	(2.035)	(2.040)	(2.034)	(2.035)
Period							
1910–1919	0.1350	0.1715	0.1365	0.1366	0.1403	0.1357	0.1267
	(0.1534)	(0.1542)	(0.1534)	(0.1534)	(0.1535)	(0.1533)	(0.1535)
1920–1928	0.7557**	0.7872**	0.7578**	0.7573**	0.7529**	0.7598**	0.7309**
	(0.1712)	(0.1719)	(0.1712)	(0.1712)	(0.1713)	(0.1711)	(0.1715)
1929–1932	2.684**	2.723**	2.689**	2.687**	2.668**	2.696**	2.649**
	(0.1405)	(0.1412)	(0.1405)	(0.1404)	(0.1406)	(0.1403)	(0.1411)
1933–1939	2.073**	2.103**	2.075**	2.073**	2.046**	2.085**	2.039**
	(0.1376)	(0.1390)	(0.1376)	(0.1376)	(0.1377)	(0.1376)	(0.1381)
1940–1945	0.7244**	0.7556**	0.7209**	0.7265**	0.6906**	0.7377**	0.6953**
	(0.2178)	(0.2190)	(0.2179)	(0.2178)	(0.2179)	(0.2177)	(0.2179)

TABLE 5.4 (*cont.*)
Models of the Failure Rates of Commercial Banks in Illinois, 1900–1993

Independent Variable	Models						
	(r_B1)	(r_B2)	(r_B3)	(r_B4)	(r_B5)	(r_B6)	(r_B7)
1946–1959	−0.2920	−0.2718	−0.3025	−0.2886	−0.3247	−0.2810	−0.3147
	(0.2627)	(0.2641)	(0.2632)	(0.2627)	(0.2628)	(0.2627)	(0.2628)
1960–1969	−1.385**	−1.414**	−1.398**	−1.386**	−1.408**	−1.383**	−1.406**
	(0.4944)	(0.4983)	(0.4946)	(0.4947)	(0.4938)	(0.4950)	(0.4948)
1970–1979	−2.037**	−2.061**	−2.043**	−2.035**	−2.039**	−2.037**	−2.058**
	(0.6809)	(0.6790)	(0.6800)	(0.6797)	(0.6764)	(0.6813)	(0.6812)
1980–1993	−0.3072	−0.5354	−0.3125	−0.3136	−0.3349	−0.2993	−0.3211
	(0.3579)	(0.3688)	(0.3580)	(0.3579)	(0.3571)	(0.3582)	(0.3580)
Log likelihood	−1680.64	−1680.93	−1682.88	−1680.38	−1654.46	−1689.10	−1677.64
(df)	(45)	(44)	(44)	(44)	(44)	(44)	(46)

Note: Data include 1,444 failures among 2,970 banks over 108,209 organization-years. Other variables are included, as shown below. The omitted period is 1900–1909.

**p<.05. *p<.10. Standard errors are in parentheses.

organization-year of historical competition experience by a bank reduced its hazard of failure by exp[−0.0038]. At the mean observed value of this variable (33, from table 5.3), this implies a multiplier of about 0.88— meaning that failure rates in these data were about 12 percent lower for banks that experienced an average amount of historical competition, compared to banks that were always local monopolists (other things being equal). But, meanwhile, other things were not equal. The rivalry generated by a bank's rivals also increased as those rivals experienced competition, increasing a bank's failure rate by exp[0.0021] with every additional year of historical competition experienced by its rivals. At the observed mean of 96 for rivals' competitive experience (see table 5.3), this estimate implies an increase in a bank's failure rate of 22 percent due to rivals' competitive experience.

Current-time competition also was important to these organizations, but the models reveal competition driving up failure rates through the effect of a bank's market share rather than the density of rivals.[72] Market shares varied widely among Illinois banks, ranging from local monopolists to banks with as little as 1/1000 of their local market. According to model $r_B 2$, local monopolists enjoyed considerably lower failure rates due to their ownership of the local market; they were almost 30 percent less likely to fail than a bank with a negligable market share.[73] This market share effect declines, by construction, most rapidly with the first few competitors. For instance, banks facing one rival, and thus having 50 percent of the market on average, enjoyed only a 15 percent decrease in their failure chances due to market share. This effect varies, of course, depending on the distribution of the market among rivals in each particular locale. But overall, as was the case for the founding models, competition increased especially with the loss of monopoly status among these banks.

A comparison of models $r_B 1$ and $r_B 2$ permits a test of the Costly Adaptation Hypothesis. Model $r_B 1$ is the same as model $r_B 2$, except that model $r_B 1$ also includes K_j, the number of distinct rival organizations faced by organization j over its history. The theory predicted that this term would increase an organization's failure rate, assuming that the costs of adaptation increase with the number of distinct historical rivals an organization has faced. Yet a comparison of these models does not support the costly adaptation hypothesis. Whether these banks' historical competition was spread over many or over few rivals made no detectable difference to their failure rates according to these specifications.

Turning to a test of the Competency-Trap Hypothesis, models $r_B 3$ through $r_B 6$ disaggregate competitive experience into distinct variables measuring recent and distant-past competitive experience (T_{Rj} and T_{Dj} from chapter 4)—as well as the effects of these terms summed over each organization's rivals. Looking across these specifications, there is no evidence in support of the Competency-Trap Hypothesis. Distant-past historical experience does not harm an organization's life chances, as predicted, but rather enhances life chances (albeit by a smaller magnitude than the effect of more recent experience). Similarly, rivals do not become weaker due to distant-past experience but become stronger (again by a smaller magnitude than the effect of more recent experience). This failure to support the Competency-Trap Hypothesis stands in contrast to earlier findings from these data,[74] which found evidence of a competency trap in models that measured competitive experience only among an organization's surviving rivals. Allowing for historical experience also from failed rivals appears to reverse the finding in support of a competency trap. This may mean that organizations that outsurvive their rivals are precisely those that, for whatever reason, avoided or overcame the competency trap.

The Myopic Learning and Costly Predation Hypotheses

All models include the cumulative hazard rate of a bank's acquisition activity over its lifetime. According to the Costly Predation Hypothesis, banks more inclined to acquire their rivals should suffer higher failure rates—at least once one has separately controlled for the market power benefits of such acquisitions (as done in these models). Predatory activity increases an organization's hazard rate, I argued, because such organizations develop the routine of reacting to competition by eliminating it, instead of developing routines to learn from competition. Further, more predatory organizations would be more likely to pursue bad matches in terms of the possible "complementarities" that might result from acquisitions, since they are driven by the objective of reducing the competition they face. Consistent with these arguments, organizations with a higher cumulative hazard of acquiring their rivals suffered a significantly higher failure rate as a result, while the cumulative hazard of acquisition by an organization's rivals did not have this effect. The increase in the failure rate resulted not, therefore, from being in a high-acquisition locale, but rather from being the organization that does the acquiring. Specifically, according to model r_B2, preying on rivals nearly tripled the failure rates of the most predatory organizations.[75] Predation has its benefits, in the form of increased market power and reduced competitive pressure, but it also clearly has its downside.

Across all models, the cumulative hazard of failure in the local banking market over an organization's history is found to increase its failure rate—the opposite of what would be predicted by the pure-selection model. Recall that in the pure-selection model, failure rates fall the more that an organization outsurvives its competition—a fall in the failure rate that tracks unobserved differences in survivability across organizations. In these models, however, a higher cumulative hazard predicts a higher failure rate. One way to explain this finding is to note that these data pool many different locales. If some locales are more hazardous than others, then they would be marked by a higher cumulative hazard rate that would, then, predict higher ensuing failure rates among organizations in these markets. Note that the increase in failure rates due to the cumulative hazard of failure is considerably lower, about two times the standard error lower, than the increase in failure due to the cumulative hazard of acquiring one's rivals. This comparison gives added weight to the Costly Predation Hypothesis.

Finally, model 7 includes two measures of the dispersion of each organization's historical competition over time, one a gini coefficient measuring the inequality of the distribution over past years of the rivalry faced by j (= 1 if all competition came in a single prior year and none in any other prior years), and the other measuring the inequality of the distribution of cohorts of rivals (= 1 if all historical rivals came from a single cohort). These terms test the Myopic Learning Hypothesis, according to which organizations exposed to a more dispersed history of competition would benefit as a result. Not only can we reject this hypothesis, but when significant the findings are opposed to what was predicted (as was the case also in the founding models). The greater the inequality of past rivalry faced by an organization, the *lower* its failure rate.

Having its competitive experience concentrated into only one or a few years was argued to create a myopic learning effect, which in turn would make organizational learning less efficacious. Instead, however, concentrating competition into only a few years corresponded to lower organizational failure rates. One possible way to account for this finding would be to look, again, at the fact that these data pool many different locales. More volatile locales, those experiencing more failures and foundings in general, would have competition spread over more years, while especially stable locales may have had competition only in a few years. Such unobserved heterogeneity across locales may have spuriously generated an effect for the historical concentration of competition. (Note that the models do include the count of failures lagged by one year, which does correspond to higher failure rates and should help to capture the effects of such heterogeneity over times and places with respect to failure rates.) In any case, as in the founding models, the Myopic Learning Hypothesis is not supported.

Other Failure Model Effects

Looking over the rest of the effects in the failure models, several findings are noteworthy. Larger banks were considerably less likely to fail, the negative size dependence in failure rates typically found in studies of organizational survival. Age dependence, meanwhile, is mildly positive, meaning that older banks were slightly more likely to fail. This pattern is consistent with the idea that older organizations fall out-of-step with the conditions of their environment.[76] Note, however, that in the context of these models, the consequences of age hinge on whether or not an organization is exposed to competition as it matures. For a monopolist in its local market, the effects of age on failure reflect the age terms reported in model r_B2. However, if a bank experienced the mean level of competition per year observed in the data, its failure rate would change with age very differently. In this way, what has been thought of as a liability of age might better be thought of, in light of the theory of Red Queen competition, as a liability of isolation.

Failure rates turn out to be lower in older markets and in more urbanized markets. Investigations into bank failures over the twentieth century often pointed to the problem of failures among rural banks, especially with their dependence on the farm economy, and more generally their reliance on a less diversified economic base.[77] Historical periods also had large effects in different directions, depending on broader social, economic, and regulatory developments of each era. Most surprising, perhaps, are the positive effects on bank failures of farm value and wages, measures of rural and urban wealth and income, respectively. Normally, studies in organizational ecology expect to see lower failure rates in contexts with greater resources, other things equal. In this case, the higher failure rates associated with income and wealth may indicate greater risk taking among bankers in such environments. Alternatively, it may be that more munificent environments were more permissive in terms of entry, so that less viable banks could come into existence to begin with in such contexts.[78]

Summary of Findings

In U.S. commercial banking over the twentieth century, two distinct logics of competition contended. Regulations restricted banks to operating in well-defined product, service, and geographic markets. When banks competed, then, they found themselves in zero-sum relation to geographically neighboring banks, contending for better customers. Where this took place, banks competed according to a logic of fiduciary effectiveness. Meanwhile, regulations also protected banks from "undue" competition, often allowing or even encouraging banks to merge with or acquire banks in the same locale. Thus banking regulations allowed banks to follow a logic of predation, eliminating rivals by acquiring or merging with them in order to avoid competition. Supporting this interpretation of the history of these markets, the statistical evidence presented here suggests that both of these logics of competition shaped the founding and failure rates of Illinois banks.

Supporting the Competitive Hysteresis Hypothesis, bank founding rates were lower in markets with incumbent banks that had competitive experience in the recent past—indicating that such experience made these banks stronger competitors. Similarly, banks with more competitive experience were less likely to fail, and their more experienced rivals generated stronger competition, again supporting the basic prediction of the Red Queen theory, that competitive experience made these organizations more viable and stronger competitors.

Meanwhile, distant-past competitive experience among incumbents increased founding rates, supporting the Competency-Trap Hypothesis—although the failure models did not reveal evidence of a competency trap. And, in markets where incumbents merged with or acquired competitors at a greater rate, founding rates were higher, as predicted by the Costly Predation Hypothesis. Similarly, acquisitions made organizations more likely to fail (controlling for the market power benefits of such acquisitions) and made them weaker competitors in terms of their effect on other's failure rates—again supporting the Costly Predation Hypothesis.

The Costly Adaptation Hypothesis was not supported in the failure models, nor was the Myopic Learning Hypothesis supported in either the failure or founding models. In fact, founding rates and failure rates were lower the more that incumbent organizations concentrated their competitive experience into fewer years (and, for founding rates, fewer cohorts of rivals). It is likely that an even distribution of competitors over time reflects greater volatility among banks that is otherwise not controlled in my models. Yet the basic predictions of the Red Queen model are supported. Clearly, organizational founding and failure in commercial banking hinged on competitive hysteresis, with the viability and competitiveness of organizations varying according to whether—and when—they endured a history of competition.

SIX

Red Queen Competition among Computer Manufacturers

OUR KNOWLEDGE OF THE COMPUTER industry has emerged over time through search and discovery. Industry experts now can detail the logics of competition that have prevailed in the industry's markets, but this understanding was slow to develop and often clear only in hindsight. Very often, computer technologies have not been well understood, even by the engineers and scientists closest to these technologies. Take, for example, the so-called Y2K bug. As the turn of the century approached, experts in the computer industry increasingly spoke of malfunctions that would likely occur in computerized systems when the date moved from 1999 to 2000. The "bug" was in so-called legacy computer programs that devoted only two digits to the year, created at a time when one could not have imagined that the program would last to the next century. When clocks turned to 2000, so went the concern, computers calibrating their operations on the date would not know how to make sense of the year "00." With computer systems embedded in so many aspects of modern life, from jet airplanes to water systems to organizational infrastructures and accounting systems to home appliances one could only imagine the catastrophe waiting to be triggered at the new millennium. The dire possibilities were reflected in the considerable resources spent to remedy the problem in advance, estimated to have amounted to as much as $600 billion in the United States.[1] Public rhetoric mirrored this spending. A search of the *New York Times* historical archives suggests that the term Y2K first appeared in that paper in 1997, when only 2 articles mentioned Y2K. In 1998, 62 *Times* articles used the term, and then mentions of Y2K skyrocketed in1999 to 316 articles. Meanwhile, many experts shared this public concern, as in one 1998 book on the subject: "It is unlikely that if unlimited human resources were available to every organization today that management could mobilize the teams to incorporate [needed] massive changes in such a short period of time. Time has run out on us all."[2] In retrospect, despite the fact that not all organizations dealt with the bug in advance, we now know that the Y2K bug did not trigger a catastrophe. But the fact that so many—experts and outsiders alike—thought that great problems would plague those who did not prepare illustrates the uncertainty surrounding computer technology even after fifty years of experience.

Looking over time, it is clear that the case of the Y2K bug is not an isolated example. Time and again, the industry's leading minds have dismissed new technologies as trivial, or have written off existing technologies as doomed, only to be shown to be incorrect by unfolding events. For instance, time would show how important is the mechanism that allows humans to interact with the computer, the so-called user interface—especially the now-ubiquitous "graphical user interface" combined with a "mouse." (Young readers may not realize that, even as recently as the 1980s, one could interact with many computers only by entering lines of text, or by punching holes in cards that would be fed physically into a machine.) Early theoretical work in cybernetics linked human thinking to the physical act of creation, and building on these ideas one of the earliest computers, MIT's "Whirlwind," employed a "light gun" in 1952 for use on a visual screen (a cathode ray oscilloscope).[3] These developments laid the groundwork for Douglas Engelbart's invention of the mouse, noted in his papers as early as 1963.[4] Yet the importance of the user interface was not understood at the time, as nearly all computers neglected the user interface. Not for another twenty years would a commercially available computer feature a mouse and graphical user interface— the Apple "Lisa" in 1983.[5] So it is that we often have not initially realized how the technologies of the computer might be valuable and consequently have developed our understanding of this value largely through experience and experimentation.

As with the technologies of the computer, so also the markets made possible by computers have often been poorly understood, at least until experience could reveal these markets. For instance, Lawrence Roberts, who led the design effort for ARPANET—the predecessor of our modern Internet—wrote in 1967 a list of reasons justifying the creation of a network among computers. Those reasons were exclusively technical and referred only to improvements in scientific activity that would be enabled by such a network. At one point, however, Roberts notes in passing: "As soon as the need became apparent, additional small computers could be located at strategic connection points within the network to concentrate messages over cross-country lines."[6] Elaborating on Roberts's ideas in 1971, the eminent computer scientists C. Gordon Bell and Allen Newell similarly pay little mind to nonscientific uses of such a network. They observe that a network could connect "a number of low data-rate users," adding, "This may not be a reason for a network per se but may justify a larger network, provided that there is some reason for having one in the first place."[7] So those who first designed what would become the Internet did not seem to be aware that this innovation would have revolutionary implications for markets. As with computer technologies, the market implications of computers, and the logics of competition that would prevail in these markets, often have been clear to us only in hindsight.

Ironically, as important as learning has been in the computer industry, its established experts and leading organizations have been notoriously resistant to new possibilities, as evidenced by the long time lags that typically occurred between when innovations first appeared and when they finally affected the industry's installed base. For instance, the microcomputer market typically is said to have begun in 1975, yet a well-established text on the economics of data processing and technology, published in 1979, made no use of the term "microcomputer."[8] When such systems were referred to in this text, it was with the term "personal computers," defined away as "general purpose computers in the under-$5,000 price range, marketed to individuals for hobby, education, entertainment, and other personal use." This source goes on to exclude these systems from its statistical figures, explaining that "the number of personal computers in use exceeded the number of [other] general purpose computers in use during 1978. However, note also that the value of these computers is so low it would hardly show if plotted on [the] figure."[9] The point here is not that the author should somehow have been more aware of what was emerging in the industry, but rather that the existing understanding of what constituted a significant computer—combined with an installed base of older computers—helped to conceal what was an oncoming revolution. Consequently, although the microcomputer may have first appeared in 1975, the interpretive frame that would identify the microcomputer market as a social fact was considerably slower to develop. In short, the logics of competition operating within the computer industry were discovered over time, with some considerable difficulty, as organizations gained experience.

My argument in this chapter is that this difficult process of discovery was driven by competition among organizations in the industry, as they evolved through the back-and-forth of Red Queen evolution. In an attempt to attract and retain customers, computer manufacturers needed to solve the myriad technical, marketing, and organizational problems involved in making computers valuable to businesses and, ultimately, consumers. In this search, each organization's successes increased the pressures faced by other organizations that also were searching for ways to attract and retain customers, through both technical and organizational means. General Electric, for instance, rose to become a significant player in the industry in the 1960s due, in part, to its innovations in "time sharing"—a technical design feature that allowed multiple users to employ simultaneously the full features of a mainframe computer system. In response, other manufacturers then were triggered to speed the development of their own time-sharing systems.[10] In other cases, innovations were organizational rather than technical, as in the creation of large-scale service and consulting organizations to help customers put their computer systems to use. The importance of such organizational innovations is underscored by the continual presence of consultants—starting as far back as the proliferation of so-called service bureaus in the 1950s—specializing in providing service and support organizations where manufacturers fell short. So both organizational and technical advances were involved in the industry's development over time. I propose that Red Queen competition among computer manufacturers accelerated this process of development.

Note that my argument is not purely about a "technology race" among organizations in the industry. Such races of course have gone on in the computer industry since its earliest years but have in many cases remained distinct from the logics of competition developing in the market. To reveal the logics of competition operating in the industry, rivalries needed to be *mediated by the market* as opposed to being purely technical contests. For instance, computer scientist Herman Luckoff described being part of the team designing the BINAC, which he portrayed as a "race to develop the first stored-program computer."[11] Yet his description of this race was largely technical. He describes in detail the difficult technological problems that needed to be solved if his team was to achieve this milestone before other scientists. Such a race is not what I have in mind. Rather, my argument is about market-mediated competition—the kind that repeatedly confronts organizations with problems that, once resolved, bring the organizations into alignment with the market's logic of competition. In the case of the BINAC, Herman Luckoff also describes product development for UNIVAC III systems in 1964, a time of market-mediated competition for the firm (then Sperry Univac). This race involved technology, the market, and organization—all in an effort to create a product that would meet the needs of customers. Luckoff notes the organizational innovation that resulted from resolving these tensions: "Marketing sold Sperry Univac products. Engineering designed Sperry Univac products. But whether or not Marketing was selling what Engineering had designed was coincidental in some cases. Consequently there was a lot of anguish when Marketing discovered what the product really was. I established a procedure under which the groups worked together formally to describe products, in which both were knowledgeable, in detail."[12] To succeed in the market, both technical and marketing problems needed to be resolved, and in so doing Sperry Univac's organization developed to perform better given its market's logic of competition.

In order to estimate the Red Queen model using data from the computer industry, I first distinguish its logics of competition. I briefly discuss these logics, to delineate the distinct markets that developed in the industry over time. Initially, I lay out the operational definitions that I used to determine what organizations to include in the study, and in sorting the organizations into distinct markets. Next, I review the logics of competition that developed in each of these markets, to illustrate the processes of organizational learning that were involved along the way. I then estimate the Red Queen model using data on organizations in each of the markets.

The Computer Industry and Its Markets

I define the computer industry in this study to include manufacturers in the United States who sold, rented, or leased general purpose, digital, electronic computers. This definition excludes organizations engaged solely in research, such as universities. Also excluded are manufacturers of the mechanical computers that predated modern electronic computers. Among electronic computers, I exclude analog systems, which express information in the form of electrical currents and voltages and allow one to model real-world systems in terms of the dynamics of these electrical properties. Such computers permit modeling a system in continuous terms without approximation and can do so easily in "real time." In contrast, electronic digital computers, by their nature operating sequentially and in discrete terms, were initially less suitable for real-time problems such as simulations of dynamic systems. Consequently, during the early years of the computer industry, electronic analog computers were often employed for such tasks, as were so-called hybrid computers that combined digital and analog processes.[13] Improvements in the performance of digital systems have allowed them to progressively increase their usefulness in areas previously thought to be the exclusive domain of analog systems, such as complex dynamic simulations. In the twenty-first century, electronic analog computers have been largely displaced by digital computers. Nonetheless, I would have liked to include analog computers, but comprehensive data on such computers are not available systematically over the industry's entire history.

   I bound the study in time and space to keep the data collection task manageable. Geographically, I confined the study to include only manufacturers in the United States. Although the industry is recently born, it turns out to be poorly documented in any one data source (see the appendix). Consequently, most studies of the industry have settled for analyzing size- or survivor-biased data. Instead, I collected data from a variety of data sources and found that if I restricted the sample space to include only U.S. manufacturers, I could combine these various sources to trace the life histories of all manufacturers that ever sold, rented, or leased an electronic, general purpose, digital computer. So defined, the industry begins in 1951 with the commercial launch of the Univac by the Eckert-Mauchly Division of Remington Rand (although this computer was not actually shipped

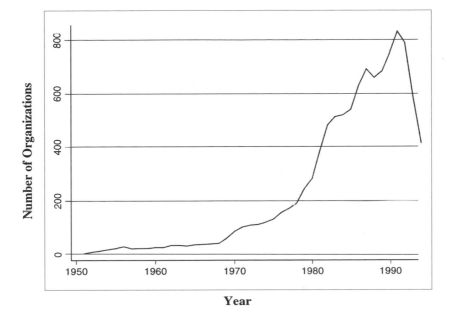

Figure 6.1. Number of U.S. computer manufacturers.

until 1952).[14] I end the study in 1994, a point when the logics of competition in the industry were about to be transformed by the Internet. (See figure 6.1, above, and figures 6.5 and 6.6, pages 150 and 151, respectively.)

Identifying distinct markets within the computer industry is difficult because computer systems have ranged historically from very large mainframes and supercomputers to small microcomputers. Complicating market distinctions further, the computer industry also has been marked by an ongoing process of technical and organizational change. Consequently, what would have been considered a powerful computer of the 1960s would be dwarfed by the processing capability of a small, inexpensive, consumer-oriented microcomputer of the 1990s. Even just a few years in this industry typically involved considerable change. For instance, the hand-held calculators used by the last of the Apollo astronauts were comparable to their vintage on-board Apollo Guidance System, an embedded minicomputer that had been designed into the Apollo systems a few years earlier.[15] Market and organizational differences, in turn, have corresponded to the variety of different technologies across the industry and over time. For instance, large mainframe manufacturers have typically operated high-budget, fundamental research laboratories and elaborate service organizations tailored to the computing needs of gigantic corporate customers. Meanwhile, microcomputer manufacturers have ranged from small "garage" start ups to efficient, large-scale, assembly, logistics, and marketing organizations providing technical support and point-to-point delivery to consumers. Clearly these various technologies, organizations, and markets involve very different logics of competition and so cannot be analyzed as a single market.

Looking at the industry from its inception in 1951 through 1994, it is possible to identify three distinct market segments: Large-scale "mainframe" computers (including supercomputers), "midrange" computers (including minicomputers, small business computers, servers, high-end workstations and other medium-sized systems), and "microcomputers," as described in figures 6.2 (page 147), 6.3 (page 148), and 6.4 (page 149). As I will explain, historical accounts suggest that each of these markets has been characterized by a relatively coherent, if evolving, logic of competition. The corporate demography of the industry supports distinguishing between these markets. As table 6.1 shows, most manufacturers remained wholly within one of these three markets, with only a minority of organizations operating across multiple markets. Next, I discuss the logics of competition that evolved within each of these three markets over time. In reviewing the institutional histories of these markets, it will be especially important to note evidence that Red Queen competition was at work as these logics evolved over time—as the organizations in this industry discovered and struggled with their rivals to market revolutionary technical developments in order to meet escalating customer demands.

Discovering Logics of Competition among Mainframe Computer Manufacturers

The early computer industry developed in a fog of uncertainty. Very few organizations had purchased or leased a computer, and so potential customers were unsure about whether the benefits of using a computer would outweigh the costs involved. Meanwhile, the initial costs of adopting computer technologies were very high, involving not only hardware costs but also the costs of programming and operating the computer as well as establishing data collection and processing procedures suitable for use with a computer. The range of possible tasks that could be tackled by a computer was unknown, although there was great speculation about the possibilities. Furthermore, few qualified computer technicians were available in the labor market, making it difficult to hire the talent needed to address these uncertainties.[16] In this environment, the use of the term "computer industry" itself was dubious. Questions about the legitimacy of the budding computer industry were raised even at IBM, where the first general-purpose IBM computer, the 701, was referred to internally as an "electronic data processing machine" rather than a computer in order

TABLE 6.1
Number of Distinct Commercial General Purpose Digital Computer Manufacturers in the U.S. by Market

	1955	1960	1965	1970	1975	1980	1985	1990	1994	Overall
Organizations in microcomputer market only	0	0	0	0	2	100	253	535	278	1662
Organizations in midrange market only	0	0	5	66	114	141	169	124	85	542
Organizations in mainframe market only	22	25	27	6	5	10	23	8	7	97
Organizations in both (and only) the microcomputer and midrange markets	0	0	0	0	0	22	79	58	28	233
Organizations in both (and only) the microcomputer and mainframe markets	0	0	0	0	0	0	1	0	0	2
Organizations in both (and only) the midrange and mainframe markets	0	0	3	13	9	5	4	13	7	41
Organizations in all three markets	0	0	0	0	1	3	9	11	7	25
Organizations in any market	22	25	35	85	131	281	538	749	412	2602

Source: Various archival documents (see appendix).

to minimize internal opposition to the project.[17] In this light, many of the early developments in the industry can be understood as a process of discovering, amidst considerable uncertainty regarding possible technologies and markets.

The First Large Mainframe Systems

Installing and using one of the earliest mainframe computers involved a set of uncertain and complex technical and organizational efforts. The first mainframe computers were elaborate systems including various components, such as the processor, storage, input, and output devices.[18] The processor was not yet a miniaturized component but rather included relatively large physical systems that performed numerical and arithmetic processes. Neither were all of the components of the early mainframes containerized in a single "box," as would be routinely done later. Rather, the various parts of the computer would be colocated in large rooms, where a team of experts would work together to operate the system. When an organization bought or leased one of these computers, the installation and operation typically were carried out by employees of the manufacturer working in coordination with the customer's computer experts. In this way, the earliest mainframe computers were inaccessible to anyone but experts, and for an organization to buy or lease such a system required that such experts be employed on their own staff.

Most general purpose digital computers since the UNIVAC's introduction in 1951 have been designed according to the so-called von Neumann architecture. The distinguishing feature of such computers is the stored-program design, where instructions and data are stored together on the same memory device, and where the unit that processes information is separate from the storage unit. When operating, the computer would "fetch" an instruction, decode the instruction, and execute the instruction, with this sequence followed unless the result of an operation required the computer to "branch" to a new instruction sequence. The stored-program design allows rapid access to all data and instructions equally quickly, enabling the system to branch to other instructions without slowing the execution of the cycle.[19] The von Neumann design distinguished computers from advanced calculators, which did not have the stored-program feature, and from most special-purpose computers, which often did not feature programmability.

As the first mainframe computers were being offered for lease or sale in the early 1950s, IBM researcher Herbert Grosch noted that the performance of computers appeared to increase as a square of the computer's cost.[20] This regularity came to be known as "Grosch's law" and was cited as a reason for the prevalence of large computers from the 1950s through the 1970s. For instance, articles on the buy-or-lease decision in the 1960s typically referred to Grosch's law as a reason to lease the use of time on a large mainframe rather than purchase a smaller machine, and similarly Grosch's law inspired the push toward systems that supported time sharing among multiple users. Grosch's law also was cited as a reason for the prevalence of large computer firms, such as IBM throughout the 1960s and into the 1970s. Textbooks published as late as 1973, well into the era of the minicomputer, continued to play down the role of smaller computers in data processing because of a belief in Grosch's law.[21] Many described early mainframe computing as proceeding through "generations" corresponding to the vacuum tube, transistor, and then integrated circuit.[22] In fact, these innovations in microelectronics weakened Grosch's law by making smaller computers cost effective,[23] such that by the 1980s the "law" no longer held.[24] Nonetheless, Grosch's law, and the belief in Grosch's law, led to an early emphasis on scale that would favor large mainframe computers and their (typically large) manufacturers.

Hardware Organizations and the Emergence of Programming Languages

Who could use a computer, and what support was needed for customers, hinged on the development of computer software. The earliest computers were used by working directly with the design of the hardware itself, programming in so-called machine language and then manually providing cards or tapes with commands and data. Machine-language programming required knowledge particular to the specific system in use and resulted in machine-specific investments. So the very first customers were typically extremely sophisticated computer users, such as the Department of Defense or large industrial firms that could employ rare, specialized computer experts. These customers then worked with teams of experts from the manufacturer during the operation of the computer. Consequently, large, vertically integrated computer manufacturers had an initial advantage in the mainframe market, since these organizations had the capability to provide the sophisticated service and support that customers required for such a system. These organizations favored leasing over selling equipment because leases enabled the manufacturers to pace the rate of new technology introduction and to keep control over what technologies were connected into these systems.

As software developed, the skills and investments involved in operating a computer became increasingly independent of the particular hardware system being used. With the development of "compilers," program commands could be written in syntax more appealing to the user and then translated into machine language. Compilers allowed for the development of "assembler" languages, which incorporated both commands and the instructions to organize program execution.[25] As assembler languages developed, user groups began to form comprising sophisticated users who sought to improve the functionality of products, sometimes to the chagrin of the manufacturers themselves.[26] These groups mark the beginning of what would ultimately become the software industry, but in the early days the future importance of software was not apparent.

Programming languages were advanced markedly by the introduction in 1957 of FORTRAN by IBM for its 704 machine, followed soon by COBOL, ALGOL, and a variety of other languages. Such languages were notable not only for their efficiency, but especially because they featured syntax that was completely removed from the workings of the machine on which the program would be run.[27] For instance, a book on the language ALGOL, published in 1962, described such programming as "machine independent," emphasizing the importance of programming languages in separating investments in programming from the specific hardware on which the programs would be executed.[28] These developments led to increasing sunk costs in software and programming, and a consequent drive among customers to remain compatible with initial investments in programming. At the same time, the machine-independent quality of these languages kept the market open to the entry of new hardware manufacturers, who continued to proliferate into the 1960s as shown in figure 6.7.

The Early Development of the Mainframe Market

Initial customers for the computer mainframe were organizations with the ability and need to pay the considerable costs involved in the development of these first systems, such as the U.S. Bureau of the Census, the U.S. Air Force, the U.S. Atomic Energy Commission, and very large industrial firms such as General Electric.[29] Such customers were sufficiently sophisticated technically that manufacturers did not need to "sell" computers to them; these customers already understood how computers could be used in valuable ways.[30] Nor were such customers particularly sensitive to costs. Consequently, the market for mainframe computers did not segment into distinct price positions but rather was made sense of in terms of the areas in which an organization might apply a computer (such as in accounting versus inventory management), technical performance, or the computer's size or architecture. Bell and Newell, writing in 1971, described "the computer space" according to these three dimensions, with only a fleeting mention of cost or price.[31] Rather than a price or value-based definition of the computer "space," industry experts typically referred to the industry according to low-data, high-difficulty problems, such as those faced by scientists, and low-difficulty, data-intensive problems more likely to be encountered in industrial applications such as accounting. This distinction broke down quickly in practice, but it prevailed nonetheless in writings about the industry and as a guide for development efforts such as the IBM 360.

The first order of business for manufacturers was to solve the variety of technical problems connected to making the mainframe computer workable. Skilled scientists and knowledgeable employees more generally were hard to come by. In the 1950s, most who understood the computer came out of universities, one of the few manufacturers, or the government agencies or the military where computers were installed. In this context, manufacturers typically were forced to solve technical problems "in house," leading them to become vertically integrated into supplying their own memory devices, input and output units, and software.[32] Considerably less attention was focused on helping less sophisticated customers productively adopt the computer. The initial growth of the mainframe market, consequently, remain largely among technically sophisticated customers who already saw the computer as valuable, and who could work alongside the manufacturers' teams of experts to install and use a computer.

Into the late 1950s and 1960s the mainframe computer market broadened, but widespread use of mainframes was hindered by limited development in computer operating systems and the user interface. In the 1970s and 1980s, these aspects of computer software would become key to broadening the appeal of computing among organizations and consumers. But the earliest operating systems began as controllers, often created by highly technical users, which coordinated the execution of batch programs to make more efficient use of a computer. Through the 1960s, these operating systems were developed to apportion the uses of a computer's resources, allow for "time sharing" among multiple users, and to provide often-cryptic error diagnostics.[33] The typical mainframe user interface also was limited, often amounting to a card reader or, in some cases, a teletype for entering commands. Even then, such commands were rarely interactive. Rather, commands were typically run in "batch mode," with users entering commands into the computer through human operators who would typically feed cards and mount tapes. Although "automatic" computers were developed that did not require an operator to mount tapes, making the transition to computer technology still involved working with a mysterious and difficult-to-penetrate technology.

Managing input, output, and the data-processing tasks involved in computerization all were difficult impediments to potential customers of the budding industry. Input to and output from a mainframe computer was a difficult computing problem in itself, often requiring small computers to manage these tasks. In fact, some of the first minicomputers would start as input/output control devices for large mainframe systems. Early systems did not typically employ video screens to display output, making access to output often very difficult. The development of high-speed printers helped considerably in this regard, but the actual output printed by mainframe systems often was difficult to decipher. In many cases, output referred to specific hardware functions or locations in the system and so required specialized knowledge to understand. Meanwhile, productively managing the employment of a computer's data-processing capabilities involved new accounting and management challenges for most organizations. Data management systems in organizations were not structured in a way that eased the transition to computerization. Neither was data retrieval straightforward; most systems required that a user have detailed knowledge of where his or her required data could be found—a notorious problem that later would give rise to the market for relational database management systems. So it was that even organizations that sought to adopt computer technology found the transition to be difficult. Altogether, these impediments to computer use amounted to a call to those who might provide solutions.

A broad community of organizations answered the call to make computers more broadly useful, and chief among these were colleges and universities. The short supply of technically skilled computer specialists was not addressed immediately by colleges and universities; not until the mid- to late 1960s did computer science departments appear, stimulated especially by developments at MIT and Stanford. Earlier on, colleges and universities helped broaden the adoption of computer technology by devising ways for their students to work with computers. These efforts helped to make it easier for less sophisticated users to take advantage of computer technology.[34] Perhaps the best-known example here would be Dartmouth's development of the programming language BASIC, which was not taken seriously by computer experts at the time but went on to spur the movement into microcomputers a decade later. Easier-to-understand error messages, as well as debugging programs, also emerged from colleges and universities as efforts to teach computer programming and resulted in more broadly useful software and output. Universities also provided a context for the formation of user groups, which were especially influential given the lack of an established "software firm" model. These groups tended to focus on the hardware of a particular company, such as "SHARE" among IBM users[35] and various DEC user groups.[36] These groups often had a grass-roots quality, attacking problems that users perceived as neglected by the manufacturers—although a much stronger social-movement quality would appear among user groups once they shifted to be defined by software communities as in the USENIX group among UNIX users or, much later, the Linux community.[37] In these ways, out of universities and voluntary associations came some of the earliest solutions to the difficult problems involved with adopting computer technology.

Commercial firms also emerged in complementary markets, smoothing the way for a broader range of organizations to make use of mainframe computers. Service bureaus emerged in the late 1950s, providing organizations with a data-processing specialist to which they could outsource their computerization needs, or to work with organizations to productively install and use computer technology on premises.[38] The availability of machine-independent software and languages increased during the 1960s and further fueled the proliferation of the service bureaus, as these organizations built up specialized abilities in service and support that the manufacturers often lacked.[39] IBM had strong service and support organizations, based on management strengths that predated the computer industry.[40] Yet, in some ways, IBM's policies appear to have spurred the market for service and support, albeit unintendedly. After the 1956 consent decree by the U.S. Department of Justice, IBM began to make its systems available for sale as opposed to only leasing its systems. This decision spurred the development of so-called leasing companies that purchased mainframe systems and then leased the use of these systems to customers, often providing service and support as part of the deal. Similarly, the IBM decision to "unbundle" software and hardware in 1968 is said to have fueled the development of the service bureau population.[41]

By the mid- to late 1960s, then, the mainframe computer market had broadened considerably compared to the early days of the industry. One industry observer, writing at the time, noted that high-profile, sophisticated uses of computers were far rarer than the use of computers for "standard tasks of accounting and financial information processing."[42] This observer goes on to note the increasing use of computers for manufacturing, transportation, communications, wholesale and retail trade, and the like among cutting-edge organizations in these markets. Another observer claims that IBM's decision to unbundle software and hardware in 1968 was driven, in part, by an effort to appeal to a broader range of potential customers.[43] As the mainframe market broadened, even organizations in low-technology industries with little or no computer expertise became customers. For instance, a window-coverings manufacturer, the Newell Company, in 1969 hired a team of computer experts from Honeywell to install and operate a mainframe computer to manage Newell's accounts.[44] By the 1970s, customers served by the mainframe computer manufacturers were so broad that many referred to the industry as "electronic data processing" rather than as the computer industry.[45]

It is well known that IBM has consistently been the mainframe market's leading manufacturer, but perhaps less known are the ways that IBM has helped stimulate the proliferation of mainframe companies generally. In some cases, pressure from U.S. antitrust authorities led to IBM policies that, in turn, increased opportunities for other businesses in the mainframe market—such as the policy to sell as well as lease IBM systems, and the unbundling decision of 1968. In other cases, IBM's position of dominance, by creating a de facto standard in mainframe computing, encouraged the entry of so-called plug-compatible mainframe manufacturers such as Amdahl.[46] Similarly, by the late 1960s, IBM's technological specifications became the basis for plug-compatible manufacturers of memories, tape drives, and processors, which in turn facilitated the development of mainframe manufacturers generally.[47] So important were these effects that plug compatibility, and charges that IBM was intentionally harming the ability of other companies to conform to its technological specifications, became the subject of additional antitrust litigation.

IBM's dominance also had the effect of creating a collective identity for non-IBM companies. It was common in the early mainframe years for companies to describe themselves in oppositional terms by comparison to IBM. For instance, Honeywell employed an oppositional framing when naming its "liberator" software, which allowed users of some Honeywell systems to emulate IBM machines for software compatibility purposes (thus "liberating" the user from IBM). More generally, industry observers routinely counterposed IBM against the other mainframe manufacturers, using phrases like "IBM and the seven dwarfs" or, after GE and RCA left the market, "IBM and the BUNCH" (referring to Burroughs, Univac, NCR, Control Data, and Honeywell). Oppositional rhetoric would be even more important in the rise of the midrange and microcomputer markets, but by the 1970s an oppositional identity appeared to have developed among non-IBM mainframe manufacturers as well.

The Second Wave in Mainframe Computing

After a period of decreasing numbers of firms in the 1970s, the mainframe computer market experienced a dramatic resurgence from the late 1970s through the 1980s. During this second wave, the number of mainframe computer manufacturers in the United States would reach its all time high, just before a sharp collapse into the 1990s as illustrated in figure 6.2. From 1980 through 1994, fifty-four organizations would enter the mainframe market. Meanwhile, the size of the mainframe market in shipments also grew from the late 1970s. According to IDC's historical shipments data, "large computer" market shipments grew by about one-third on an annual basis from 1975 to 1980, with slower but steady growth through the 1980s and early 1990s. So both the density and mass of the mainframe market experienced a surge in the late 1970s and 1980s—a second wave of mainframe computing.

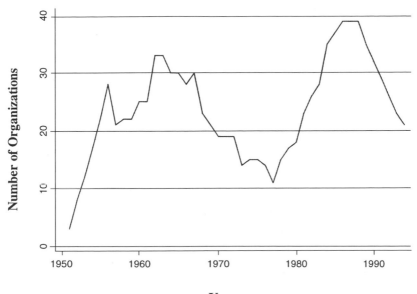

Figure 6.2. Number of U.S. mainframe computer manufacturers.

For many industry insiders, the ongoing health of the mainframe market was consistent with their expectations for the industry. By the 1970s, mainframe computing had become accepted as a requirement for modern organizations—even among low-technology businesses. And although the mainframe market had experienced an ongoing shakeout over its history, and a reduction in the total number of organizations during the first half of the 1970s, a number of firms were healthy. For instance, Burroughs President R. W. Macdonald spoke of a bullish future, looking forward from 1975, with reference to the company's history of success in the mainframe market: "Our revenue has doubled every five years, and today, at $1.5 billion, is four times its level of ten years ago. Our net earnings have increased by 14 times during the 10-year period, and this is the best record of growth in the mainframe computer industry. Our manpower worldwide has increased from about 34,000 to more than 51,500. We are operating 54 plants in ten countries and two more plants are under construction."[48] What Macdonald did not know, of course, was that fundamental transformations were about to take place in the industry. As Macdonald made his bullish statement regarding mainframes in 1975, the technological basis of distributed computing was being developed at Xerox PARC, the first microcomputer was being shipped by a small inventor, and Microsoft had just been formed.

Year

Figure 6.3. Number of U.S. midrange computer manufacturers.

Now with the benefit of hindsight, we know that 1975 was a threshold, and many may find the resurgence of mainframe manufacturers after that point to be unexpected. The typical retelling of the industry's history describes a transformation to distributed computing and client-server architectures in the 1980s. Like mainframes, these systems allow users to share computer resources that reside centrally, but unlike mainframes they also allow computing power to reside in multiple locations—and to be employed by users regardless of their locations. Observers routinely described the shift to distributed computing using terms like "paradigm shift" and "disruption," even before the Internet. Looking back from the twenty-first century, one can easily imagine that mainframe computers would have been displaced entirely by client-server systems, since nowadays many organizations use exclusively the latter for their computing needs. Yet the mainframe market remained vibrant in the 1980s, attracting considerable entrepreneurial energy and technical innovation, even as distributed computing and client-server architectures were taking hold.

One likely reason for the mainframe's continued strength was the fact that the initial innovations in distributed computing emphasized networking capabilities combined with delivering more computing power to the desktop. These innovations were notably distinct from the technical

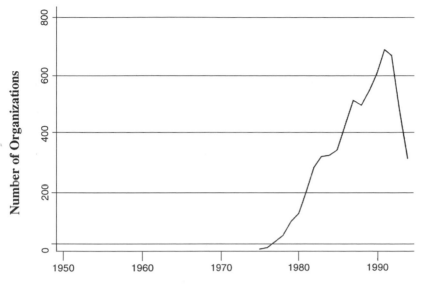

Figure 6.4. Number of U.S. microcomputer manufacturers.

functionality of a large-scale, centralized mainframe computer. Networking hardware stemmed from various developments but was advanced greatly by Robert Metcalf's development of the Ethernet at Xerox PARC in the mid 1970s.[49] Metcalf would go on to found 3COM in 1981, bringing to market in the 1980s, along with many other firms, technologies that would enable networked computing. In this context, the 1980s saw organizations such as SUN and SGI, as well as established midrange firms such as DEC, bring workstations to desktops.[50] The servers in these early systems were not as advanced as would be the case several years later and so were not a substitute for the large-scale mainframe. Said one expert looking back on the era:

> During the 1980s, distributed computing was serving a market completely unrelated to mainframe computing. I associate mainframe computing with commercial, enterprise applications like accounting, payroll, ERP,[51] transaction processing—the stuff corporations use to run their business. During the 80s, UNIX workstations were tools on engineers' desktops and PCs were tools on business people's desktops. My rough memory is that when many of these client-server firms started, they only sold workstations. Later, they pretended to sell "servers," but the servers were pretty much just workstations packaged in taller racks.

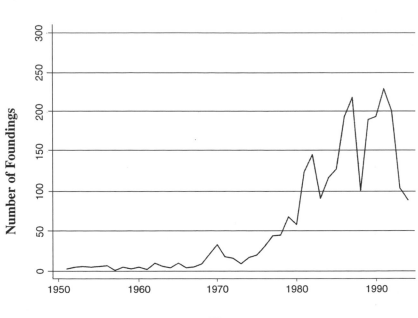

Figure 6.5. Annual entries into the U.S. computer industry.

It took a while before they really started designing in the high-end RAS (reliability, availability, serviceability) required to compete against mainframes.[52]

Thus, even as distributed computing was taking off in the 1980s, the mainframe remained distinctly able to meet the data management needs of large-scale organizations.

A second reason for the continued strength of the mainframe market was that the movement to distributed computing was complementary in many ways with mainframe computing. Workstations were a means for people throughout an organization to access information that might, ultimately, reside in a mainframe system. The technical challenges and opportunities involved in integrating mainframe computing into distributed computing systems were the subject of considerable research and advancement among computer scientists during this period. For instance, a series of annual ACM/IEEE conferences on supercomputers began in 1988, featuring research on a wide variety of technical topics, many of which were concerned in some way with how mainframe storage and processing technologies could be designed to work within distributed computing environments.[53] In this way, until the client-server architecture and systems matured to the point where mainframes could be dis-

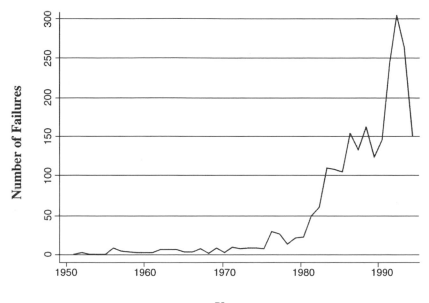

Figure 6.6. Annual failures of U.S. computer manufacturers.

placed, the move to distributed computing if anything complemented mainframe computers.

One particularly intriguing development was the explosion of super-computing in the second wave of the mainframe market. Technologists distinguish supercomputers according to their performance, size, and architectures. Some of these systems rely on exceptionally fast and expensive processors. Others take advantage of so-called parallel or massively parallel architectures, wherein problems are subdivided into many smaller parts that can be handled separately but simultaneously—typically by larger numbers of less expensive and less powerful microprocessors. The 1980s saw a flowering of various approaches to supercomputing, building on advances in microprocessor technologies, networking technologies that enabled parallel processing, and innovations in computer architectures. Such machines are normally associated with Seymour Cray, who worked on advanced machines at Control Data in the 1960s. Many dub Cray's release of the Cray I in 1975–76 to be the beginning of the supercomputer era. In fact, very few supercomputers entered the market until the 1980s, a period when many designs were attempted and only some resulted in marketable computers. Of the fifty-four organizations entering the mainframe market from 1980 to 1994 (see fig. 6.7), nearly half (twenty-four) manufactured supercomputers.

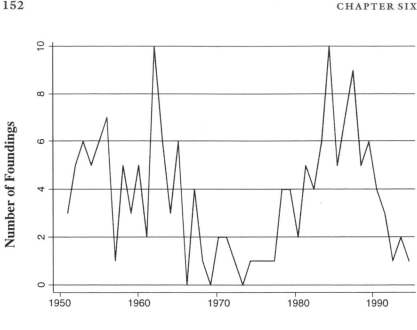

Figure 6.7. Entries into the U.S. mainframe computer market.

Competition as a Sampling Process among Mainframe Computer Organizations

So the mainframe market's development wove together various technical and institutional factors. In this process, mainframe manufacturers were discovering what was—even when seen in retrospect—a complicated mesh of market requirements, institutional constraints, and technical impera-tives. The logic of competition implied by these factors continued to de-velop over time, challenging those organizations that attempted to com-pete in this context. As figure 6.8 illustrates, this process was sufficiently difficult that mainframe manufacturers faced an ongoing shakeout throughout the market's history. By competing, these organizations con-tinually sampled the market's logic of competition and adjusted accord-ingly—potentially improving their performance, but in the process affect-ing their rivals all the more.

How organizational size affected competition was much debated in the history of the mainframe market. Much of this debate centered around IBM and its antitrust prosecutions. IBM's success as a large, vertically integrated manufacturer often was held out as evidence that scale and scope drive innovation—especially in complex technology markets. IBM's scale and vertical integration, it was argued, gave it the wherewithal to

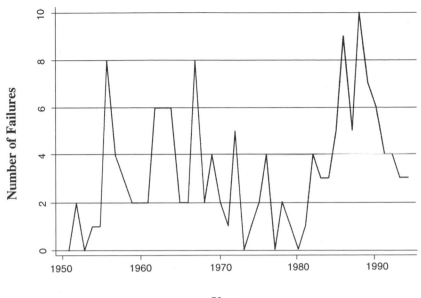

Figure 6.8. Failures of U.S. mainframe computer manufacturers.

efficiently coordinate the different interdependent parts of what was a complex technological system. Some might discount this argument looking back from the twenty-first century, because we have seen so many smaller organizations successfully innovate. Furthermore, the pro-IBM argument was typically attributed to Franklin Fisher, IBM's chief economist, who wrote on the topic in 1983 immediately after defending the company.[54] For instance, Fisher and his colleagues saw IBM's success compared to the failure of General Electric, a more decentralized firm, as evidence of the superiority of central control in this market. Yet this idea, at least in general, also had support broadly among various other institutional economists. Decades earlier, Schumpeter had argued that the market power of large organizations gave them incentives for long-term research and development, and other institutional economists writing in the era emphasized other advantages due to size.[55]

Yet amidst IBM's size and centralized control, competition within the mainframe market emerged from various directions. In part, competition emerged due to antitrust constraints, but competition was triggered also through technological developments that invited new manufacturers into the market. On the antitrust front, a consent decree ended the IBM policy of (mostly) leasing rather than selling its equipment; a policy, it was feared, that might have allowed IBM to control the market's pace of technological advance. Similarly, a consent decree ended IBM's policy of bundling software and hardware, further encouraging the creation of machine-independent software. Meanwhile, as the market for components, peripherals, and machine-independent software developed, vertical integration became less of an advantage for mainframe manufacturers.[56] Growing demand for mainframe computing invited new foundings, and teams of researchers designing new approaches to computing answered this call. A stream of new mainframe manufacturers entered the industry throughout the 1950s and 1960s, as illustrated in figure 6.7. Some of these were established firms entering based on their own innovations, and some were start-ups formed around teams of researchers coming up with new computer designs. Some start-ups became "restarts," acquisitions—often by established firms trying to get in to the mainframe market—of small, innovative organizations that had created a new computer design but failed when trying to grow the firm into a full-scale mainframe manufacturer. In these ways, new competitors and new technologies appeared in the mainframe market throughout its first two decades.

As the market for mainframe computing broadened in the 1960s, more manufacturers began to focus on increasing their service and support capabilities. Established, large-scale organizations did not typically have elaborate information technology capabilities at that time. This shortcoming was enough to prevent an organization from successfully installing and making use of a mainframe system. Such systems required specialized technicians to mediate the interaction of the user and the system. Furthermore, specialized knowledge was required to make use of software in any form—especially in a form tailored to the needs of the customer organization. And to make optimal use of a mainframe system, new organizational routines would be required to collect, manage, and retrieve useful data. These various capabilities were in short supply. Although service bureaus sometimes were relied upon to fill the need for service and support, manufacturers found themselves at a competitive disadvantage if they could not help customers to install and make good use of their systems.[57] Scientific Data Systems' annual report in 1965 was telling in this regard:

> The character of the computer market changed substantially last year as the result of advances in both the understanding of the technology and in the manner in which computers should be employed. . . . During the past year increasing emphasis has been placed by management on providing complete service to SDS customers both before and after installation. To this end, technical staffs and applications programming, systems engineering, customer training and maintenance have more than doubled in size and in the scope of their activities.[58]

In these efforts, Scientific Data Systems was not alone. All those competing in this market learned, through competition, that an extensive customer service and support organization was required to win the business of the typical customer. When many of these manufacturers were first founded, the focus was typically on solving the daunting technical problems involved in mainframe computing. But through competing over customers, these manufacturers discovered the importance of customer service and support.

Similarly, competition pushed manufacturers to develop their technologies: the components, peripherals, and system architectures associated with mainframe computers. Components were improved dramatically as they incorporated transistor technology, a Bell Labs innovation released to the computer market after a 1956 consent decree.[59] Transistors allowed new manufacturers to build systems without using vacuum tubes, increasing performance and reliability.[60] Many competitors based their systems on innovations in new storage devices, memory technologies, input-output peripherals, and processor designs. In the ensuing competition, established firms and new firms alike released a variety of new technologies. For instance, Honeywell, IBM, and other firms featured internally modularized systems that could be configured differently for different users. Such "microprogramming" was key to the IBM 360 line of computers but over time became common as many manufacturers developed such cost effective, modular architectures in an effort to compete.

Technological competition continued in the mainframe market even after the broad acceptance of the IBM 360/370 line of computers. Investments in these systems, in terms of both hardware and software, were sunk costs that inhibited customers from switching to new systems.[61] Nonetheless, new technologies and competitors continued to appear in the mainframe market in two ways. First, some innovations built upon the installed base of 360 systems. Software emulators allowed customers to run programs written for the IBM 360 on other systems, in turn allowing customers to migrate to new hardware manufactured by other firms without losing the value of their existing software.[62] Meanwhile, various hardware manufacturers introduced systems that conformed to the technical specifications of the 360.[63] In these ways, competition occurred within the technological specifications established by IBM's 360 system.

Competitors and technologies that were not compatible with the IBM 360 were at a disadvantage. From the perspective of Red Queen competition, IBM's success with the 360 could be expected to generate fewer, but more significant, competitive entries in its wake. In order to succeed despite the broad acceptance of the IBM 360 line, new innovations by IBM's rivals had to be exceptionally valuable from a customer's perspective. For example, time-sharing—a feature that allows multiple users to operate si-multaneously on a mainframe system—would come to be commonplace in mainframe computing since it allows mainframes to be more cost effec-tive. This feature, however, was not at first designed into IBM's machines, including the initial 360 line. Other firms, such as General Electric, did offer time-sharing systems and so made inroads into the mainframe mar-ket and eventually stimulated a competitive response by IBM.[64] In another example, the supercomputers introduced by Cray starting in 1975 at-tracted the high end of the mainframe market, establishing Cray as the benchmark for high-speed (and high-priced) processing. So it was that IBM's successes based on its 360/370 line effectively raised the bar in Red Queen competition, making it necessary for new innovations by rivals to be exceptional in order to be accepted in the market. More generally, the mainframe market remained technically innovative and competitive, with the manufacturers developing their products, services, and technologies in response to one another.[65]

Estimates of the Founding and Failure Models for Mainframe Manufacturers

The institutional history of the mainframe market suggests that these or-ganizations engaged in the kind of reciprocal feedback described by the theory—competition triggering learning, further intensifying competi-tion. But a brief review of examples is necessarily selective and does not constitute a test of a theory's predictions. For such a test, I conduct a systematic analysis of the data on these organizations to see whether esti-mates of the model show evidence of Red Queen competition among these organizations as the theory predicts.

The data on computer manufacturers, and the method used to collect these data, are described in the appendix. Table 6.1 describes the numbers of general purpose electronic digital computer manufacturers in the United States over the period 1951–1994. A total of 2,602 organizations existed in this industry over that time period. Tables 6.2 and 6.4 describe the data on mainframe manufacturers as arranged in order to estimate the founding and failure models. Some 165 organizations would enter into the manufacture of mainframe computers during this period, and 146 of these would exit the market at some point prior to 1995.

Estimates of the founding models for mainframe manufacturers are re-ported in table 6.3. The table includes four models. Model $\lambda_{mn}1$ is a base-line specification, including density terms, exogenous factors likely to af-fect the founding rate, the mass of mainframe organizations (shipments), lagged foundings and failures, and the (average) cumulative hazard of fail-

TABLE 6.2
Description of the Data Used in the Mainframe Manufacturer Founding Analysis

Variables	Mean	Std Dev	Min	Max
Mainframe manufacturer entries/1,000	0.0038	0.0026	0	0.0100
Mainframe manufacturer entries last year /1,000	0.0037	0.0027	0	0.0100
Lagged mainframe manuf. failures/1,000	0.0033	0.0026	0	0.0100
Mainframe market shipments/106	0.0059	0.0045	0	0.0123
Real U.S. gross domestic product	3069	1,193	0	5,135
U.S. prime interest rate	7.256	3.716	0	18.87
Cumulative hazard of failure since organization's birth	0.8877	0.5062	0	1.910
Mainframe market density/1,000	0.0199	0.0076	0	0.0340
Mainframe market density squared / 1,000	0.4534	0.2866	0	1.156
Historical competition faced by org. in mainframe market/1,000	3.376	1.901	0	6.242
Recent historical competition faced in mainframe market/1,000	1.625	0.8717	0	3.102
Distant-past historical competition faced in mainframe market/1,000	1.751	1.107	0	3.278
Gini based on density	0.1935	0.0609	0	0.2971
Gini based on founding	0.2976	0.1056	0	0.4572

Source: Various archival documents (see appendix).

ure over the lives of the incumbents to test for a pure-selection effect. This model also includes the historical competition measure, $\Sigma_k T_k$, which is the sum of the organization-years of competition faced historically by incumbent organizations (denoted by **k**) as of any given year. Model $\lambda_{mn}2$ is the same as model $\lambda_{mn}1$, except that density is specified without the squared term. Model $\lambda_{mn}3$ decomposes the historical competition term, $\Sigma_k T_k$, distinguishing recent versus distant-past exposure to competition to test the Competitive Hysteresis and Competency-Trap Hypotheses. Finally, model $\lambda_{mn}4$ also includes the average gini coefficients, **G**, measuring how dispersed over time the incumbents' history of competition has been, to test the Myopic Learning Hypothesis.

Looking first at models $\lambda_{mn}3$ and $\lambda_{mn}4$, there is consistent evidence in support of both the Competitive Hysteresis and Competency-Trap Hypotheses. The more that incumbent mainframe firms have been exposed to competition in recent years, the stronger the competition they generate, consistent with Red Queen theory. Put differently, founding rates fell as incumbent organizations built up recent competitive experience. As this experience became outdated, however, its effect on the founding rate reversed completely. In support of the Competency-Trap

TABLE 6.3
Estimates of the Founding Rate of U.S. Mainframe Computer Manufacturers, 1951–1994

Independent Variable	($\lambda_{mn}1$)	($\lambda_{mn}2$)	($\lambda_{mn}3$)	($\lambda_{mn}4$)
Prior year mainframe manufacturer entries/1,000	−0.0370 (0.0568)	−0.0595 (0.0483)	−0.1142** (0.0539)	−0.2326** (0.0703)
Prior year mainframe manufacturer failures/1,000	0.0058 (0.0416)	0.0096 (0.0413)	0.0713 (0.0485)	0.1010* (0.0547)
Sum of sizes of mainframe organizations (annual shipments)/1,000	−0.0001 (0.0001)	−0.0001 (0.0001)	−0.0002 (0.0001)	−0.0002 (0.0001)
Real U.S. gross domestic product	0.0004 (0.0003)	0.0005 (0.0003)	0.0005** (0.0003)	0.0006* (0.0003)
U.S. prime interest rate	0.0624* (0.0361)	0.0716** (0.0338)	0.0237 (0.0401)	0.0126 (0.0425)
Avg. cumulative hazard of failure in the mainframe market since incumbents' births	−2.628** (0.6669)	−2.285** (0.4773)	−2.690** (0.5020)	−1.212 (0.8713)
Number of mainframe manufacturers/1,000	36.67 (49.62)	44.58 (25.02)	48.52 (31.15)	190.8** (60.71)
Number of mainframe manufacturers/1,000, squared	−1.407 (1.864)			
Historical competition faced by organization in mainframe market/1,000	0.2971 (0.3419)	0.1264 (0.2555)		
Recent historical competition faced by organization in mainframe market/1,000			−0.8962* (0.4921)	−1.924** (0.6701)
Distant-past historical competition faced by organization in mainframe market/1,000			1.258** (0.5215)	1.181** (0.5438)
Inequality of past rivalry faced by organization (average gini)				−5.563* (3.070)
Inequality of past rival cohorts faced by organization (average gini)				−3.175 (3.012)
Constant	1.097** (0.4744)	1.185** (0.4458)	1.142** (0.4560)	1.134** (0.4925)
Log likelihood	−80.66	−80.94	−77.93	−74.03
(df)	(9)	(8)	(9)	(11)

Note: The data include 165 market entries over 44 years, modeled as annual event counts. For coefficient estimates, standard errors are in parentheses.
* $p < .10$
** $p < .05$

TABLE 6.4
Description of the Data Used in the Mainframe Manufacturer Failure Analysis

Variables	Mean	Std Dev	Min	Max
Dealio entrant	0.6013	0.4899	0	1
Real U.S. gross domestic product	3,254	1,135	0	5,135
U.S. prime interest rate	7.562	3.475	0	18.87
Market tenure, small organization	0.4313	0.4955	0	1
Market tenure, medium-sized organization	0.3910	0.4882	0	1
Market tenure, large-sized organization	0.1777	0.3825	0	1
Mainframe market shipments/10⁶	0.0065	0.0045	0	0.0123
Mainframe manufacturer entries/1,000	0.0043	0.0027	0	0.0100
Lagged mainframe manuf. failures/1,000	0.0038	0.0026	0	0.0100
Mainframe market density at entry/1,000	0.0183	0.0088	0	0.0340
Cumulative hazard of failure since organization's birth	0.8681	1.056	0	5.263
Computer industry density/1,000	0.2208	0.2134	0	0.6030
Computer industry density squared/1,000	94.24	119.0	0	363.6
Microcomputer market density/1,000	0.1352	0.1691	0	0.4780
Midrange market density/1,000	0.0926	0.0830	0	0.2170
Mainframe market density/1,000	0.0225	0.0065	0	0.0340
Duration in microcomputer	1.082	3.045	0	20.00
Duration in midrange	3.429	6.049	0	32.00
Historical competition faced by org. in mainframe market/1,000	0.1340	0.1610	0	0.8140
Recent historical competition faced in mainframe market/1,000	0.0649	0.0548	0	0.2423

TABLE 6.4 (*cont.*)
Description of the Data Used in the Mainframe Manufacturer Failure Analysis

Variables	Mean	Std Dev	Min	Max
Distant-past historical competition faced in mainframe market/1,000	0.0690	0.1099	0	0.5717
Number of distinct rivals faced in mainframe market/1,000	0.0344	0.0264	0	0.1390
Historical competition faced by org. in micro-computer market/1,000	0.2304	0.7155	0	4.336
Historical competition faced by org. in midrange market/1,000	0.3856	0.7493	0	3.484
Mainframe rivals' historical exposure to competition/1,000	3.387	1.692	0	5.947
Mainframe rivals' recent exposure to competition/1,000	1.678	0.7797	0	2.909
Mainframe rivals' distant exposure to competition/1,000	1.709	0.9824	0	3.216
Sum of ages of mainframe rivals/1,000	3.385	2.623	0	8.071
Gini based on density	0.2041	0.1636	0	0.6667
Gini based on founding	0.2988	0.2057	0	0.6667

Source: Various archival documents (see appendix).

Hypothesis, the more distant-past competitive experience among incumbents, the more inviting was the market to new entries. So mainframe organizations developed in line with the theory of Red Queen competition, becoming stronger competitors and so deterring entry by enduring competition, but ultimately weakening as this competitive experience became outdated.

This pattern of effects held despite the many other factors included in these models. In particular, models $\lambda_{mn}1$ through $\lambda_{mn}3$ show evidence of a pure-selection effect. Higher average values of the cumulative hazard of failure in the market over each incumbent's life to date had a negative effect on the founding rate going forward. This means that incumbents who had survived while others failed appear to have generated stronger competition, lowering founding rates in the market. This effect does not hold in model $\lambda_{mn}4$, but that model shows an unbelievably explosive posi-

tive effect of density—a term that is considerably smaller and nonsignificant in the other specifications. (Recall that this already large coefficient
is exponentiated, implying a massive increase in the founding rate with
increased density.) It appears that including the gini coefficients along
with the other terms may be generating collinearity, so results that hold
only in that specification are suspect. For instance, one of the gini coefficients has a negative and marginally significant effect on foundings, weakly
supporting the Myopic Learning Hypothesis. That is, it appears that incumbents who faced competitors broadly dispersed over time generated
stronger competition. Besides the weak significance level, however, this
effect should also be interpreted skeptically because of model $\lambda_{mn}4$'s erratic
behavior in the other coefficients.

Turning now to the organizational failure models, these estimates are
shown in tables 6.5 and 6.6. Look first at the baseline model $r_{mn}1$ in table
6.5. The density of mainframe manufacturers has a strong positive effect
on the organizational failure rate, an effect that remains robust across different specifications. (Also, in models not shown, I estimated quadratic
density effects, but these did not improve over the monotonic specification.) This density effect is evidence of competition among mainframe
manufacturers in the founding process, such that founding rates declined
as the number of mainframe manufacturers increased. Model $r_{mn}2$ includes
all the terms in model $r_{mn}1$ as well as T_j, the historical competition faced
by the focal organization (j) in the mainframe market. Model $r_{mn}3$ then
includes K_j, the number of distinct historical rivals faced by a given organization j, to test the Costly Adaptation Hypothesis. And models $r_{mn}4$ and
$r_{mn}5$ then separately specify recent- and distant-past historical experience
for the organization, to test the Competitive Hysteresis and Competency-
Trap Hypotheses.

Comparing these models, the historical timing of competitive experience clearly is important, as the theory predicts. Only in models $r_{mn}4$ and
$r_{mn}5$ does historical competition have significant effects. Consistent with
the Competitive Hysteresis Hypothesis, mainframe manufacturers with
recent historical experience competing are considerably less likely to fail.
This effect reverses with the passage of time, however. As the Competency-
Trap Hypothesis predicts, organizations with more competitive experience in the distant past are more likely to fail. So competitive experience
made mainframe manufacturers more viable, at least until this experience
was rendered outdated. Meanwhile, the number of distinct historical rivals
is not significant in either of the specifications where it is included, so I do
not find evidence in support of the Costly Adaptation Hypothesis among
mainframe manufacturers.

The models in table 6.6 are the same as model $r_{mn}5$, but with additional
terms. Model $r_{mn}6$ includes the gini coefficients, G_j, measuring the disper-

TABLE 6.5

Estimates of the Failure Rates of U.S. Mainframe Computer Manufacturers, 1951–1994

Independent Variable	$(r_{mn}1)$	$(r_{mn}2)$	$(r_{mn}3)$	$(r_{mn}4)$	$(r_{mn}5)$
Number of mainframe manufacturers at entry/1,000	-10.96 (13.35)	-11.04 (13.43)	-7.810 (13.59)	-4.753 (13.82)	-4.765 (13.78)
Cumulative hazard of failure in mainframe market since the organization's birth	0.4530 (0.3986)	0.0218 (1.020)	0.3381 (1.046)	-0.8605 (1.205)	-0.8663 (1.084)
Historical competition faced by organization in mainframe market/1,000	2.931 (6.375)		7.385 (7.011)		
Recent historical competition faced by organization in mainframe market/1,000				-21.49 (15.48)	-21.60* (11.64)
Distant-past historical competition faced by organization in mainframe market/1,000				21.84** (9.867)	21.86** (9.760)
Number of distinct historical rivals faced by organization in mainframe market/1,000			-39.26 (26.46)	-0.3554 (32.49)	
Dealio entrant	0.0470 (0.1964)	0.0598 (0.1977)	0.0772 (0.1981)	0.0960 (0.1985)	0.0959 (0.1985)

TABLE 6.5 (*cont.*)
Estimates of the Failure Rates of U.S. Mainframe Computer Manufacturers, 1951–1994

Independent Variable	$(r_{mn}1)$	$(r_{mn}2)$	$(r_{mn}3)$	$(r_{mn}4)$	$(r_{mn}5)$
Number of mainframe manufacturers/ 1,000	66.74**	62.18**	79.94**	75.46**	75.32**
	(24.75)	(26.55)	(30.07)	(30.50)	(27.98)
Number of midrange computer manufacturers/1,000	0.5436	0.5566	−0.7913	−1.295	−1.289
	(3.005)	(3.012)	(3.128)	(3.120)	(3.067)
Number of microcomputer manufacturers/1,000	−0.4489	−0.4497	0.1765	−0.0096	−0.0135
	(1.444)	(1.446)	(1.525)	(1.511)	(1.468)
Sum of sizes of microcomputer organizations (shipments)/1,000	−0.0031	−0.0129	−0.0102	0.0238	0.0239
	(0.1111)	(0.1129)	(0.1152)	(0.1166)	(0.1163)
Prior year mainframe manufacturer entries/1,000	−61.52	−59.31	−76.81	−85.42*	−85.34*
	(45.22)	(45.46)	(47.41)	(47.54)	(46.89)
Prior year mainframe manufacturer failures/1,000	−21.48	−18.32	−9.95	21.08	21.13
	(43.67)	(44.12)	(44.39)	(46.92)	(46.75)
Organization also is in midrange computer market	−0.2721	−0.2784	−0.3217	−0.3369	−0.3367
	(0.2257)	(0.2261)	(0.2286)	(0.2300)	(0.2292)
Organization also is in microcomputer market	−0.5129	−0.5085	−0.5277	−0.6402	−0.6404
	(0.4555)	(0.4561)	(0.4642)	(0.4805)	(0.4801)

TABLE 6.5 (*cont.*)
Estimates of the Failure Rates of U.S. Mainframe Computer Manufacturers, 1951–1994

Independent Variable	$(r_{mn}1)$	$(r_{mn}2)$	$(r_{mn}3)$	$(r_{mn}4)$	$(r_{mn}5)$
Real U.S. gross domestic product	0.0001	0.0001	0.0002	0.0001	0.0001
	(0.0005)	(0.0005)	(0.0005)	(0.0005)	(0.0005)
U.S. prime interest rate	−0.0583	−0.0565	−0.0627	−0.0647	−0.0647
	(0.0478)	(0.0479)	(0.0483)	(0.0481)	(0.0480)
Market tenure, all organizations					
0–1 year	−2.508**	−2.476**	−3.061**	−2.989**	−2.985**
	(1.042)	(1.039)	(1.179)	(1.174)	(1.109)
1–3 years	−2.360**	−2.338**	−2.200**	−2.008*	−2.008*
	(1.043)	(1.040)	(1.086)	(1.082)	(1.081)
3–5 years	−2.417**	−2.407**	−2.308**	−1.575	−1.574
	(1.070)	(1.065)	(1.111)	(1.153)	(1.141)
5–10 years	−2.353**	−2.373**	−2.269**	−1.140	−1.136
	(1.111)	(1.108)	(1.152)	(1.262)	(1.230)
10–15 years	−3.482**	−3.529**	−3.476**	−1.987	−1.983
	(1.430)	(1.428)	(1.458)	(1.603)	(1.548)
15+ years	−3.138*	−3.200**	−3.358**	−2.157	−2.152
	(1.611)	(1.613)	(1.671)	(1.796)	(1.732)

TABLE 6.5 (*cont.*)
Estimates of the Failure Rates of U.S. Mainframe Computer Manufacturers, 1951–1994

Independent Variable	$(r_{mm}1)$	$(r_{mm}2)$	$(r_{mm}3)$	$(r_{mm}4)$	$(r_{mm}5)$
Market tenure, medium-sized organizations					
0–1 year	−0.0832	−0.0921	−0.0744	−0.0483	−0.0484
	(0.4744)	(0.4743)	(0.4768)	(0.4763)	(0.4761)
1–3 years	−0.3447	−0.3524	−0.3457	−0.3278	−0.3277
	(0.3524)	(0.3524)	(0.3515)	(0.3524)	(0.3524)
3–5 years	−0.7156*	−0.7058	−0.6949	−0.6699	−0.6699
	(0.4307)	(0.4309)	(0.4309)	(0.4304)	(0.4303)
5–10 years	−0.9328**	−0.9060**	−0.9626**	−0.9124**	−0.9119**
	(0.3722)	(0.3769)	(0.3773)	(0.3769)	(0.3742)
10–15 years	0.1261	0.1894	0.0817	0.0798	0.0805
	(0.9389)	(0.9462)	(0.9346)	(0.9204)	(0.9180)
15+ years	−1.699*	−1.658*	−1.917*	−2.276**	−2.275**
	(0.9783)	(0.9856)	(1.022)	(1.118)	(1.115)
Market tenure, large organizations					
0–5 years	−1.294*	−1.294*	−1.303*	−1.290*	−1.290*
	(0.7425)	(0.7422)	(0.7423)	(0.7423)	(0.7423)
5–10 years	−2.423**	−2.372**	−2.371**	−2.361**	−2.361**
	(1.032)	(1.038)	(1.037)	(1.038)	(1.038)
10+ years	−2.225**	−2.197**	−2.429**	−2.890**	−2.890**
	(0.9542)	(0.9615)	(1.005)	(1.173)	(1.173)
Log likelihood	−224.105	−223.998	−222.884	−220.684	−220.684
(df)	(28)	(29)	(30)	(31)	(30)

Note: The data include 146 failures from a risk set of 165 organizations over 1,041 organization-years. Other variables also are included in each model, as shown in the continuation of the table. For coefficient estimates, standard errors are in parentheses.

* p < .10
** p < .05

TABLE 6.6
Estimates of the Failure Rates of U.S. Mainframe Computer Manufacturers, 1951–1994

Independent Variable	$(r_{mn}6)$	$(r_{mn}7)$	$(r_{mn}8)$
Number of mainframe manufacturers at entry/1,000	4.816	-4.874	-3.526
	(16.35)	(13.72)	(13.59)
Cumulative hazard of failure in mainframe market since the organization's birth	-1.243	-0.8735	-0.8581
	(1.099)	(1.085)	(1.080)
Historical competition faced by organization in mainframe market/1,000			
Recent historical competition faced by organization in mainframe market/1,000	-26.96**	-22.03*	-23.33**
	(12.41)	(11.74)	(11.68)
Distant-past historical competition faced by organization in mainframe market/1,000	27.46**	22.20**	22.11**
	(10.16)	(9.831)	(9.831)
Number of distinct historical rivals faced by organization in mainframe market/1,000			
Mainframe rivals' historical exposure to competition/1,000		0.0934	
		(0.3323)	
Recent mainframe rivals' historical exposure to competition/1,000			1.055
			(0.8235)
Distant-past mainframe rivals' historical exposure to competition/1,000			-0.8847
			(0.8388)
Inequality of past rivalry faced by organization (gini)	1.702		
	(1.410)		
Inequality of past rival cohorts faced by organization (gini)	-0.5851		
	(1.349)		

TABLE 6.6 (*cont.*)
Estimates of the Failure Rates of U.S. Mainframe Computer Manufacturers, 1951–1994

Independent Variable	$(r_{mn}6)$	$(r_{mn}7)$	$(r_{mn}8)$
Number of mainframe manufacturers/1,000	68.92**	65.85	17.43
	(29.72)	(43.51)	(56.69)
Number of midrange computer manufacturers/1,000	-1.908	-1.381	3.261
	(3.124)	(3.078)	(4.784)
Number of microcomputer manufacturers/1,000	-0.2794	0.3620	-0.9142
	(1.590)	(1.975)	(2.227)
Sum of sizes of mainframe organizations (annual shipments)/1,000	0.0499	0.0043	0.0223
	(0.1187)	(0.1351)	(0.1350)
Prior year mainframe manufacturer entries/1,000	-78.42*	-76.29	-60.07
	(47.07)	(56.81)	(57.75)
Prior year mainframe manufacturer failures/1,000	31.73	17.03	-19.20
	(47.01)	(49.17)	(56.11)
Dealio entrant	0.1167	0.0926	0.1086
	(0.1985)	(0.1988)	(0.1998)
Organization also is in midrange computer market	-0.3124	-0.3487	-0.3774
	(0.2328)	(0.2330)	(0.2342)
Organization also is in microcomputer market	-0.6838	-0.6320	-0.6414
	(0.4839)	(0.4814)	(0.4821)
Real U.S. gross domestic product	0.0001	0.0000	0.0003
	(0.0005)	(0.0006)	(0.0006)

TABLE 6.6 (*cont.*)

Estimates of the Failure Rates of U.S. Mainframe Computer Manufacturers, 1951–1994

Independent Variable	$(r_{mn}6)$	$(r_{mn}7)$	$(r_{mn}8)$
U.S. prime interest rate	-0.0673	-0.0613	-0.0583
	(0.0479)	(0.0496)	(0.0496)
Market tenure, all organizations			
0–1 year	-3.148**	-2.805**	-2.802**
	(1.135)	(1.260)	(1.243)
1–3 years	-2.187**	-1.811	-1.747
	(1.103)	(1.270)	(1.254)
3–5 years	-1.700	-1.358	-1.245
	(1.154)	(1.358)	(1.346)
5–10 years	-0.9925	-0.9236	-0.8094
	(1.238)	(1.429)	(1.420)
10–15 years	-1.733	-1.765	-1.631
	(1.552)	(1.718)	(1.708)
15+ years	-1.968	-1.936	-1.769
	(1.744)	(1.883)	(1.888)
Market tenure, medium-sized organizations			
0–1 year	-0.0218	-0.0467	-0.0687
	(0.4769)	(0.4763)	(0.4763)
1–3 years	-0.3521	-0.3216	-0.3294
	(0.3510)	(0.3531)	(0.3529)
3–5 years	-0.6478	-0.6773	-0.6749
	(0.4309)	(0.4312)	(0.4312)

TABLE 6.6 (*cont.*)
Estimates of the Failure Rates of U.S. Mainframe Computer Manufacturers, 1951–1994

Independent Variable	$(r_{mn}6)$	$(r_{mn}7)$	$(r_{mn}8)$
5–10 years	−0.8995**	−0.9134**	−0.8987**
	(0.3730)	(0.3741)	(0.3747)
10–15 years	0.1027	0.0739	0.0446
	(0.9154)	(0.9178)	(0.9135)
15+ years	−2.378**	−2.269**	−2.354**
	(1.148)	(1.114)	(1.118)
Market tenure, large organizations			
0–5 years	−1.344*	−1.283*	−1.279*
	(0.7434)	(0.7430)	(0.7431)
5–10 years	−2.343**	−2.350**	−2.335**
	(1.037)	(1.038)	(1.039)
10+ years	−2.961**	−2.898**	−2.992**
	(1.223)	(1.172)	(1.183)
Log likelihood	−218.979	−220.644	−219.849
(df)	(32)	(31)	(32)

Note: The data include 146 failures from a risk set of 165 organizations over 1,041 organization-years. Other variables also are included in each model, as shown in the continuation of the table. For coefficient estimates, standard errors are in parentheses.

* p < .10
** p < .05

sion of each organization's historical competition, to test the Myopic Learning Hypothesis. Neither gini coefficient is significant, however, so the Myopic Learning Hypothesis is not supported in terms of the failure prospects of mainframe manufacturers. Additionally, models $r_{mn}6$ and $r_{mn}7$ include the historical competition faced by an organization's rivals, $\Sigma_k T_k$, to test for the rivalry side of the Competitive Hysteresis Hypothesis. This term is not significant, nor is it significant when specified in model $r_{mn}7$ to allow for the historical timing of competitive experience—a specification that was significant in the mainframe founding models.

Looking at the other terms in the various mainframe failure models, organizational size has its expected effect, with larger organizations being less likely to fail. To see this, note that the piecewise age effects are negative for medium-sized organizations and are more strongly negative for large organizations. The effects of organizational age, however, hinge on the operation of the Red Queen. The pattern of age dependence changes when one compares models $r_{mn}1$ through $r_{mn}3$, which do not allow for competitive hysteresis and the competency trap, with models $r_{mn}4$ and $r_{mn}5$, which do. Allowing for these Red Queen effects, the effects of organizational age change considerably, even reversing direction for small mainframe manufacturers. Changes over time in the survival chances of mainframe organizations do not follow a set pattern of change with the ticking of the clock. Rather, they depend on whether these organizations have endured competition, and on how recently they have done so.

Perhaps the most profound reaction to the evolution of the mainframe market was the development of a completely distinct approach to computing. Midway through the 1960s, smaller, less expensive systems of a distinctly different design appeared on the market. The organizations that manufactured these systems, and the customers who used them, differed fundamentally from those in the mainframe market. The midrange computing market, starting with the minicomputer and evolving into the client-server systems of the distributed computing era, would develop a new and distinct logic of competition.

Discovering Logics of Competition among Midrange Computer Manufacturers

In the early 1960s, as mainframe manufacturers were centrally controlling the development and use of their systems, a "hacker culture" was forming in universities and technology firms around the United States. The term "hacker," at that time, described those rare individuals who were competent at working with computers. These individuals would be intimately familiar with both hardware and software and needed access to a computer and the ability to work with the machine—likely at the level of machine-level or assembly language. Writing in the 1980s, Steven Levy recalled the "hacker code of ethics" from his days in the Tech Model Railroad Club at MIT:

Access to computers should be unlimited and total.
All information should be free.
Mistrust authority—Promote decentralization.
Hackers should be judged by their hacking, not bogus criteria such as degrees, age, race, or position.
You can create art and beauty on a computer.
Computers can change your life for the better.[66]

Looking back from the twenty-first century, these ideals have more in common with the current "open source" community of Linux programmers than they do with the 1950s' world of mainframe computing. In fact, what Levy refers to as a hacker culture was the beginning of an alternative logic of competition in the industry that would grow up around the powerful, yet directly accessible, midrange computer.

DEC, Data General (founded by former DEC engineers), and the many minicomputer firms that followed these organizations looked very different from the mainframe manufacturers of the era.[67] These were technology firms, typically with a research culture centered on the technology of computing. These organizations were not vertically integrated but instead focused only on designing and building a new kind of computer, often relying on components and software from elsewhere. Neither were these organizations known for elaborate sales and service organizations. Instead, the early minicomputer firms were technologists building for technologists. Consequently, the minicomputer manufacturers typically followed DEC's lead of selling rather than leasing systems, so that users could alter or augment their systems freely. Rather than "owning" service and support, the early minicomputer firms also were known for freely disseminating documentation on the technical details of their systems to users, another DEC innovation.[68] This presumed, of course, that users were likeminded technologists, working in technology firms or in the role of a technologist within a nontechnology firm. Competing for such customers, the first minicomputer firms would discover the initial market for midrange computing.

Discovering the Early Midrange Computer Market

The first midrange computer, the minicomputer, was a distinct break with the mainframe computer in ways that opened up a new market with a new logic of competition. The market for minicomputers exploded in the mid-1960s, due to the combination of the small size, low price, and high performance (relative to price) of these systems. Key to these differences was the minicomputer's very different architecture. Minicomputers typically were designed to operate without using input/output channels, the separate processors used by mainframe systems to manage the transfer of data into and out of the computer.[69] Instead, minis featured "direct memory access," an architecture that allows data to be transferred from an input device directly to memory—limiting what can be done in input and output but improving performance.[70] Costs were further reduced by designing the system to require shorter word lengths, where a "word" is a group of (typically binary) digits that are processed together by a computer. For instance, the PDP-5 and PDP-8 minicomputers had a 12-bit word length, as compared to word lengths of 36 bits or more among mainframe computers of the same era. The innovative genius was then in the system's architecture, designed so that the computer's instruction set could still perform well despite the smaller word lengths. Performance was also enhanced by designing minicomputers explicitly to take advantage of microelectronic components—at first transistors, and later integrated circuits. So designed, minicomputers violated "Grosch's law," in that with these systems one could access cost-effective computing power even at a small scale.[71] Thus the new architecture and lower cost of the minicomputer opened up a new market, bringing affordable computing power to a broad range of customers with lower-scale computing needs.

I count the first minicomputer, and with it the midrange computer market, as beginning with the PDP-5 offered by DEC for $27,000 in 1963. The PDP-5 was the first minicomputer if one uses both low price and architecture together as the defining attributes of the minicomputer. Because the actual term "minicomputer" was not used until the 1965 release of the PDP-8, many regard that system as the first, but the PDP-5 was similarly a minicomputer in terms of both price and architecture. Other candidates for the first such computer have been offered, by looking only at price and size, or only at architecture. Based only on architecture, DEC founder Ken Olsen would later refer to the Whirlwind as the first mini because of some of its design features—but the Whirlwind was a huge and expensive mainframe system.[72] Similarly, some point to Seymour Cray's CDC 160, developed from 1960 to 1962, as the first mini because of its architecture, but its $60,000 price tag kept it out of what would become the market for minicomputers.[73] Levy calls the PDP-1 the first minicomputer because he focuses on the ability to directly interact with the computer: "PDP-1. Digital Equipment's first minicomputer, and in 1961 an interactive godsend to the MIT hackers and a slap in the face to IBM fascism."[74] But at a price of $100,000 (reflecting, in part, this computer's longer 18-bit word length), this computer was a godsend only to those who could enjoy the largess of an MIT. By contrast, looking only at size and price, some credit the $30,000 Burroughs E-101 as starting this mar-

ket as far back as 1954,[75] but neither was this a stored-program system nor
did it feature the performance-enhancing architecture that would create
the midrange market a decade later.

Unknown to the pioneers of early minicomputing, the midrange market
would develop in various directions from the 1960s to the 1990s, with
competition among manufacturers helping them to discover the logics that
would drive success and failure. Initially, it was not clear whether there
would be much demand for these systems. There was an attempt by DEC
early on to target the technically savvy user who would value direct interaction with a computer, but who could not have such access in a world of
large-scale mainframe systems. The "PDP" in the name of the DEC minicomputers stood for "programmed data processor," a name chosen to distance these machines from the term "computer," which was associated
with large, expensive systems that a user could not work with directly. The
minicomputer's user interface also set it apart from mainframe systems,
because it allowed direct interaction with the system—at first through tele-
types, but ultimately through a keyboard with a video screen.[76]

As competition drove down prices in the late 1960s, access to minicomputers by technologists grew. Technically sophisticated users were able to
modify these systems, adding components often from other manufacturers
or adapting systems to suit their needs.[77] In this way, the first minicomputers played to the fancy of those users who wanted to be involved in system
design. The modular architecture of the minicomputer also allowed customers to build these systems—as delivered, modified, or in part—into
their own machines. This so-called embedded computer market had
begun with the first minicomputers in the early 1960s, when they were
used as input/output processors within mainframe systems. But embedded uses of midrange computers broadened and grew over the 1960s, and
continued to flourish into the twenty-first century in one or another form.
Some of these installations were high visibility, such as the Apollo space-
ship guidance system. But the bulk of the embedded uses of minicomputers drew little media attention, since the ultimate branded product or
system would not typically refer to the minicomputer within.[78] For instance, well-known medical device firms such as General Electric and Varian embedded minicomputers into their large-scale diagnostic imaging
equipment—often unbeknownst to the hospitals that purchased the
equipment. Minicomputers also invaded the market for specialized, analog
computer systems that had been used to coordinate activities in real time.
Manufacturers across a variety of industries, for example, embedded minicomputers in their automated production systems. What started as an appealing technology for the limited market of computer-savvy technologists
grew into a broad market for embedded midrange systems.

Another early market discovered for minicomputers was the small- to
medium-sized business computer niche. During the 1960s, the perception

grew that computers were necessary in order for organizations to be competitive. One sees this claim in 1960s-era management textbooks, which
told of a competitive advantage for small firms that adopted computerized
data-processing systems, and my review of the industry literature found
such claims echoed repeatedly. For instance, a team of Harvard Business
School professors reported, in 1967, that "small companies will face increased competition from other small competitors" that adopt computerized information systems.[79] Although it remains unclear whether this
claim was true at the time,[80] the perception that computerization was necessary for smaller firms was an important social fact that drove many
smaller organizations into the market for computers.

Small-firm demand grew for the minicomputer also because computer
outsourcing had not worked well for many of these organizations. By the
late 1960s, service bureaus and other forms of outsourcing had proven to
be ineffective without considerable, additional overhead costs to tailor
these services to the needs of the individual firms.[81] Mainframes, complete
with the service and support provided by their manufacturers or leasing
companies, would solve the problem, but only at a scale far beyond the
reach of most small- to medium-sized businesses. Minicomputers gave
these customers efficient computing capability at a more appropriate scale
and required only that they employ a relatively small cadre of technologists
to integrate the system into their businesses.

In-house operation of minicomputer systems was eased by the growing
community of software developers. User groups were central players in the
minicomputer era, since the manufacturers of these systems encouraged
users to work with and alter these systems. Often, new product development by the minicomputer manufacturers was shaped by ideas and innovations born in user groups. In DEC's cultish early days, user groups took
on a strong social movement quality, identifying themselves in opposition
to IBM and the other large mainframe manufacturers.[82] Similarly, after
the rapid success of its Nova minicomputer introduced in 1969, Data General's customer base grew while, alongside, its user groups encouraged
the development of software for the company's products. Although these
development efforts often were shared collectively among Data General
"followers," a number of these software development efforts led to the
establishment of software firms marketing products that enhanced the use
of Data General equipment. The social movements surrounding the minicomputer thus encouraged the growth of a broader organizational community supporting the market for these systems.

Advances in the midrange market during the 1970s were fueled by
competition, as organizations flooded into this market. Figures 6.9 and
6.10 illustrate the founding and failure activity in this market continuing
from the late 1960s onward. During the 1970s, the midrange computer
market saw intense competition among manufacturers, as advances in mi-

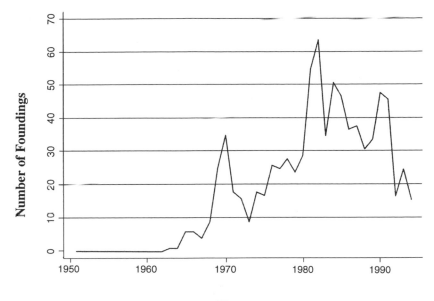

Figure 6.9. Entries into the U.S. midrange computer market.

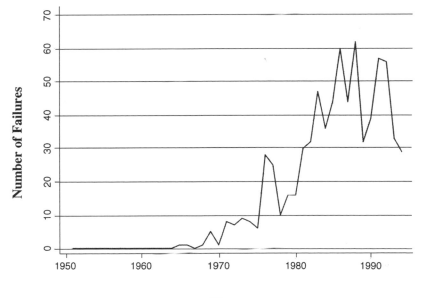

Figure 6.10. Failures of U.S. midrange computer manufacturers.

croelectronics enabled the production of ever more sophisticated mini-computers. The market was fine-grained, with high equipment replacement rates giving midrange manufacturers more chances to receive performance feedback from the competitive environment. Consequently, designs were rapidly transformed over the decade, moving from architectures based on the integrated circuits in the early 1970s to microprocessor-based "superminicomputers" in the late 1970s. As microprocessors were adopted, computer architecture changed markedly. No longer was the instruction set designed among multiple components in a "processor;" rather, the processor would be a single chip. Consequently, the organizational capabilities required for innovation shifted to microelectronic innovation by the end of the 1970s, just as the move to distributed computing was about to begin.

From Distributed Computing to the "Enterprise Space"

Beginning in the 1980s, the microprocessor combined with networking technology to revolutionize computing, with organizational consequences that would be revealed over another decade of competition. Entering the 1980s, microprocessors replaced processors made up of multiple components. In so doing, microprocessors made it possible to distribute computing power into separate, desktop-sized machines. These early workstations were considerably more powerful, and more expensive, than the microcomputers of the time. Meanwhile, networking firms were starting up, making possible high-volume, high-speed data transmission from workstations to servers—or among workstations. 3Com, for instance, started in 1981, bringing Ethernet technology to the market. Computer networking was also stimulated by developments in software. Novell, founded in 1983, introduced networking software that allowed computers to transfer and share files with one another and with peripherals such as printers. As these "local area networks" proliferated, incompatibilities among the multiple "protocols" in these systems created the opportunity for network router companies specializing in helping such networks communicate. For instance, Cisco Systems was founded in 1984, initially to enable communication among the (often incompatible) networks at Stanford University. Combined, the development of workstations with their own processors linked into local area networks was a dramatic departure from the earlier minicomputer-based period in midrange computing.

As companies entered the workstation market in the early 1980s, their products were known as "graphics computers"; only later, in retrospect, would we refer to these machines as "workstations" within "client-server" systems. To the user, the most notable difference in these new computers was the workstation itself and its user interface. Historically, users interacted with minicomputers using terminals that lacked a microprocessor. (Some of these "dummy terminals" can be seen as props in the classic science fiction film *2001 A Space Odyssey*.) Using such terminals, one entered lines of text, or for those with a good modem, screens of text. These terminals did not, themselves, execute commands, but rather were like a teletype merely transferring the keyed commands of the user through to the computer, which resided in a central location. By contrast, the early workstations had impressive graphics capabilities for their time and could process commands themselves. The first of these workstations were installed in companies with high-end processing needs, such as computer-aided design firms, and at college campuses.

Before long, what started as a niche market for graphics computers came to be known as the workstation market, and a number of manufacturers entered amidst considerable uncertainty. Figure 6.9 shows a flurry of midrange computer manufacturers entering in the early 1980s, many of which were workstation manufacturers moving into the rapidly growing market for client-server computing systems. SUN Microsystems and Silicon Graphics (SGI), for instance, were founded in 1982 and saw their first successes shortly thereafter. Faced with great uncertainty about the budding new markets for these powerful systems, workstation manufacturers experimented with pricing, new products, features, technologies, and approaches to organizing and delivering products and services to customers.[83] Consequently, what would later appear to be the strategies of these firms in fact emerged from their experience in the market.[84] By the end of the 1980s, early experiments gave way to established product lines. Some ran on variants of the Unix operating system. (I found hundreds of Unix variants in my data.) Others ran on their own operating systems, as was the case for DEC's VMS operating system. The midrange computing boom of the 1980s produced a variety of approaches to distributed computing.

Competition among these organizations intensified as products proliferated in the workstation market, leading to improved workstations, servers, and system architectures.[85] The original challenge of creating client-server systems gave way, by the 1990s, to the challenge of scalability. Unlike mainframe systems, client server systems could start relatively small and grow incrementally. At some point, however, these systems reached a scale past which additional growth could not be sustained. To tackle this challenge, some manufacturers designed systems that could, it was hoped, scale up to meet the needs of very large organizations with massive data requirements and global distributed computing needs. Such systems were expected to perform reliably, a challenge that many of the budding client-server manufacturers failed to meet. Over time, however, competition among these manufacturers gave rise to high-reliability, large-scale computing on par with many mainframes. Ultimately, competition among client-server manufacturers led to computing in the "enterprise space," a term that I could not find used in journalistic print until 1998—beyond the ending point of the study—but that quickly found favor within the industry.

The historical evidence shows that the midrange computer market emerged from a discovery process. Manufacturers discovered the market's logic of competition by competing. From 1963 through 1994, this included the broadening of the minicomputer market, the opening of a small and medium-sized business computing market, the development of superminicomputers, the discovery and development of workstations and distributed computing architectures, and finally the scaling of these client-server systems to deal with large-scale computing demands. I have cited examples to support the argument that competition played an important role in this discovery process. Next I test this hypothesis systematically by estimating the Red Queen model on the midrange computer manufacturer data.

Estimates of the Founding and Failure Models for Midrange Computer Manufacturers

The data collection procedures for the midrange computer manufacturers are described in the appendix. As prepared for the estimation of the organizational founding and failure models, the midrange manufacturer data are described in tables 6.7 and 6.9. Of the 841 market entries from the first in 1963 through 1994, 743 exit by the end of the sample period. This considerable volatility gives ample evidence to estimate the Red Queen models, in terms of both foundings and failures. Table 6.8 shows the estimates of various specifications of the founding rate for the midrange manufacturers. Tables 6.10 and 6.11 show estimates of the failure rate models for these organizations.

Considering first the founding rate, the models in table 6.8 show evidence in support of the Competitive Hysteresis Hypothesis. In models $\lambda_{md}1$ and $\lambda_{md}2$, the historical competition faced by incumbent organizations in the midrange market, $\Sigma_k T_k$, has a negative and significant effect on the founding rate of midrange manufacturers. This indicates stronger competition from incumbents with more competitive experience, lowering the entry rate of new manufacturers. The Competency-Trap Hypothesis does not receive support, however. Models $\lambda_{md}3$ and $\lambda_{md}4$ break out the historical competition term according to recent-versus distant-past experience, and these terms are not significant, nor are their effects significantly different from one another. Neither does the Myopic Learn-

TABLE 6.7
Description of the Data Used in the Midrange Computer Manufacturer Founding Analysis

Variables	Mean	Std Dev	Min	Max
Midrange computer manufacturer entries/1,000	0.0263	0.0164	0.001	0.0640
Midrange computer manufacturer entries last year/1,000	0.0258	0.0170	0	0.0640
Lagged midrange computer manuf. failures/1,000	0.0223	0.0206	0	0.0620
Midrange computer market shipments/10^6	0.0941	0.0961	0	0.2465
Real U.S. gross domestic product	3,603	887.6	2,128	5,135
U.S. prime interest rate	8.638	3.3679	4.5	18.87
Cumulative hazard of failure since organization's birth	0.4330	0.3827	0	1.370
Midrange computer market density/1,000	0.1133	0.0696	0	0.2170
Midrange computer market density squared/1,000	17.52	15.00	0	47.09
Historical competition faced by org. in midrange computer market/1,000	84.77	79.50	0	204.3
Recent historical competition faced in midrange computer market/1,000	5.46	45.21	0	122.1
Distant-past historical competition faced in midrange computer market/1,000	34.31	35.54	0	95.32
Gini based on density	0.1886	0.0839	0	0.3518
Gini based on founding	0.2053	0.0823	0	0.3337

Source: Various archival documents (see appendix).

ing Hypothesis receive support. Neither of the gini coefficients in model $\lambda_{md}4$ have a significant effect on the founding rate, so I do not find evidence that the dispersion of experience makes incumbent organizations more competitive with respect to deterring entry to the midrange market.

Other effects in the midrange founding models are noteworthy. The density of midrange manufacturers is never statistically significant, neither in the quadratic nor in a monotonic specification. Evidence of competition with respect to foundings, then, can be found only from organizations that have experienced a history of having competed. Meanwhile, founding rates also are lower the more that incumbent organizations have survived while others have failed. This pure-selection effect holds in all models, including those with the Red Queen effects. Another robust finding is the positive effect of prior-year failures on current-year foundings among midrange manufacturers. This renewal effect was found, as well, for banks

TABLE 6.8
Estimates of the Founding Rate of U.S. Midrange Computer Manufacturers, 1963–1994

Independent Variable	$(\lambda_{md}1)$	$(\lambda_{md}2)$	$(\lambda_{md}3)$	$(\lambda_{md}\ddagger)$
Prior year midrange manufacturer entries/1,000	0.0058 (0.0062)	0.0061 (0.0061)	0.0103 (0.0081)	0.0024 (0.0092)
Prior year midrange manufacturer failures/1,000	0.0233** (0.0069)	0.0228** (0.0067)	0.0204** (0.0073)	0.0237** (0.0082)
Sum of sizes of midrange organizations (annual shipments)/10⁶	0.0040 (0.0050)	0.0050 (0.0040)	0.0040 (0.0040)	0.0030 (0.0040)
Real U.S. gross domestic product	0.0031** (0.0008)	0.0030** (0.0005)	0.0032** (0.0006)	0.0037** (0.0007)
U.S. prime interest rate	0.0196 (0.0205)	0.0203 (0.0202)	0.0193 (0.0204)	-0.0036 (0.0284)
Avg. cumulative hazard of failure in midrange market since incumbents' births	-5.356** (1.022)	-5.308** (1.010)	-5.133** (1.024)	-5.845** (1.214)
Number of midrange manufacturers/1,000	-3.291 (7.080)	-1.086 (2.510)	-5.111 (5.735)	-0.8493 (6.741)
Number of midrange manufacturers/1,000, squared	0.0103 (0.0308)			
Historical competition faced by organization in midrange-market/1,000	-0.0149** (0.0056)	-0.0140** (0.0049)		
Recent historical competition faced by organization in midrange market/1,000			-0.0037 (0.0141)	-0.0099 (0.0138)

TABLE 6.8 (*cont.*)
Estimates of the Founding Rate of U.S. Midrange Computer Manufacturers, 1963–1994

Independent Variable	$(\lambda_{md}1)$	$(\lambda_{md}2)$	$(\lambda_{md}3)$	$(\lambda_{md}4)$
Distant-past historical competition faced by organization in midrange market/1,000			-0.0263 (0.0166)	-0.0255 (0.0164)
Inequality of past rivalry faced by organization (average gini)				-4.250 (3.944)
Inequality of past rival cohorts faced by organization (average gini)				1.953 (4.868)
Constant	-5.761** (1.893)	-5.316** (1.320)	-5.979** (1.592)	-6.794** (1.666)
Log likelihood	-101.40	-101.46	-101.15	-98.996
(df)	(9)	(8)	(9)	(11)

Note: The data include 841 market entries over 32 years, modeled as annual event counts. For coefficient estimates, standard errors are in parentheses.
* p < .10
** p < .05

TABLE 6.9
Description of the Data Used in the Midrange Computer Manufacturer Failure Analysis

Variables	Mean	Std Dev	Min	Max
Dealio entrant	0.3345	0.4719	0	1
Real U.S. gross domestic product	4,003	663	2,128	5,135
U.S. prime interest rate	9.873	3.248	4.500	18.87
Market tenure, small organization	0.4364	0.4960	0	1
Market tenure, medium-sized organization	0.4604	0.4985	0	1
Market tenure, large-sized organization	0.1032	0.3043	0	1
Midrange computer market shipments/10^6	0.1353	0.0848	0	0.2465
Midrange computer manufacturer entries/1,000	0.0345	0.0144	0	0.0640
Lagged midrange computer manuf. failures/1,000	0.0314	0.0182	0	0.0620
Midrange computer market density at entry/1,000	0.1276	0.0630	0	0.2170
Cumulative hazard of failure since organization's birth	0.5649	0.6627	0	4.008
Computer industry density/1,000	0.3409	0.1762	0.025	0.6030
Computer industry density squared/1,000	147.2	116.2	0.625	363.6
Microcomputer market density/1,000	0.2116	0.1636	0	0.4780
Midrange market density/1,000	0.1531	0.0480	0	0.2170
Mainframe market density/1,000	0.0225	0.0071	0.0100	0.0340
Duration in microcomputer	1.324	2.888	0	2.00
Duration in mainframe	1.153	4.830	0	42.00
Historical competition faced by org. in midrange computer market/1,000	0.5750	0.6674	0	3.484
Recent historical competition faced in midrange computer market/1,000	0.3449	0.3091	0	1.278
Distant-past historical competition faced in midrange computer market/1,000	0.2301	0.3744	0	2.2181
Number of distinct rivals faced in midrange computer market/1,000	0.1952	0.1550	0	0.7020
Historical competition faced by org. in microcomputer market/1,000	0.2713	0.6758	0	4.337

TABLE 6.9 (*cont.*)
Description of the Data Used in the Midrange Computer Manufacturer Failure Analysis

Variables	Mean	Std Dev	Min	Max
Historical competition faced by org. in mainframe market/1,000	0.0218	0.0896	0	0.8140
Midrange computer rivals' historical exposure to competition/1,000	115.7	63.98	0	19.4
Midrange computer rivals' recent exposure to competition/1,000	69.82	36.73	0	118.6
Midrange computer rivals' distant exposure to competition/1,000	45.90	28.92	0	88.33
Sum of ages of midrange computer rivals/1,000	9.744	6.612	0	22.57
Gini based on density	0.2087	0.1808	0	0.7500
Gini based on founding	0.2304	0.1856	0	0.587

Source: Various archival documents (see appendix).

in chapter 5 and has appeared in organizational founding models from time to time over years of research.[86] The typical interpretation of this effect is that when organizations exit a market, resources freed up in the process accelerated the rate of organizational founding.

Turning to the failure models for midrange manufacturers, note the estimates in tables 6.10 and 6.11. The models in table 6.10 show that the cumulative hazard of failure over an organization's lifetime significantly reduces the organization's failure rate. This finding is consistent with a pure-selection model of increasing viability. Also, these results show that the historical competition faced by an organization, T_j, also significantly decreases an organization's failure rate, supporting the Competitive Hysteresis Hypothesis. Yet when the two terms are together in model $r_{md}2$, neither is significant—largely because of a substantial increase in their standard errors when they are modeled together. The historical competition term, however, becomes even stronger in table 6.11 once the other terms suggested by the theory are included in the model. For this reason, I include the historical competition term rather than the cumulative hazard of failure in the table 6.11 models. In table 6.11, models $r_{md}5$ and $r_{md}6$ reveal no support for the Competency-Trap Hypothesis, since breaking out T according to the historical timing of experience does not generate significant results nor does it improve the fit of the model. Also, the number of distinct historical rivals faced by an organization, K_j, is not significant in either model $r_{md}5$ or model $r_{md}6$, so the Costly Adaptation Hypothesis is not supported.

Models $r_{md}7$ through $r_{md}9$ in table 6.11 look at how a history of competing affects the strength of competition generated by an organization's

TABLE 6.10
Estimates of the Failure Rates of U.S. Midrange Computer Manufacturers, 1963–1994

Independent Variable	$(r_{md}1)$	$(r_{md}2)$	$(r_{md}3)$	$(r_{md}4)$
Cumulative hazard of failure in midrange market since the organization's birth		-0.5081 (0.4407)	-0.8251** (0.1923)	-0.7828** (0.1880)
Historical competition faced by organization in midrange market/1,000		-0.3515 (0.4191)		
Number of midrange manufacturers at entry/1,000	-4.142** (1.429)	-1.676 (1.679)	-1.294 (1.588)	-2.560* (1.492)
Number of mainframe manufacturers/1,000	-21.09 (14.88)	-21.28 (15.36)	-24.17 (14.95)	-17.21 (14.94)
Number of midrange computer manufacturers/1,000	8.164** (2.621)	5.605* (3.001)	4.685** (2.754)	7.240** (2.649)
Number of microcomputer manufacturers/1,000	1.306* (0.7729)	1.356* (0.7813)	1.293* (0.7790)	1.429* (0.7766)
Sum of sizes of midrange organizations (annual shipments)/1,000	0.0027 (0.0037)	0.0042 (0.0038)	0.0046 (0.0037)	0.0034 (0.0037)
Prior year midrange manufacturer entries/1,000	-3.010 (5.941)	-1.993 (6.013)	-1.375 (5.965)	-2.992 (5.945)
Prior year midrange manufacturer failures/1,000	-1.613 (4.392)	-0.6411 (4.384)	-0.5300 (4.371)	-0.8989 (4.398)
Dealio entrant	-0.0943 (0.0814)	-0.1064 (0.0813)	-0.1051 (0.0813)	-0.1078 (0.0813)

TABLE 6.10 (*cont.*)
Estimates of the Failure Rates of U.S. Midrange Computer Manufacturers, 1963–1994

Independent Variable	$(r_{md}1)$	$(r_{md}2)$	$(r_{md}3)$	$(r_{md}4)$
Organization also is in mainframe computer market	-0.4209** (0.1827)	-0.4229** (0.1833)	-0.4076** (0.1824)	-0.4405** (0.1827)
Organization also is in microcomputer market	-0.1707* (0.0971)	-0.1564 (0.0973)	-0.1611 (0.0972)	-0.1531 (0.0972)
Real U.S. gross domestic product	0.0003 (0.0004)	0.0002 (0.0004)	0.0002 (0.0004)	0.0002 (0.0004)
U.S. prime interest rate	-0.0511** (0.0164)	-0.0510** (0.0163)	-0.0515** (0.0163)	-0.0502** (0.0164)
Market tenure, all organizations				
0–1 year	-3.232** (1.514)	-3.169** (1.528)	-3.021 (1.518)	-3.381** (1.516)
1–3 years	-2.704* (1.514)	-2.429 (1.530)	-2.285 (1.520)	-2.666* (1.516)
3–5 years	-2.574* (1.519)	-2.006 (1.540)	-1.874 (1.530)	-2.270 (1.522)
5–10 years	-2.649* (1.521)	-1.704 (1.553)	-1.583 (1.543)	-2.005 (1.530)
10–15 years	-2.572* (1.540)	-0.9600 (1.602)	-0.8590 (1.592)	-1.326 (1.570)
15+ years	-3.359** (1.568)	-0.8960 (1.685)	-0.8230 (1.672)	-1.345 (1.639)

TABLE 6.10 (*cont.*)
Estimates of the Failure Rates of U.S. Midrange Computer Manufacturers, 1963–1994

Independent Variable	$(r_{md}1)$	$(r_{md}2)$	$(r_{md}3)$	$(r_{md}4)$
Market tenure, medium-sized organizations				
0–1 year	−0.0080	−0.0387	−0.0397	−0.0328
	(0.2008)	(0.2009)	(0.2009)	(0.2008)
1–3 years	−0.2488*	−0.2597**	−0.2564**	−0.2623*
	(0.1324)	(0.1325)	(0.1324)	(0.1324)
3–5 years	−0.4993**	−0.5161**	−0.5113**	−0.5207**
	(0.1664)	(0.1666)	(0.1665)	(0.1665)
5–10 years	−0.7322**	−0.6741**	−0.6810**	−0.6726**
	(0.1648)	(0.1652)	(0.1651)	(0.1652)
10–15 years	−0.9300**	−0.9190**	−0.9195**	−0.9228**
	(0.2761)	(0.2760)	(0.2760)	(0.2760)
15+ years	−1.233**	−1.341**	−1.362**	−1.331**
	(0.4658)	(0.4678)	(0.4690)	(0.4673)

TABLE 6.10 (*cont.*)

Estimates of the Failure Rates of U.S. Midrange Computer Manufacturers, 1963–1994

Independent Variable	$(r_{md}1)$	$(r_{md}2)$	$(r_{md}3)$	$(r_{md}4)$
Market tenure, large organizations				
0–1 year	−0.0882	−0.1344	−0.1391	−0.1206
	(0.4701)	(0.4704)	(0.4704)	(0.4702)
1–3 years	−1.531**	−1.548**	−1.543**	−1.551**
	(0.4575)	(0.4576)	(0.4576)	(0.4576)
3–5 years	−1.605**	−1.609**	−1.603**	−1.616**
	(0.5123)	(0.5124)	(0.5123)	(0.5124)
5–10 years	−1.365**	−1.318**	−1.321**	−1.321**
	(0.3501)	(0.3502)	(0.3502)	(0.3502)
10–15 years	−2.520**	−2.616**	−2.601**	−2.625**
	(0.7350)	(0.7349)	(0.7347)	(0.7348)
15+ years	−1.883**	−1.933**	−1.888**	−1.982**
	(0.7923)	(0.7941)	(0.7922)	(0.7931)
Log likelihood	−1063.47	−1054.16	−1054.54	−1054.74
(df)	(30)	(32)	(31)	(31)

Note: The data include 743 exits from a risk set of 41 organizations over 4,466 organization-years. Other variables also are included in each model, and are shown in the continuation of the table. For coefficient estimates, standard errors are in parentheses.

* p < .10
** p < .05

TABLE 6.11
Estimates of the Failure Rates of U.S. Midrange Computer Manufacturers, 1963–1994

Independent Variables	$(r_{md}5)$	$(r_{md}6)$	$(r_{md}7)$	$(r_{md}8)$	$(r_{md}9)$	$(r_{md}10)$
Number of midrange manufacturers at entry/1,000	-2.367 (1.905)	-1.890 (1.958)	-2.658* (1.498)	-2.558* (1.501)	-2.593* (1.484)	-2.137 (1.532)
Historical competition faced by organization in midrange market/1,000		-0.6920 (0.5880)	-0.7860** (0.1880)	-0.7680** (0.1890)	-0.7890** (0.1880)	-0.9100** (0.1980)
Recent historical competition faced by organization in midrange market/1,000		0.5830 (1.319)				
Distant-past historical competition faced by organization in midrange market/1,000		-1.146 (0.7210)				
Number of distinct historical rivals faced by organization in midrange market/1,000	-0.4450 (2.728)	-1.760 (2.992)				
Total historical competition faced by rivals in midrange market/1,000			0.0110 (0.0080)		0.0130** (0.0040)	0.0110 (0.0080)
Recent historical competition faced by rivals in midrange market/1,000			-0.0110 (0.0210)			
Distant-past historical competition faced by rivals in midrange market/1,000					0.0420 (0.0290)	
Inequality of past rivalry faced by organization (gini)						-1.875 (1.200)
Inequality of past rival cohorts faced by organization (gini)						2.342* (1.221)

TABLE 6.11 (*cont.*)
Estimates of the Failure Rates of U.S. Midrange Computer Manufacturers, 1963–1994

Independent Variables	$(r_{md}5)$	$(r_{md}6)$	$(r_{md}7)$	$(r_{md}8)$	$(r_{md}9)$	$(r_{md}10)$
Number of mainframe manufacturers/1,000	−17.26	−19.362	−43.14*	−29.915	−47.04**	−41.78*
	(14.94)	(15.07)	(24.19)	(26.82)	(−20.56)	(−24.22)
Number of midrange computer manufacturers/1,000	7.319**	6.505**	1.487	9.583		0.2100
	(2.695)	(2.787)	(4.885)	(8.749)		(−4.89)
Number of microcomputer manufacturers/1,000	1.430*	1.456*	0.7140	−0.6840	0.5440	0.8560
	(0.7770)	(0.7780)	(0.9370)	(1.557)	(0.7540)	(0.9400)
Sum of sizes of midrange organizations (shipments)/1,000	0.0030	0.0040	0.0060	0.0060	0.0060	0.0050
	(0.0040)	(0.0040)	(0.0040)	(0.0040)	(0.0040)	(0.0040)
Prior year midrange manufacturer entries/1,000	−3.172	−2.532	−0.4740	−7.189	0.6550	0.4550
	(6.047)	(6.073)	(6.246)	(8.658)	(5.035)	(6.269)
Prior year midrange manufacturer failures/1,000	−0.8280	−1.784	−3.330	0.6540	−3.531	−2.826
	(4.416)	(4.492)	(4.704)	(5.859)	(4.647)	(4.723)
Dealio entrant	−0.1070	−0.1070	−0.1090	−0.1120	−0.1100	−0.1080
	(0.0810)	(0.0810)	(0.0810)	(0.0810)	(0.0810)	(0.0810)
Organization also is in microcomputer market	−0.1530	−0.1510	−0.1540	−0.1530	−0.1530	−0.1610*
	(0.0970)	(0.0970)	(0.0970)	(0.0970)	(0.0970)	(0.0970)
Organization also is in mainframe computer market	−0.4390**	−0.4350**	−0.4450**	−0.4460**	−0.4490**	−0.4300**
	(0.1830)	(0.1830)	(0.1830)	(−.1830)	(−.1830)	(−.1830)
Real U.S. gross domestic product	0.0002	0.0002	0.0004	−0.0010	−0.0005	0.0004
	(0.0004)	(0.0004)	(0.0062)	(0.0010)	(0.0005)	(0.0006)
U.S. prime interest rate	−0.0500**	−0.0520**	−0.0400**	−0.0350*	−0.0370**	−0.0340*
	(0.0160)	(0.0170)	(0.0180)	(0.0180)	(0.0150)	(0.0180)

TABLE 6.11 (*cont.*)
Estimates of the Failure Rates of U.S. Midrange Computer Manufacturers, 1963–1994

Independent Variables	$(r_{md}5)$	$(r_{md}6)$	$(r_{md}7)$	$(r_{md}8)$	$(r_{md}9)$	$(r_{md}10)$
Market tenure, all organizations						
0–1 year	-3.396**	-3.198**	-0.9380	-0.010	-0.476	-1.016
	(1.519)	(1.529)	(2.315)	(2.452)	(1.741)	(2.304)
1–3 years	-2.623*	-2.452	-0.2120	0.708	0.254	-0.354
	(1.539)	(1.547)	(2.321)	(2.456)	(1.740)	(2.309)
3–5 years	-2.229	-2.165	0.1930	1.107	0.663	-0.046
	(1.542)	(1.544)	(2.330)	(2.462)	(1.741)	(2.320)
5–10 years	-1.968	-1.930	0.4570	1.366	0.929	0.277
	(1.546)	(1.547)	(2.334)	(2.465)	(1.742)	(2.326)
10–15 years	-1.296	-1.203	1.142	2.051	1.620	1.074
	(1.581)	(1.583)	(2.364)	(2.493)	(1.762)	(2.354)
15+ years	-1.326	-1.063	1.143	2.049	1.628	1.213
	(1.643)	(1.659)	(2.422)	(2.547)	(1.822)	(2.412)
Market tenure, medium-sized organizations						
0–1 year	-0.0330	-0.0330	-0.0290	-0.026	-0.028	-0.031
	(0.2010)	(0.2010)	(0.2010)	(0.201)	(0.201)	(0.201)
1–3 years	-0.2620**	-0.2640**	-0.2620**	-0.263**	-0.262**	-0.271**
	(0.1320)	(0.1320)	(0.1320)	(0.132)	(0.132)	(0.133)
3–5 years	-0.5200**	-0.5180**	-0.5160**	-0.513**	-0.516**	-0.523**
	(0.1670)	(0.1670)	(0.1670)	(0.167)	(0.167)	(0.167)
5–10 years	-0.6720**	-0.6740**	-0.6750**	-0.668**	-0.675**	-0.667**
	(0.1650)	(0.1650)	(0.1650)	(0.165)	(0.165)	(0.165)
10–15 years	-0.9240**	-0.9290**	-0.9250**	-0.9170**	-0.926**	-0.918**
	(0.2760)	(0.2760)	(0.2760)	(0.2760)	(0.276)	(0.276)
15+ years	-1.330**	-1.389**	-1.352**	-1.339**	-1.350**	-1.346**
	(0.4670)	(0.4710)	(0.4680)	(0.4680)	(0.468)	(0.468)

TABLE 6.11 (*cont.*)
Estimates of the Failure Rates of U.S. Midrange Computer Manufacturers, 1963–1994

Independent Variables	(r$_{md}$5)	(r$_{md}$6)	(r$_{md}$7)	(r$_{md}$8)	(r$_{md}$9)	(r$_{md}$10)
Market tenure, large organizations						
0–1 year	-0.1210	-0.1200	-0.1180	-0.1180	-0.119	-0.117
	(0.4700)	(0.4700)	(0.4700)	(0.4700)	(0.470)	(0.470)
1–3 years	-1.551**	-1.559**	-1.552**	-1.548**	-1.552**	-1.568**
	(0.4580)	(0.4580)	(0.4580)	(0.4580)	(0.458)	(0.458)
3–5 years	-1.615**	-1.615**	-1.609**	-1.610**	-1.608**	-1.616**
	(0.5120)	(0.5120)	(0.5120)	(0.5120)	(0.512)	(0.512)
5–10 years	-1.321**	-1.320**	-1.322**	-1.319**	-1.321**	-1.312**
	(0.3500)	(0.3500)	(0.3500)	(0.3500)	(0.350)	(0.350)
10–15 years	-2.626**	-2.637**	-2.624**	-2.613**	-2.622**	-2.625**
	(0.7350)	(0.7350)	(0.7350)	(0.7350)	(0.735)	(0.735)
15+ years	-1.981**	-2.054**	-2.003**	-1.985**	-2.000**	-1.978**
	(0.7930)	(0.7960)	(0.7930)	(0.7940)	(0.793)	(0.795)
Log likelihood	-1054.73	-1054.13	-1053.80	-1053.17	-1053.85	-1050.92
(df)	(32)	(33)	(32)	(33)	(31)	(34)

Note: The data include 743 exits from a risk set of 841 organizations over 4,466 organization-years. Other variables also are included in each model, and are shown in the continuation of the table. For coefficient estimates, standard errors are in parentheses.

* p < .10
** p < .05

rivals. Neither rivals' historical competition nor their historical competition distinguishing recent- versus distant-past experience, significantly affect an organization's failure rate. Including these terms, however, eliminated the competitive effect of midrange density. This suggests that competition may depend on rivals' exposure to competition, and that this effect was appearing spuriously as density-dependent competition. In fact, when density is removed in model $r_{md}9$, the standard error of the coefficient of rivals' historical competition, $\Sigma_k T_k$, falls by half while the coefficient remains relatively stable. (Compare models $r_{md}7$ and $r_{md}9$.) So it appears that the strength of competition depends on rivals' competitive experience, rather than on simply the numbers of rivals without regard for experience. This result is additional support for the Competitive Hysteresis Hypothesis. The Competency-Trap Hypothesis is not supported, however, given that separating the effects of rivals historical competition according to recent- versus distant-past in model $r_{md}8$ does not improve the model. Finally, the Myopic Learning Hypothesis is not supported, and in fact the estimates of the effects of the gini coefficients in model $r_{md}10$ show that organizations with greater dispersion (across cohorts) in their experience had higher failure rates—the opposite of what is predicted by the myopic learning argument.

The midrange failure rate models reveal several other interesting effects. Some of the models show higher failure rates for midrange manufacturers due to the density of microcomputer firms. This evidence of overlap between these markets is not robust across all specifications, however. Across all the midrange failure models, organizational size consistently has a negative effect on the failure rate in the usual way. Age dependence, however, seems to hinge on whether the models include the competitive history terms. As was the case for the mainframe failure models, midrange failure rates follow different patterns of age dependence with and without including the Red Queen terms. In particular, small midrange manufacturers appear to have a relatively constant failure rate with respect to age in model $r_{md}1$, which includes none of the competitive history effects. In the other models, which do include competitive history terms, age dependence is positive for small midrange manufacturers. In line with Red Queen theory, this pattern suggests that variation over time in the failure rates of these organizations depends not just on their ages, but also on whether they experience competition as they age.

These results support the conclusion that the development of the midrange manufacturers was driven by their competition with one another. Just as technical developments opened up the opportunity for midrange computer firms to establish a new market with its own logic of competition, so again in the 1970s would technological change open up another new market. While the microprocessor was used at the high end to create supercomputers, and in the midrange market to distribute computing through local area networks, at the low end it reduced the technical requirements for making a computer. Ironically, the ultimate competition for the midrange market would come from a market that initially no one in the established computer world would take seriously—the low-end hobby machines of the early microcomputer market.

Discovering Logics of Competition among Microcomputer Manufacturers

The microprocessor simplified computer design, so much so that even someone with limited technical ability could design a computer. Prior to the microprocessor, the art of computer design was to build the computer's "instruction set," the logical sequence followed as a computer operates, into the architecture of computer components so that they would execute commands efficiently. This challenge was rendered moot by the microprocessor, since the execution of the instruction set was contained within this single integrated circuit. With the development of low-end microprocessors in the 1970s, the most difficult problem of any computer's architecture was solved. So it was that hobbyists would initiate a new approach to computing, and start a process of discovery that would rapidly develop into a mass market with its own logic of competition.

Competing for Legitimacy

The first mention I can find of a microprocessor-based microcomputer is the Scelbi 8H, a kit available in 1973.[87] Most credit the first microcomputer to be the Altair, announced in the January 1975 edition of *Popular Electronics* and available from MITS, a small assembler run by Ed Roberts in Albuquerque, New Mexico. The Altair was extremely limited in its capabilities, operated by flipping switches and coming with no programming. What made this computer important was its role as a catalyst to the growing community of computer enthusiasts around the United States. Computer hobby clubs were forming nationwide, typically focusing on what could be done on kit computers like the Altair. Perhaps the best known was the Homebrew Computer Club, originally meeting in the Menlo Park garage of Gordon French in 1975, but growing quickly to include a San Francisco "branch" that met in Berkeley.[88] Budding entrepreneurs, tinkerers, and self-proclaimed hackers attended the Homebrew meetings, run by Lee Felsenstein, an engineer, Berkeley counterculture figure, and underground print journalist. Freiberger and Swaine describe a typical meeting:

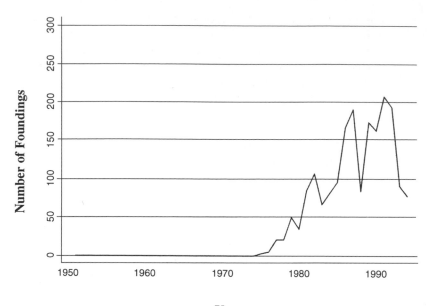

Year

Figure 6.11. Entries into the U.S. microcomputer market.

The meetings didn't follow Robert's Rules of Order with Felsenstein running them: he gave them their own special structure. First came a mapping session, during which Felsenstein recognized people who briefly proffered their interests, questions, rumors, or plans. Felsenstein sometimes had quick answers to their questions or witty comments on their plans. A formal presentation followed, generally of someone's latest invention. Finally, there was the Random Access session, in which everyone scrambled around the auditorium to meet those they felt had interests in common with them. It worked brilliantly, and numerous companies were formed. A remarkable amount of information was exchanged at those meetings, and much information had to be exchanged; they were all in unfamiliar territory.[89]

As figure 6.11 illustrates, dozens of new companies were formed during this period to produce microcomputers—a development that received scant attention from the legitimate computing world. Amdahl had released a plug-compatible 8-bit microprocessor in 1975, which would power some of these new machines. In that same year, Bill Gates formed Micro-soft to adapt the BASIC programming language for use on the Altair.[90] (The hyphen in Micro-soft would be dropped later.) But not knowing what we know now, the established computer industry had little regard for these developments. The early microcomputers were so simple

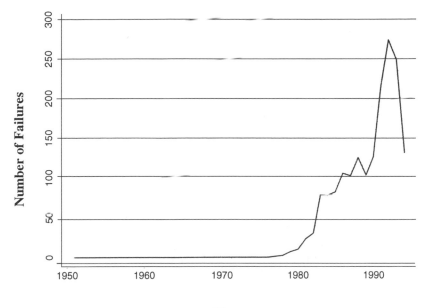

Year

Figure 6.12. Failures of U.S. microcomputer manufacturers.

and limited that they hardly merited mention alongside the likes of a su-
perminicomputer or an IBM mainframe. Instead, established computer
firms were focused on even greater capabilities in high-end computing,
where there was a promise of significant technical and business opportunities. So it was that Steve Wozniak would design the "Apple I" while attending meetings of the Homebrew Computer Club but ultimately would
start Apple Computer after his employer, Hewlett-Packard, refused to develop the product.

Debates over the legitimacy of commercial microcomputing erupted
within the movement, too. On the one hand, a collectivist ideology grew
out of the various hobby clubs, strengthened by the strongly oppositional
position taken by these organizations against the commercial establishment. Keith Britton, an original Homebrew Computer Club member, describes the oppositional self-image typical of those in the early microcomputer clubs: "There was a strong feeling that we were subversives. We
were subverting the way the giant corporations had run things. We were
upsetting the establishment, forcing our mores into the industry. I was
amazed that we could continue to meet without people arriving with bay-
onets to arrest the lot of us."[91] The business implications of this framing
hinged on the question of paying for software. Recall that one of the main

tenants of the "hacker code of ethics" was that "all information should be free." This belief remained alive and well into the microcomputer era and became especially significant with the development of the electronic bulletin board in 1978. This innovation was key to the collectivist camp within the microcomputer movement because it allowed anyone with a computer, modem, and telephone line to exchange computer files. Ward Christensen and Randy Suess of "Cache," the Chicago Atari Computer Hobbyists Exchange, set up a modem-accessible disk running the operating system CP/M, and such boards then proliferated nationally.[92] In this light, the budding entrepreneurs of the time were a bourgeois contradiction to a more collectivist "freeware" movement. Bill Gates, notably, authored in 1976 his "open letter to hobbyists" in which he framed the argument that software should be paid for as a way to maintain quality. This letter spawned a debate within the microcomputer movement over the legitimacy of commercial software development versus the free sharing of software, and more generally about the legitimacy of commercial microcomputing. This debate would not be settled within the microcomputing community. Even into the twenty-first century, the "open source" movement, centering especially on the Linux programming environment, would stand in contradiction to commercial software development.

The wave of microcomputer firms entering around 1980 introduced various technical advances, progressively improving on what microcomputers could do and thereby increasing market acceptance. Surrounded by uncertainty about the market and technologies of the microcomputer, these new organizations were experimenting. Computer manufacturers both innovated and imitated one another in order to cope with the uncertainty of the times.[93] Much is made of Apple Computer's mouse and graphical user interface having been inspired by existing technologies at Xerox PARC. In fact, most microcomputer companies' technologies were not original, but rather were derivative in many ways from earlier work or even outsourced to other firms entirely. Even the Xerox mouse was based on a considerable history of research elsewhere—in particular the Whirlwind "light pen" and Douglas Engelbart's invention of the mouse noted in his papers as early as 1963.[94] Among microcomputer manufacturers, competing as they were to build a new mass market, innovations were rewarded that yielded a computer that was at once appealing to novices and affordable. Typically, this meant assembling systems using processors, operating systems, and other technologies (such as the mouse) regardless of where these originated.[95] The early logic of competition in microcomputing was taking shape: The most competitive manufacturers would deliver easy-to-use products at low cost before their rivals, using modularized components from other firms as much as necessary.

It was in this context that IBM entered the microcomputer business in 1981. Considering the legitimacy problems facing the microcomputer, many took serious note of the market for the first time because of IBM's arrival. In fact, Apple Computer publicly welcomed IBM's entry into the market for precisely this reason.[96] IBM's entry thus helped give the market legitimacy, but at the same time it established a set of technological standards around which others could design so-called IBM clone computers. The result was the surge of microcomputer manufacturer foundings in the wake of IBM's entry, shown in figure 6.11. By the early 1980s, a combination of technical advance, market acceptance, and participation by the likes of IBM made it clear that the microcomputer market was a reality.

Competition and Standards in Microcomputing

Even as firms proliferated into microcomputing in the 1980s, increasingly the systems produced by these organizations conformed to a few standard operating systems and architectures. Initially, the standards question was seen as "IBM versus Apple," but by the 1990s the IBM standard was commonly referred to as "Wintel"—short for Windows and Intel. The rise of a few standards in microcomputing, and the dominance of one of these standards, raises the question of how computing standards shaped competition. As is often discussed in the analysis of the computer industry, incentives tend to favor concentration into a small number of such standards. There are advantages to using a computer system that is compatible with the systems of others, for purposes of exchanging software and files. Independent software vendors will tend to produce software for widely used standards, and of course consumers and businesses benefit from having such software available. Consequently, prevalence per se is likely to be self-reinforcing for a computer standard, a fact that has often been given to explain the rapid rise of the Wintel standard.

Yet the rise of the Wintel standard emerged from a set of decisions made in response to immediate competitive pressures, and not because the firms were playing out the calculus of a standards battle. To enter the market competitively, IBM designed a 16-bit system to run the then-industry-standard operating system, CP/M. (A look at textbooks from 1982 shows considerable discussion of CP/M, the prevailing standard operating system, and few mentions of DOS.[97]) But CP/M was an 8-bit technology, and its developer was behind schedule for the release of a 16-bit version. Consequently, IBM turned to a small software developer, Microsoft, who agreed to develop a 16-bit operating system based on CP/M in order to raise some quick revenue and gain legitimacy from an association with the computer giant.[98] As new competitors proliferated and the market was fast developing around other systems, time was of the essence to IBM and, consequently, to its partners. Microsoft moved fast by purchasing 86-DOS from Seattle Computer Products, an operating system that mimicked CP/M, and built its 16-bit DOS operating system from that product.[99]

Similarly, competitive pressures pushed Microsoft and Apple to cooperate during this period, a fact that often is overlooked. Virtually hundreds of new computer companies were entering the market, each representing a possible inroad to another technological standard. These entries thus intensified the competition felt by both Microsoft and Apple, leading to moves that later would be hard to reconcile with the logic of a standards-based strategy. For instance, although Apple's strategy is often described as having been "closed" or "proprietary," my data show that some of its first computers ran Microsoft's MS DOS. And, as Apple felt competitive pressures to speed the development of the Apple Lisa, it contracted with Microsoft for development help. Microsoft, too, was under competitive pressure. In an effort to accelerate its move toward a graphical user interface, Microsoft would license some aspects of the Apple interface—yet only a few years later Apple would sue (to no avail), claiming that Microsoft had violated its copyright by imitating the "look and feel" of the Apple user interface. In these ways, the intense competition of the early 1980s put considerable time pressure on microcomputer manufacturers and so shaped their decisions regarding technology standards.

In retrospect, we now know that some of these decisions would have long-term, strategic implications, but at the time these implications were less clear. Difficult as it is to imagine given what we now know, even the boundary around what is an operating system was unclear. Textbooks on computing written in the mid-1980s, for instance, typically discussed the Apple Macintosh graphical user interface as a graphics feature rather than an operating system, while discussions of operating systems would focus strictly on DOS, CP/M, and Unix.[100] With the successful release of the Apple Macintosh, Steve Jobs would move on to start a new company, NeXT, and in so doing would introduce yet another operating system incompatible with those rising in the market. Despite considerable hype, this computing system would never take off, suffering the fate of many such proprietary systems of the era.[101] Not until the early 1990s would NeXT fail outright, and Jobs would suffer stinging criticisms from analysts enjoying the benefit of hindsight.[102]

As standards became established, competition would intensify both within and between standards. Within the Wintel standard, hundreds of manufacturers competed to produce and distribute these systems quickly and at the lowest possible cost for a given level of quality. This competition gave rise to innovations among these manufacturers in distribution, some going with direct-to-consumer approaches that would flourish later with the coming of the Internet. Competition kept the pressure on manufacturers to keep on the cutting edge in terms of new product releases, and in turn put pressure on their component suppliers, to improve their products. Some who have analyzed microcomputer manufacturers during this period have found that these companies either released new products in rapid succession or failed.[103] In this way, the rise of a dominant standard did not end competition in the industry. If anything, competition intensified among those firms that conformed to the standard.

In the 1990s competition would develop between alternative microcomputer standards as well. The pressure to move the "IBM" standard to a graphical user interface came from the Apple Macintosh. Similarly, the push to miniaturize these technologies to enable portable computing took place between these standards. Along the way, a surprisingly large number of nonstandard approaches to microcomputing would be tried, and though these attempts typically failed, they introduced to the market improvements and features that intensified pressures on all microcomputer firms to improve. As my study period ends in the mid-1990s, improvements in microcomputing had developed to the point where high-end microcomputers competed increasingly with the workstations of the client-server world. For example, software for image manipulation and editing enabled Macintosh computers in 1994 to perform tasks that had been the exclusive domain of midrange workstations from the likes of SGI. The upward migration of microcomputing had begun, and with it increased competition foreshadowing the oncoming movement of microcomputers into the client-server world of network computing.

Over the twenty years from 1975 through 1994, the microcomputer market emerged from its beginnings as a pastime for hobbyists into a mass market served by hundreds of manufacturers. In fact, over that period thousands of organizations tried to manufacture microcomputers commercially, and most failed. Their competitive struggle can be thought of, as I have briefly reviewed here, in terms of the specific technological changes and strategic moves made along the way. The unifying thread through this history, however, is the role of competition—triggering attempts to improve and in the process helping these organizations discover the market's logic of competition. Like the mainframe and midrange markets, the microcomputer market was shaped in its evolution by an ongoing competition among the organizations that attempted to survive in that market. My theory suggests that the consequent successes and failures should have followed a predictable pattern, conforming to the model of Red Queen competition.

TABLE 6.12
Description of the Data Used in the Microcomputer Manufacturer Founding Analysis

Variables	Mean	Std Dev	Min	Max
Lagged microcomputer manufacturer entries/1,000	0.0922	0.0693	0	0.2080
Lagged microcomputer manuf. failures/1,000	0.0804	0.0849	0	0.2730
Microcomputer market shipments/10^6	4.6420	4.6153	0	15.69
Real U.S. gross domestic product	4,149	614.6096	3,222	5,135
U.S. prime interest rate	9.9800	3.3642	6	18.87
Avg. cumulative hazard of failure since incumbents' births	0.3414	0.3299	0	1.2110
Microcomputer market density/1,000	0.2295	0.1649	0	0.4780
Microcomputer market density squared/1,000	78.49	78.77	0	228.5
Historical competition faced by incumbents in microcomputer market/1,000	228.6	253.6	0	698.6
Recent historical competition faced by incumbents in microcomputer market/1,000	161.4	172.6	0	485.9
Distant-past historical competition faced by incumbent in microcomputer market/1,000	67.19	82.72	0	229.6
Average gini based on density	0.1547	0.0753	0	0.2567
Average gini based on founding	0.1582	0.0735	0	0.2498

Estimates of the Founding and Failure Models for Microcomputer Manufacturers

A number of other studies of the microcomputer market exist, and most if not all rely on the IDC database. As described in the appendix, however, I found many firms that were not included in the IDC data, and so by including data from multiple sources I am reasonably confident that this dataset does not suffer from sample-selection bias. The data do have the limitation that they only include U.S. microcomputer manufacturers, however. These manufacturers are described in tables 6.12 and 6.14. A total of 1,922 entries to the U.S. microcomputer market occur from 1975 through 1994, and 1,739 of these exit the market before the end of the study period.

Table 6.13 shows the estimates of the microcomputer manufacturer founding models. Comparing models $\lambda_{mc}1$ and $\lambda_{mc}2$ reveals support for the Competitive Hysteresis Hypothesis. Model $\lambda_{mc}1$ reveals a quadratic density effect, with numbers of microcomputer manufacturers initially in-

TABLE 6.13
Estimates of the Founding Rate of U.S. Microcomputer Manufacturers, 1975–1994

Independent Variable	($\lambda_{mc}1$)	($\lambda_{mc}2$)	($\lambda_{mc}3$)
Prior year microcomputer manufacturer entries/1,000	−0.00007 (0.0014)	−0.0079* (0.0048)	−0.0039 (0.0049)
Prior year microcomputer manufacturer failures/1,000	0.0100** (0.0032)	0.0160** (0.0048)	0.0168** (0.0047)
Sum of sizes of microcomputer organizations (annual shipments)/10^6	0.0005** (0.0001)	0.0004** (0.0001)	0.0005** (0.0001)
Real U.S. gross domestic product	0.0013** (0.0005)	0.0020** (0.0006)	0.0024** (0.0006)
U.S. prime interest rate	0.0585** (0.0219)	0.0246 (0.0293)	0.0027 (0.0331)
Avg. cumulative hazard of failure in microcomputer market since incumbents' births	−10.07** (1.251)	−10.65** (1.295)	−12.96** (1.661)
Number of microcomputer manufacturers/1,000	12.05** (1.789)	16.41** (3.037)	13.29** (3.556)
Number of microcomputer manufacturers/ 1,000, squared	−0.0218** (0.0055)	−0.0109 0.0083	−0.0149* (0.0086)
Historical competition faced by incumbents in microcomputer market/1,000	−0.0014 (0.0016)		
Recent historical competition faced by incumbents in microcomputer market/1,000		−0.0184* (0.0099)	−0.0155 (0.0097)
Distant-past historical competition faced by incumbents in microcomputer market/1,000		0.0204 (0.0125)	0.0170 (0.0124)
Inequality of past rivalry faced by incumbents (average gini)			−4.470 (3.648)
Inequality of past rival cohorts faced by incumbents (average gini)			8.610** (4.131)
Constant	−2.232 (1.470)	−4.328** (1.964)	−5.794** (2.048)
Log likelihood	−79.70	−77.96	−74.73
(df)	(9)	(10)	(12)

Note: The data include 1,922 market entries over 20 years, modeled as annual event counts. For coefficient estimates, standard errors are in parentheses.
* p < .10
** p < .05

creasing founding rates, but then ultimately decreasing founding rates at high numbers. This is the familiar pattern consistent with the theory of density-dependent legitimation and competition, in which the negative effect of the squared term picks up the competitive effect of increasing numbers of organizations. Given these estimates, however, the competitive effect is relatively weak in magnitude—too weak, in fact, to offset fully the positive first-order effect of density over the observed range. Model

TABLE 6.14
Description of the Data Used in the Microcomputer Manufacturer Failure Analysis

Variables	Mean	Std Dev	Min	Max
Dealio entrant	0.2803	0.4492	0	1
Real U.S. gross domestic product	4,501	453	3,222	5,135
U.S. prime interest rate	9.527	2.821	6	18.87
Market tenure, small organization	0.3198	0.4664	0	1
Market tenure, medium-sized organization	0.5770	0.4941	0	1
Market tenure, large-sized organization	0.1032	0.3043	0	1
Microcomputer market shipments/10^6	6.896	3.746	0	15.69
Lagged microcomputer manufacturer entries/1,000	0.1335	0.0559	0	0.2080
Lagged microcomputer manuf. failures/1,000	0.1198	0.0750	0	0.2730
Microcomputer market density at entry/1,000	0.2738	0.1390	0	0.4780
Cumulative hazard of failure since organization's birth	0.4872	0.5899	0	3.505
Computer industry density/1,000	0.4693	0.1115	0.111	0.6030
Computer industry density squared/1,000	232.6	95.00	12.32	363.6
Microcomputer market density/1,000	0.3357	0.1194	0	0.4780
Microcomputer market density squared/1,000	127.0	73.04	0	228.5
Midrange market density/1,000	0.1698	0.0307	0.107	0.2170
Mainframe market density/1,000	0.0261	0.0051	0.01	0.0340
Duration in midrange	1.1242	3.608	0	32
Duration in mainframe	0.3859	3.219	0	42
Historical competition faced by org. in microcomputer market/1,000	0.6629	0.8123	0	4.337
Recent historical competition faced in microcomputer market/1,000	0.4750	0.4903	0	2.126
Distant-past historical competition faced in microcomputer market/1,000	0.1879	0.3437	0	2.211
Number of distinct rivals faced in microcomputer market/1,000	0.3314	0.3087	0	1.374
Historical competition faced by org. in midrange market/1,000	0.1471	0.4728	0	3.484
Historical competition faced by org. in mainframe market/1,000	0.0071	0.0587	0	0.8140
Microcomputer rivals' historical exposure to competition/1,000	347.5	226.1	0	664.8

TABLE 6.14 (*cont.*)

Description of the Data Used in the Microcomputer Manufacturer Failure Analysis

Variables	Mean	Std Dev	Min	Max
Microcomputer rivals' recent historical exposure to competition/1,000	249.0	155.0	0	468.6
Microcomputer rivals' distant historical exposure to competition/1,000	98.53	72.63	0	209.2
Sum of ages of microcomputer rivals/1,000	9.000	5.996	0	20.25
Gini based on density	0.1848	0.2031	0	0.6778
Gini based on founding	0.1917	0.2053	0	0.5604

$\lambda_{mc}2$, however, shows a much stronger competitive effect—one that depends not just on the number of incumbents, but on the historical competition faced by these incumbents ($\Sigma_k T_k$). As these organizations endured competition, they became stronger competitors, consequently reducing entries into their market. This effect reduces the competitive effect that had been attributed to density. Consistent with the Competitive Hysteresis Hypothesis, the strength of competition over founding among microcomputer manufacturers hinged on incumbents' exposure to competition.

By contrast, the Competency-Trap Hypothesis does not receive support. The effect of distant-past historical competition is nonsignificant. So I do not find that distant-past competitive experience made organizations stronger at deterring entry, but neither do I find that outdated experience made them weaker as predicted by the competency trap argument. Neither is the Myopic Learning Hypothesis supported. In fact, the estimates in model $\lambda_{mc}3$ show higher founding rates the more that incumbents have had a widely dispersed range of competitive experience (among cohorts). This is the opposite of what was predicted by the Myopic Learning Hypothesis.

In other effects, the pure-selection argument receives support. The cumulative hazard of failure over the incumbents' lives consistently and strongly depresses founding rates. Organizations that are survivors of a rigorous selection process reduce the chances that new organizations will enter their market. The mass of microcomputer manufacturers is positive and significant across all models and can be interpreted as a positive effect of larger organizations on the founding rates of new organizations. Finally, as was the case with banks and midrange computer manufacturers, there is evidence of a renewal process among microcomputer manufacturers. Failures of microcomputer manufacturers in one year predict foundings of such firms in the next, an effect that likely indicates the freeing up of resources for new foundings when organizations fail.

The organizational failure model estimates are reported for the microcomputer manufacturers in tables 6.15 and 6.16. Because the microcomputer manufacturers became numerically overwhelming, I first experimented with whether to specify their failure rates as density dependent including all computer manufacturers, or to distinguish between the different market densities. Models $r_{mc}1$ through $r_{mc}4$ in table 6.15 assess different density specifications and show that monotonic densities by market demonstrate interesting differences in the strength of competition generated by the different organizations. Microcomputer manufacturers exhibit density-dependent competition with one another across all models in tables 6.15 and 6.16. Midrange manufacturers also generate competition felt by microcomputer firms. On further investigation, I found that this competition was not coming strictly from midrange manufacturers that were also producing microcomputers. That is, this is an effect across the markets and suggests that the increasing overlap between these markets noted in the historical review had measurable effects on the life chances of these organizations. Especially interesting among these estimates are the negative and significant effects of mainframe density, which appear in the more complete specifications of table 6.16. This result is consistent with a partitioning of the market, where gains by mainframe manufacturers released other parts of the market to the microcomputer manufacturers.[104]

The specifications in table 6.16 show support for the Competitive Hysteresis Hypothesis. Looking across the models, the historical competition faced by an organization, T_j, decreased its failure rate, especially when specified in terms of recently experienced competition. The same could not be said, however, for the competitive experience of one's rivals. Rivalry did not intensify as rivals had more competitive experience. Consequently, the Competitive Hysteresis Hypothesis receives only partial support. Note also that distant-past historical experience did not significantly affect an organization's failure rate, so the Competency-Trap Hypothesis is not supported. Nonetheless, historical recency does matter in these models, in that only recently experienced competition is survival enhancing. Meanwhile, the Costly Adaptation Hypothesis receives support in these models. The number of distinct historical rivals faced by an organization, K_j, positively affected these manufacturers' failure rates. Thus, historical competition was life enhancing, but not if it was spread over too many different rivals. This pattern suggests that the costs of adaptation attenuate the benefits of the Red Queen as an organization attempts to adapt to too many distinct rivals. Finally, the pure-selection argument received support, with a negative and significant effect of the cumulative hazard of failure over an organization's lifetime—but this effect vanished once the Red Queen effects were included in the models.

TABLE 6.15

Estimates of the Failure Rates of U.S. Microcomputer Manufacturers, 1975–1994

Independent Variable	$(r_{mc}1)$	$(r_{mc}2)$	$(r_{mc}3)$	$(r_{mc}4)$
Number of computer manufacturers/ 1,000	4.272** (0.7727)	4.376** (2.019)		
(Number of computer manufacturers) squared/1,000		-0.0001 (0.0023)		
Number of mainframe manufacturers/ 1,000			-18.90 (15.78)	-20.21 (14.04)
Number of midrange computer manufacturers/1,000			8.466** (3.685)	8.443** (3.703)
Number of microcomputer manufacturers/1,000			2.505 (2.319)	2.881** (1.034)
(Number of microcomputer manufacturers) squared/1,000			0.0006 (0.0032)	
Sum of sizes of microcomputer organizations (shipments)/1,000	0.0003** (0.00004)	0.0003** (0.00005)	0.0002** (0.00005)	0.0002** (0.00005)
Prior year microcomputer manufacturer entries/1,000	-0.7793 (1.091)	-0.7727 (1.097)	-0.1715 (1.203)	-0.1743 (1.203)
Prior year microcomputer manufacturer failures/1,000	5.096** (0.9293)	5.084** (0.9525)	6.199** (1.319)	6.123** (1.253)
Number of microcomputer manufacturers at entry/1,000	0.0905 (0.5070)	0.0929 (0.5088)	0.0581 (0.5138)	0.0603 (0.5136)
Cumulative hazard of failure in microcomputer market since the organization's birth	-0.3078** (0.1315)	-0.3083** (0.1318)	-0.2974** (0.1325)	-0.2982** (0.1324)

TABLE 6.15 (*cont.*)
Estimates of the Failure Rates of U.S. Microcomputer Manufacturers, 1975–1994

Independent Variable	$(r_{mc}1)$	$(r_{mc}2)$	$(r_{mc}3)$	$(r_{mc}4)$
Dealio entrant	-0.1485**	-0.1485**	-0.1477**	-0.1478**
	(0.0574)	(0.0574)	(0.0574)	(0.0574)
Organization also is in midrange	-0.2413**	-0.2414**	-0.2418**	-0.2416**
computer market	(0.0873)	(0.0873)	(0.0873)	(0.0873)
Organization also is in mainframe	-0.4436	-0.4437	-0.4381	-0.4385
computer market	(0.3123)	(0.3123)	(0.3123)	(0.3123)
Real U.S. gross domestic product	-0.0026**	-0.0026**	-0.0018**	-0.0017**
	(0.0004)	(0.0004)	(0.0006)	(0.0006)
U.S. prime interest rate	0.0194	0.0193	0.0379	0.0366
	(0.0245)	(0.0245)	(0.0313)	(0.0307)
Market tenure, all organizations				
0–1 year	5.665**	5.628**	2.182	2.095
	(1.066)	(1.249)	(2.557)	(2.522)
1–3 years	6.127**	6.091**	2.646	2.559
	(1.061)	(1.243)	(2.554)	(2.518)
3–5 years	6.356**	6.320**	2.867	2.780
	(1.071)	(1.249)	(2.559)	(2.524)
5–10 years	6.421**	6.385**	2.924	2.838
	(1.086)	(1.256)	(2.567)	(2.533)

TABLE 6.15 (*cont.*)
Estimates of the Failure Rates of U.S. Microcomputer Manufacturers, 1975–1994

Independent Variable	$(r_{mc}1)$	$(r_{mc}2)$	$(r_{mc}3)$	$(r_{mc}4)$
Market tenure, all organizations				
10–15 years	6.911**	6.876**	3.398	3.314
	(1.161)	(1.313)	(2.603)	(2.571)
15+ years	7.075**	7.041**	3.555	3.471
	(1.365)	(1.493)	(2.702)	(2.671)
Market tenure, medium-sized organizations				
0–1 year	-0.1582	-0.1580	-0.1609	-0.1602
	(0.0987)	(0.0988)	(0.0988)	(0.0988)
1–3 years	-0.3115**	-0.3114**	-0.3108**	-0.3105**
	(0.0802)	(0.0802)	(0.0802)	(0.0802)
3–5 years	-0.6115**	-0.6113**	-0.6093**	-0.6088**
	(0.1215)	(0.1215)	(0.1216)	(0.1215)
5–10 years	-0.7571**	-0.7568**	-0.7620**	-0.7617**
	(0.1392)	(0.1393)	(0.1394)	(0.1394)
10–15 years	-0.7672**	-0.7670**	-0.7707**	-0.7711**
	(0.3796)	(0.3796)	(0.3797)	(0.3796)
15+ years	-1.206	-1.206	-1.206**	-1.206
	(1.225)	(1.225)	(1.225)	(1.225)

TABLE 6.15 (*cont.*)
Estimates of the Failure Rates of U.S. Microcomputer Manufacturers, 1975–1994

Independent Variable	$(r_{mc}1)$	$(r_{mc}2)$	$(r_{mc}3)$	$(r_{mc}4)$
Market tenure, large organizations				
0–1 year	−0.5926**	−0.5917**	−0.5996**	−0.5980**
	(0.2180)	(0.2186)	(0.2186)	(0.2184)
1–3 years	−0.9596**	−0.9593**	−0.9626**	−0.9620**
	(0.1794)	(0.1795)	(0.1795)	(0.1795)
3–5 years	−1.031**	−1.030**	−1.033**	−1.032**
	(0.2299)	(0.2300)	(0.2299)	(0.2299)
5–10 years	−2.783**	−2.783**	−2.787**	−2.787**
	(0.4600)	(0.4601)	(0.4601)	(0.4601)
10–15 years	−3.613**	−3.613**	−3.612**	−3.613**
	(1.047)	(1.047)	(1.047)	(1.047)
15+ years	−2.710**	−2.709**	−2.723**	−2.722**
	(1.227)	(1.227)	(1.227)	(1.227)
Log likelihood	−2398.43	−2398.43	−2397.76	−2397.77
(df)	(29)	(30)	(32)	(31)

Note: The data include 1739 exits from a risk set of 1922 organizations over 6510 organization-years. Other variables also are included in each model and are shown in the continuation of the table. For coefficient estimates, standard errors are in parentheses.

* p < .10
** p < .05

TABLE 6.16
Estimates of the Failure Rates of U.S. Microcomputer Manufacturers, 1975–1994

Independent Variable	$(r_{mc}5)$	$(r_{mc}6)$	$(r_{mc}7)$	$(r_{mc}8)$	$(r_{mc}9)$
Number of microcomputer manufacturers at entry/1,000	-0.1383	-0.1748	-0.2895	-0.2206	-0.4142
	(0.5274)	(0.6235)	(0.6220)	(0.6325)	(0.6279)
Cumulative hazard of failure in microcomputer market since the organization's birth	0.1776	0.1850	0.0978	0.0720	0.1851
	(0.3095)	(0.3168)	(0.2873)	(0.2856)	(0.2959)
Historical competition faced by organization in microcomputer market/1,000	-0.3448*	-0.3769			
	(0.1996)	(0.3548)			
Recent historical competition faced by organization in microcomputer market/1,000	-1.825**	-1.967**	-1.989**		
	(0.5790)	(0.5854)	(0.6892)		
Distant-past historical competition faced by organization in microcomputer market/1,000	0.5018	0.4446	0.5993		
	(0.4383)	(0.4409)	(0.4666)		
Number of distinct historical rivals faced by organization in microcomputer market/1,000	0.0887	1.588*	1.755*	1.780*	
	(0.8093)	(0.9249)	(0.9255)	(1.008)	
Microcomputer rivals' historical exposure to competition/1,000				0.0015	
				(0.0010)	
Inequality of past rivalry faced by organization (gini)					0.3842
					(0.9787)
Inequality of past rival cohorts faced by organization (gini)					-0.2876
					(1.004)

TABLE 6.16 (*cont.*)
Estimates of the Failure Rates of U.S. Microcomputer Manufacturers, 1975–1994

Independent Variable	$(r_{mc}5)$	$(r_{mc}6)$	$(r_{mc}7)$	$(r_{mc}8)$	$(r_{mc}9)$
Number of mainframe manufacturers/1,000	-26.03*	-26.34*	-27.33*	-7.286	-26.69**
	(14.49)	(14.76)	(14.71)	(19.62)	(14.82)
Number of midrange computer manufacturers/1,000	8.635**	8.693**	9.140**	8.524**	8.946**
	(3.728)	(3.765)	(3.791)	(3.685)	(3.830)
Number of microcomputer manufacturers/1,000	3.441**	3.442**	3.734**	1.933	3.723**
	(1.084)	(1.084)	(1.081)	(1.606)	(1.088)
Sum of sizes of microcomputer organizations (annual shipments)/1,000	0.0002**	0.0002**	0.0002**	0.0002**	0.0002**
	(0.00005)	(0.00005)	(0.00005)	(0.00006)	(0.00005)
Prior year microcomputer manufacturer entries/1,000	-0.4415	-0.4210	-0.8400	0.0090	-0.8038
	(1.213)	(1.227)	(1.235)	(1.363)	(1.237)
Prior year microcomputer manufacturer failures/1,000	6.236**	6.226**	6.562**	5.172**	6.449**
	(1.261)	(1.264)	(1.275)	(1.543)	(1.309)
Dealio entrant	-0.1543**	-0.1543**	-0.1514**	-0.1516**	-0.1515**
	(0.0575)	(0.0575)	(0.0575)	(0.0575)	(0.0575)
Organization also is in midrange computer market	-0.2492**	-0.2492**	-0.2582**	-0.2616**	-0.2608**
	(0.0875)	(0.0875)	(0.0875)	(0.0876)	(0.0879)
Organization also is in mainframe computer market	-0.4500	-0.4500	-0.4655	-0.4646	-0.4604
	(0.3124)	(0.3124)	(0.3125)	(0.3125)	(0.3128)
Real U.S. gross domestic product	-0.0017**	-0.0017**	-0.0016**	-0.0020**	-0.0016**
	(0.0006)	(0.0006)	(0.0006)	(0.0007)	(0.0006)
U.S. prime interest rate	0.0343	0.0344	0.0310	0.0429	0.0293
	(0.0310)	(0.0310)	(0.0313)	(0.0311)	(0.0315)

TABLE 6.16 (*cont.*)

Estimates of the Failure Rates of U.S. Microcomputer Manufacturers, 1975–1994

Independent Variable	$(r_{mc}5)$	$(r_{mc}6)$	$(r_{mc}7)$	$(r_{mc}8)$	$(r_{mc}9)$
Market tenure, all organizations					
0–1 year	1.914	1.907	1.605	2.924	1.676
	(2.535)	(2.535)	(2.549)	(2.636)	(2.571)
1–3 years	2.367	2.340	2.087	3.379	2.145
	(2.531)	(2.544)	(2.556)	(2.638)	(2.579)
3–5 years	2.584	2.558	2.446	3.733	2.521
	(2.537)	(2.548)	(2.561)	(2.641)	(2.585)
5–10 years	2.620	2.595	2.411	3.683	2.494
	(2.547)	(2.558)	(2.570)	(2.647)	(2.590)
10–15 years	3.056	3.031	2.499	3.737	2.542
	(2.587)	(2.597)	(2.615)	(2.682)	(2.632)
15+ years	3.116	3.092	2.254	3.463	2.281
	(2.690)	(2.698)	(2.722)	(2.781)	(2.734)
Market tenure, medium-sized organizations					
0–1 year	-0.1795*	-0.1776*	-0.1866*	-0.1892*	-0.1877*
	(0.0994)	(0.1009)	(0.1009)	(0.1010)	(0.1010)
1–3 years	-0.3163**	-0.3171**	-0.3116**	-0.3148**	-0.3134**
	(0.0803)	(0.0806)	(0.0806)	(0.0806)	(0.0806)
3–5 years	-0.5988**	-0.5989**	-0.5852**	-0.5848**	-0.5832**
	(0.1217)	(0.1217)	(0.1218)	(0.1218)	(0.1218)
5–10 years	-0.7494**	-0.7491**	-0.7696**	-0.7706**	-0.7685**
	(0.1397)	(0.1397)	(0.1399)	(0.1399)	(0.1399)

TABLE 6.16 (*cont.*)
Estimates of the Failure Rates of U.S. Microcomputer Manufacturers, 1975–1994

Independent Variable	$(r_{mc}5)$	$(r_{mc}6)$	$(r_{mc}7)$	$(r_{mc}8)$	$(r_{mc}9)$
Market tenure, medium-sized organizations					
10–15 years	-0.8102**	-0.8094**	-0.8151**	-0.8208**	-0.7967**
	(0.3783)	(0.3784)	(0.3835)	(0.3828)	(0.3870)
15+ years	-1.206	-1.206	-1.102	-1.108	-1.095
	(1.225)	(1.225)	(1.226)	(1.226)	(1.226)
Market tenure, large organizations					
0–1 year	-0.6124**	-0.6105**	-0.6137**	-0.6132**	-0.6087**
	(0.2181)	(0.2188)	(0.2186)	(0.2184)	(0.2188)
1–3 years	-0.9819**	-0.9830**	-0.9677**	-0.9760**	-0.9706**
	(0.1799)	(0.1802)	(0.1802)	(0.1802)	(0.1803)
3–5 years	-1.032**	-1.033**	-1.023*	-1.022*	-1.024**
	(0.2299)	(0.2300)	(0.2300)	(0.2300)	(0.2301)
5–10 years	-2.789**	-2.789**	-2.815**	-2.816**	-2.820**
	(0.4601)	(0.4601)	(0.4602)	(0.4602)	(0.4604)
10–15 years	-3.676**	-3.676**	-3.660**	-3.665**	-3.648**
	(1.047)	(1.047)	(1.049)	(1.049)	(1.050)
15+ years	-2.719**	-2.720**	-2.597**	-2.601**	-2.591**
	(1.227)	(1.227)	(1.228)	(1.228)	(1.228)
Log likelihood	-2396.24	-2396.24	-2391.39	-2390.25	-2391.20
(df)	(32)	(33)	(34)	(35)	(36)

Note: The data include 1739 exits from a risk set of 1922 organizations over 6510 organization-years. Other variables also are included in each model, as shown in the continuation of the table. For coefficient estimates, standard errors are in parentheses.

* $p < .10$
** $p < .05$

Summary of Findings

Each of the three markets within the computer industry began as an ill-defined collection of technologies, brought forward by entrepreneurs with little understanding of who would use them and why. But by competing, organizations came to discover and understand their customers, products, and technologies. Especially interesting in this transformation was that each market started from largely noncommercial beginnings. The mainframe market was initially a scientific domain, and only with experience did manufacturers discover how to bring these computers to commercial customers. The midrange and microcomputer markets each began as social movements, with participants seeing themselves in contradiction to the commercial establishment. Yet the technologies brought forward by these movements found commercial application. Large markets grew as manufacturers competed, and in the process discovered how to match customer, technology, and product. In short, the logics of competition that we would come to understand in each market was discovered by competing.

This recounting of the computer industry's development is supported, as well, by the estimates of the Red Queen models. Especially strong was support for the theory's main prediction, the Competitive Hysteresis Hypothesis. Across all three markets, manufacturers with more exposure to competition were more likely to survive, and they generated stronger competition, reducing the founding rates in their market. Weaker support was found for the theory's second prediction, the Competency-Trap Hypothesis. Only among mainframe manufacturers was outdated experience a liability. For the other markets, however, recency was important to making experience beneficial. One possible reason for this difference is the much longer history in the mainframe market. Perhaps with the passage of time, competency traps will be more apparent in the industry's other markets as well. (I will revisit the competency trap in the next chapter.) The Costly Adaptation Hypothesis received support only among microcomputer manufacturers. Again, this is the one market where this hypothesis has the greatest chance of succeeding, because in microcomputer manufacturing so many organizations populate the market. Given that the Costly Adaptation Hypothesis identifies the costs involved with adapting to numerous historical rivals, one would expect it to hold in microcomputers if at all. Receiving the least support was the Myopic Learning Hypothesis, which appeared as predicted only in the mainframe founding models. As was the case in chapter 5's banking study, the Myopic Learning Hypothesis appears to find little support in the computer industry.

Summarizing other effects, the pure-selection argument received considerable support across these markets. Simply outsurviving others is an indication of an organization's fitness, regardless of exposure to competition. Importantly, the findings in support of Red Queen theory are largely robust to controlling for the pure-selection effect. Renewal processes were revealed in midrange computers and microcomputers. The robustness of these markets thus is due, in some part, to the regeneration of new foundings from the resources freed up by earlier failures. Much is said in the technology world about the need to tolerate failure in order to get the occasional success. This finding suggests that failure may have a much more direct affect on creating new technology organizations than we have heretofore realized. Lastly, it appears that the computer industry experienced some resource partitioning, in that the more that mainframe manufacturers proliferate their market, the better off are the microcomputer manufacturers, while midrange manufacturers compete not only among themselves, but with the microcomputer manufacturers as well.

What I have not considered in this chapter are the movements of organizations among these three markets. While such changes were not common, they did occur. In particular, with the development of microcomputing, many midrange manufacturers tried their hand at producing microcomputers. The theory of Red Queen evolution has important implications for organizations engaging in such wholesale strategic change. I explain these implications, and test them using data on these computer manufacturers, in the next chapter.

SEVEN

The Red Queen and Organizational Inertia

OFTEN, SUCCESSFUL ORGANIZATIONS move into new markets only to fail. This notorious pattern can happen for two very different reasons: because organizations do the wrong things in the new market, or they do the right things but so disrupt themselves in the process that they fail nonetheless. Some examples help to illustrate this distinction. In 1994 the American Craft Brewing Company (Ambrew) was founded, one of 166 craft breweries founded that year in the United States as the microbrewery craze gained momentum.[1] Unlike most microbrewers, however, leadership at Ambrew aimed to export the American microbrewery model to other countries. Ambrew's leadership had considerable experience both in craft brewing in the United States and in international beverage distribution. They planned not to run American breweries, but rather to build a network of twenty independent microbreweries that they would start in countries worldwide. With the microbrewery movement gaining momentum in the United States, leadership at Ambrew was able to act fast. Top management assembled a board comprising members from several of their target market countries, providing the company with country-specific knowledge and networks as well as financial backing. In 1995 their first brewery, the South China Brewing Company, opened in Hong Kong— claiming to be the first microbrewery in the Asia-Pacific region. The year 1996 saw the company go public, allowing it in 1997 to establish breweries in Ireland and Mexico and purchase brewing equipment for twenty breweries in total.

The theory among Ambrew's founders was that the sentiments behind the American microbrewery movement were not limited to the United States. Furthermore, only a very small operation would be needed in each country because the company's collective scale would be achieved by "rolling out" the model across multiple countries. Products and brands, meanwhile, would appeal to local tastes—such as the "Red Dawn Ale" brewed by the South China Brewing Company in the year the British handed over rule of Hong Kong to China. Others in management thought that the American identity of the organization would be helpful for marketing, under the idea that all things American sell well in some countries. Finally, the brewing process was to be controlled centrally by Ambrew, while the organizations in each country would otherwise be decentralized to take advantage of local knowledge.

Once under way, however, this theory turned out to be in error in many ways. In general, the logics of competition in the brewing markets of different countries turned out to be very different. The obvious differences, such as regulatory differences or differences in distribution channels, were understood by Ambrew's management. More subtle differences were not, however, and led to various mismatches between Ambrew's strategy and the imperatives of the various national environments. For instance, distribution in Hong Kong relied on the company's own truck, which would leave the product in kegs outside the delivery doors of restaurants and bars. This approach might have worked well in many locations, but in Hong Kong the heat quickly spoiled the beer. Similarly, drinking customs in Ireland, Mexico, and Hong Kong differ greatly from those in the United States, with respect to whether drinking can take place at home, the degree to which drinking in public is driven by local versus global status distinctions among brands, and the like. Further problems were caused by the company's centralized quality control system, which was so far from each facility that in some cases serious quality problems emerged in the production process. Meanwhile, the company's reliance on public capital markets left it vulnerable when, in 1997, microbrewery stocks generally fell with perceived overcapacity in the U.S. markets. This event, combined with initial shortcomings in Ambrew's results in its first three breweries, saw its stock plummet. Soon afterward, the company declared bankruptcy.

What makes Ambrew's story interesting is that the organization's efforts were, in fact, such a success—the ultimate financial outcomes notwithstanding. The company's plan was executed to the letter, at least in three countries, in a relatively short period of time. The strategy failed because it was not aligned with the logics of competition in Hong Kong, Mexico, or Ireland. In short, this organization failed because the *content* of its activities—its strategy and organization—were "incorrect" given its environment.

By contrast, a company can fail as well for a distinctly different reason— when the *process* of moving into a new market is so disruptive that the organization cannot survive. For instance, the Japanese gaming software company Atlus grew during the 1980s and 1990s to become very successful in the Japanese anime video role-playing game (RPG) market, with hits like "Megami Tensei" (The Transformation of the Goddess) gaining popularity in Japan and ultimately in the United States as well.[2] Over time, this company established a cultlike following among gamers who favored Atlus's elaborate animation, complex and fantastic characters, and the storyline that connected successive game releases. With such a following, game console makers such as Nintendo and Sony favored Atlus games, making the company a sweetheart of this niche market.

But getting to this point had not been easy for Atlus, and its struggle in the very competitive gaming industry is a story of ongoing adaptability. A substantial initial investment was needed to develop such extravagant games, a problem made worse by the long lag between initial investment and revenues typical among software publishers. Consequently, for its first decade, Atlus struggled to raise capital—sometimes landing private equity, but often relying on revenues from faddish gaming products, such as the distribution of coin-operated game machines and billiard tables to Japanese pachinko parlors and game centers. At one point in the late 1980s, the cash-strapped company was on the verge of giving itself up to acquisition when its founder, Naoya Harano, began installing karaoke machines in closed rooms within amusement centers and pool halls. These "karaoke boxes" became a hit, especially among Japanese women, who would line up for the opportunity to sing with their friends in private. With revenues from such exploits, Atlus continued to develop its RPG games to be some of the most competitive in this niche of the gaming industry.

Unlike Ambrew, Atlus had no problem with the content of its strategy being out of step with its environment. Harano and his management team demonstrated an uncanny ability to make the right call when it comes to fads and fashions in gaming. His pioneering move into role-playing games led the market by a decade, and his choice to dedicate long-term software development efforts there is consistent with what has proved to be a stable and growing software publishing market in gaming. Meanwhile, Harano's timing moving in—and then back out—of billiards and karaoke boxes exactly preceded those markets' moves, so that Atlus was never left with inventory when those gaming fashions moved on. The content of Atlus's strategy was consistently well fit to the changing and emerging markets on which Atlus focused.

Again revealing an eye for the latest appealing fad, the company introduced in 1995 yet another amusement machine, again needing to raise revenue to fund its software development work. "Print Club," the brainchild of a secretary at Atlus, was a phenomenal hit. Consisting of a booth containing a camera, this machine allowed patrons to pose alone or with a friend for immediately developed photo stickers. Within a year and a half of its introduction, this machine exploded into the market, suddenly growing the company's sales by 350 percent and promising even greater growth rates if the expansion could be financed and organized. The company went public to raise capital and formed an alliance with Sega, a firm more capable of developing and organizing a major product rollout. Yet the explosive growth into a market so different from gaming software was extremely difficult for Atlus, and although Print Club continued to succeed, Atlus itself faced numerous organizational difficulties. For instance, technically simple maintenance problems became an organiza-

218   CHAPTER SEVEN

tional nightmare, as they were multiplied across thousands of installations throughout Japan. Ultimately, a desperate Atlus was purchased by a Japanese toy maker.

The problem for Atlus was that the *process* of suddenly organizing the design, manufacture, distribution, and maintenance of thousands of coin-operated photography kiosks was an impossible task. The organization was, after all, a software development firm. The organizational capabilities involved in hiring, coordinating, and retaining good software engineers as they create a complex game that both works and is on the cutting edge of this changing market are very different from what it takes for the photographic kiosk market. So Atlus's failure was due to a dramatic disruption in its organizational processes brought on as it exploded into the photographic kiosk market. The content of change, for Atlus, was not a problem. If anything, the content of Atlus's strategy was so right that the ensuing fantastic growth rate made the process of moving into that market all the more disruptive to the organization.

More generally, research on organizational change demonstrates that the process of change can be disruptive, so much so that organizational failure rates typically rise during periods of change even when the content of change is adaptive.[3] In this chapter, I consider the possibility that the process of change is especially disruptive when organizations have developed through Red Queen competition.

The Competition-Inertia Hypothesis

A fundamental argument in modern organization theory is that the process of change is especially hazardous the more that the change disrupts established organizational routines, roles, procedures, capabilities, and identities.[4] Put differently, the more capable and established an organization, the more that changing the organization is disruptive.[5] Being well adapted implies the ability to perform well but also acts to constrain attempts to alter organizational activities.[6] Organizational change is difficult and hazardous precisely when organizations are well adapted to their environment.[7]

For example, the Korean company Hyundai entered the very competitive American automobile market in the late 1980s as a low-price competitor.[8] Arguably, Hyundai at that time was one of the world's leaders when it came to manufacturing and exporting low-cost automobiles. Its reputation as a low-cost automobile manufacturer was cemented by the company's competitive success in the United States. Once in the U.S. market, however, the company changed its strategy to make and sell high-quality automobiles into that market. After roughly a decade of change, Hyundai's products were receiving top ratings for quality by independent rating organizations. The process of getting to this new strategy, however, is another story.

This new strategy required a very different kind of organization, making the process of change at Hyundai especially disruptive. To operate as a multinational corporation, leadership changed as the company moved away from a traditional family governance system, leading to considerable internal strife. Production processes in the company changed with the implementation of quality-centered manufacturing and design systems, and a shift to production in North America that included a major, failed manufacturing plant expansion in Quebec. Failures to match its new products with a suitable U.S. marketing strategy led to finger pointing between the U.S. and Korean parts of the company. Taken together, these difficulties in the process of changing this organization and its strategy involved every part of the company—its product line, manufacturing facilities, leadership, and organization. The process of executing these changes was so disruptive that at times the U.S. expansion of Hyundai was in jeopardy. In the end, although the content of change at Hyundai has arguably been a success, the execution process clearly was difficult.

The process of change is hazardous, as well, the more that the change requires altering an organization's identity.[9] Changing identities turns out to be especially difficult when one lacks social status, as in French gastronomy where the movement of higher-status chefs to nouvelle cuisine was especially influential.[10] The identity problem plagued Hyundai as well, in its attempt to move into high-quality automobile production. Even as U.S. ratings of quality were quite high for Hyundai's products by 2003, public perceptions of the company's reputation were slower to change, despite aggressive marketing tactics such as the establishment of an especially generous warranty program. More generally, the difficulties involved in the process of change result not only from the technical issues involved in altering organizational practices, but also from the fact that identities are slow to change, and the more firmly established the identity, the more disruptive is the process of changing that identity.

One of the central implications of Red Queen theory is that adaptation results from competition. Atlus honed its skills, procedures, and other development activities within the very competitive environment of gaming software publishing. Hyundai manufactured at low-cost in the late 1980s—a time of cost reduction moves worldwide by organizations in the automobile industry. That competitive history shaped Hyundai, making it especially good at low cost production and distribution. More generally, as an organization develops through the process of Red Queen evolution, it becomes more in-tune with the environment's logic of competition, and so more capable of operating well within that logic.

This result implies, however, that the more an organizations adapts to its environment through Red Queen evolution, the more difficult it will be for the organization to change to another environment entirely. Hyundai's difficulty in establishing a high-quality reputation is a direct result of this organization having so thoroughly established its low-cost (and low-quality) reputation. In another example, earlier I mentioned the Newell company as a case of an organization that had become successful manufacturing and distributing staple products such as window coverings through mass retailers in the United States, building on their strengths in organizing for efficiency and distribution using state-of-the-art information technologies to minimize inventories. Having competed well in this competitive context for some years, one might wonder whether this organization could now compete in non-U.S. markets where mass retailing is just taking off, such as China. The difficulty in making such a move is that many of the lessons learned in the U.S. context would likely not apply in China, making for less success should Newell try to build on its U.S. experiences. The point is not that Newell or Hyundai cannot change, but rather that for them to change they must endure considerable disruption due to the fact that they became so thoroughly adapted through competition in the past. In general, these arguments suggest the hypothesis:

> **Competition-Inertia Hypothesis: The more an organization experiences a history of competition in one context, the more hazardous it will be for the organization to move into another context.**

One implication of this hypothesis is that organizations do not become inert in isolation, but rather they do so in the company of their competitors. As one organization competes and becomes well adapted to its context, and so less able to change significantly, its competitors are in the same situation. This raises again the problem of organizations collectively descending into competency traps, as discussed in chapter 3. If organizations turn to one another as social referents, then they may learn from one another.[11] Such learning, however, promises to reinforce inertia as competing organizations collectively become both better adapted to one environment and especially vulnerable to disruption should they change to another. Hyundai is certainly not the only car company facing the challenge of increasing quality, nor is Newell the only domestic U.S. organization confronted by the problem of globalization.

My computer industry data are well suited to testing the Competition-Inertia Hypothesis. That three very different markets appeared in the industry over time allows for a test. Some 260 manufacturers with experience in midrange or mainframe computing made the move to produce microcomputers over the period of this study. Looking at the individual cases, these organizations were formidable competitors, typically making this move on the basis of their success—yet many of them failed in the process. That raises the question: Were microcomputer manufacturers more likely to fail if they had first experienced competition in the mid-range and mainframe markets?

Modeling the Inertial Consequences of the Red Queen

To model the Competition-Inertia Hypothesis, it is necessary to decide on what is the appropriate comparison to be made in the specification of the statistical model. Three choices are possible, but only one makes sense as a test of the hypothesis. First, it is possible to look at changes over time within a given organization. That is, we could compare how well an organization is faring before versus after a change. This comparison could not be made in a model of failure rates but could be accomplished by estimating models of organizational performance or growth. But such a comparison would be inappropriate here for two reasons. First, it would be plagued by the fact that over-time change within each organization's life will likely reflect regression to the mean.[12] Second, such an over-time comparison would conflate the content and process implications of the organizational change. For instance, if the organization's viability improved due to the move, this might have been because it moved into a more munificent environment—a content effect that might disguise a disruptive process effect.[13]

Another possibility would be to compare the changed organizations with those that did not make the change. For instance, we could compare midrange manufacturers that moved into microcomputing with midrange manufacturers that did not make such a move. This comparison again suffers the problem of conflating the content and process effects of change, however. It would not be possible to know whether the observed difference is due to the inherent differences in viability that result from being in the different markets, or whether it is due to the disruption suffered by the organization that made the change.

A better comparison, and the one I model here, is to compare all those in the "destination" market—in this case the microcomputer market—to see whether those organizations that competed in another market in the past suffer as a result. This comparison holds constant the content effects of change, in that all the organizations are in the same market. What differs is that some of these organizations were born as microcomputer manufacturers, while others traveled there through a very different competitive context. If my hypothesis is correct, that prior history of competing elsewhere will increase an organization's failure rate, evidence of a disruptive change process.

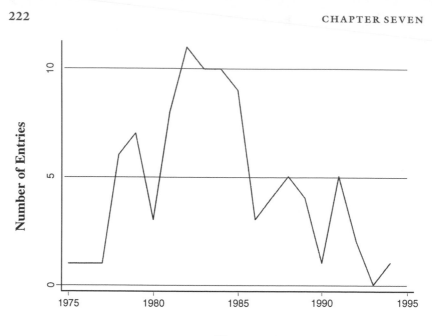

Figure 7.1. Microcomputer market entries by midrange firms.

The Red Queen and Inertia among Computer Manufacturers

As chapter 6 explains, the computer industry has been marked by a sequence of revolutions. The agent of change in one revolution rapidly becomes the defender of the status quo in the next. For instance, Data General, the company featured in Kidder's 1981 Pulitzer Prize–winning *Soul of a New Machine*, grew explosively during the 1970s by designing, manufacturing, and selling state-of-the-art minicomputers. Kidder brings alive the all-consuming culture created by rapidly building a company of smart, young technologists who were not inhibited by a preexisting conception of how a computer company ought to function. Within a few years, however, the industry would again be transformed, and now the "upstart" firms like Data General would be the status quo. Data General would introduce a microcomputer in 1983, and as a company it would reach an apex in 1988. As the microcomputer market boomed, however, Data General declined precipitously. By 1998 what was left of the company would disappear entirely. Looking back, one former Data General engineer— who left the company in the 1980s to start his own microcomputer firm— attributed the ultimate failure to Data General's earlier track record of success: Management "were reading their own press clippings. Managers stopped listening because they thought they were smart."[14]

At work in this example is more than technology. Rather, the different markets featured radically different logics of competition, as explained in chapter 6. For a company like Data General, moving into the microcomputer market was not difficult as a technical matter. The company's problem was not that it was rigid, nor that it was incapable technically. Rather, it was extremely well suited to the logic of competition surrounding the minicomputer. It was, after all, one of the revolutionary firms that discovered that market through the process of competing there. So the difficulties at Data General in microcomputer market, by this scenario, did not come from management being intransigent. Rather, they engaged the new market with the same set of routines and organizational capabilities that they fought so hard to create in the last revolution, which made the change especially disruptive.

Data General is not alone in this regard. The computer industry has repeatedly seen revolutionary new technologies and organizations appear, only to replace them with the next wave of revolutionary change. Going back in time, the revolutionaries in one year often have become the reactionary establishment of the next. In the 1950s, for example, machine-code programmers resisted the use of compilers in more advanced mainframe systems, since this innovation rendered moot the techniques and skills they had honed during the first years of the industry.[15] In another example, DEC, a legendary innovator that was once the subject of guru books on being an agent of change, stumbled in the production of microcomputers by engaging that market with the same approach that had worked so well in midrange computing.[16]

My argument here contrasts to the existing view of organizational inertia. As it stands, the literature predicts that the more established an organization, in terms of its age or size, the more it will suffer disruption should it attempt to move into a different context. In fact, my argument is not about disruption being greater when organizations are established per se. I propose that disruption is stronger the more adapted an organization is to some other context's logic of competition, and that being adapted in this way results from having competed in that context. Computer firms with considerable competitive experience in the midrange or mainframe markets can be expected to suffer especially high rates of failures should they move into microcomputers. This prediction should hold regardless of the ages or sizes of these manufacturers.

Revisiting the Microcomputer Manufacturer Failure Models

To test this hypothesis, I re-estimate the organizational failure rate models for microcomputer manufacturers. I begin with the same specification used in the microcomputer manufacturer failure rate models in chapter

6. Among the organizations in the microcomputer data, 260 had prior experience in the midrange or mainframe markets. For these organizations, I created measures of their competitive experience in those markets and included these terms in the microcomputer failure rate models. Separately, I also controlled for duration effects and for the effects of simply being in multiple markets.

Two models are reported in table 7.1. Comparing models $r_{mc}10$ and $r_{mc}11$, it is clear that prior competitive experience in the midrange or mainframe markets dramatically increased the chances that an organization would fail should it enter the microcomputer market. These effects are substantively very strong. The weaker of the effects, that for prior competitive in the midrange market, shows that (on average) firms were 67 percent more likely to fail in the microcomputer market due to their prior competitive experience in the midrange market. Recall that this same competitive experience made these organizations better off in the midrange and mainframe markets, but such experience was especially disruptive to the move into microcomputing.

The Red Queen and the Rise and Fall of Organizations

As a rule, organizations are rewarded for remaining relatively inert, and considerable research shows that constant change is disruptive to the point of being life threatening for organizations.[17] This idea surfaces in the study of technology and organizations, especially in the Schumpeterian tradition that emphasizes the difficulties of changing organizations to meet new challenges.[18] The fact of organizational inertia is even featured in the business press, where periodicals and popular books describe how the successful organizations often fail because of their inability to adapt.[19] Clearly, organizations tend toward stability and inertia, so much so that their very existence can be threatened by change. This fact needs to be reconciled with the adaptive view of organizations that is at the heart of Red Queen evolution.

One way to reconcile these facts is to distinguish between types of change, so that radical, all-at-once change is understood to be disruptive, while more gradual adaptation can occur without as much disruption. This view appears in the theory of structural inertia, where less extreme changes are predicted to generate a shorter, and so less threatening, period of disruption.[20] For instance, Barnett and Freeman demonstrate that incremental product growth by semiconductor firms has typically been survival enhancing, while sudden multiproduct expansion has been temporarily life threatening—evidence of disruption due to dramatic change.[21] Some have described these two kinds of change as typical of eras or cycles in the lives of

TABLE 7.1
Estimates of the Organizational Exit Rate from the U.S. Microcomputer Market:
Hysteretic Effects of Competition in Other Markets

Independent Variable	$(r_{mc}10)$	$(r_{mc}11)$
Number of microcomputer manufacturers at entry/1,000	−0.4228 (0.6297)	−0.2023 (0.6334)
Cumulative hazard of failure in microcomputer market since organization's birth	0.1125 (0.2909)	−0.1694 (0.3006)
Recent historical competition faced by organization in microcomputer market/1,000	−2.014** (0.5922)	−1.881** (0.6015)
Distant-past historical competition faced by organization in microcomputer market/1,000	0.5382 (0.4411)	0.7105 (0.4521)
Number of distinct historical rivals faced by organization in microcomputer market/1,000	1.868** (0.9458)	1.831* (0.9600)
Organization's time in midrange market	−0.0231 (0.0143)	−0.3543** (0.0697)
Organization's time in mainframe market	0.0516** (0.0237)	−0.5416** (0.1930)
Historical competition faced by organization in midrange market/1,000		2.161** (0.4295)
Historical competition faced by organization in mainframe market/1,000		37.71** (11.56)
Number of mainframe manufacturers/1,000	−27.39* (14.71)	−27.41* (14.72)
Number of midrange computer manufacturers/1,000	9.264** (3.789)	9.280** (3.784)
Number of microcomputer manufacturers/1,000	3.798** (1.083)	3.502** (1.085)
Sum of sizes of microcomputer organizations (annual shipments)/1,000	0.0002** (0.00005)	0.0002** (0.00005)
Prior year microcomputer manufacturer entries/1,000	−0.8783 (1.236)	−0.7317 (1.235)
Prior year microcomputer manufacturer failures/1,000	6.606** (1.275)	6.573** (1.274)
Dealio entrant	−0.1560** (0.0576)	−0.1761** (0.0579)
Organization also is in midrange computer market	−0.1426 (0.1118)	0.0621 (0.1229)
Organization also is in mainframe computer market	−1.007** (0.4970)	−2.482** (0.7838)

TABLE 7.1 (*cont.*)
Estimates of the Organizational Exit Rate from the U.S. Microcomputer Market:
Hysteretic Effects of Competition in Other Markets

Independent Variable	$(r_{mc}10)$	$(r_{mc}11)$
Real U.S. gross domestic product	−0.0016**	−0.0017**
	(0.0006)	(0.0006)
U.S. prime interest rate	0.0307	0.0341
	(0.0313)	(0.0312)
Market tenure, all organizations		
0–1 year	1.508	1.872
	(2.548)	(2.546)
1–3 years	1.959	2.367
	(2.556)	(2.554)
3–5 years	2.329	2.781
	(2.560)	(2.558)
5–10 years	2.283	2.755
	(2.570)	(2.568)
10–15 years	2.473	2.669
	(2.615)	(2.614)
15+ years	2.048	2.744
	(2.723)	(2.724)
Market tenure, medium-sized organizations		
0–1 year	−0.1869*	−0.1717*
	(0.1009)	(0.1011)
1–3 years	−0.3158**	−0.3001**
	(0.0806)	(0.0807)
3–5 years	−0.5936**	−0.5877**
	(0.1218)	(0.1218)
5–10 years	−0.7688**	−0.7591**
	(0.1399)	(0.1403)
10–15 years	−0.9450**	−0.5630
	(0.3939)	(0.3983)
15+ years	−1.065	−0.9414
	(1.226)	(1.226)

organizations, as in Tushman and Romanelli's "convergence and reorientation" model of organizational evolution.[22] However described, both disruptive and adaptive change can and do occur, with the former being sudden and extreme while the latter tends toward incrementalism.

Stories such as this abound and reinforce the idea that organizational adaptation and disruption are distinct—one occurring during periods of gradual change, and the other when organizations change significantly and rapidly. Although this portrayal is correct in many ways, it overlooks an important causal relationship between adaptation and inertia. My re-

TABLE 7.1 (*cont.*)
Estimates of the Organizational Exit Rate from the U.S. Microcomputer Market: Hysteretic Effects of Competition in Other Markets

Independent Variable	($r_{mc}10$)	($r_{mc}11$)
Market tenure, large organizations		
0–1 year	−0.6178**	−0.6163**
	(0.2187)	(0.2192)
1–3 years	−0.9708**	−0.9488**
	(0.1802)	(0.1803)
3–5 years	−1.045**	−1.016**
	(0.2303)	(0.2305)
5–10 years	−2.866**	−2.842**
	(0.4612)	(0.4645)
10–15 years	−3.860**	−4.264**
	(1.054)	(1.190)
15+ years	−2.776**	−5.156**
	(1.257)	(1.597)
Log likelihood (df)	−2388.33	−2367.75
	(36)	(38)

Note: The data include 1739 exits from a risk set of 1922 organizations over 6510 organization-years. The effects of current-time variables and market tenure are included in each model, and are shown on the following table. For coefficient estimates, standard errors are in parentheses.
* $p < .10$
** $p < .05$

sults in this chapter suggest that disruption occurs because of adaptation, rather than instead of adaptation. Through the process of Red Queen evolution, an organization discovers and adapts to the logic of competition in its environment. As a result of this adaptation, moving into a very different context and competing on the basis of a very different logic is extremely disruptive.

In this way, the theory of Red Queen competition not only offers an explanation of why organizations become well suited to a given environment, but also helps to explain why organizations fail to sustain such success as times change. With the birth of new markets and the changing of old ones, logics of competition are altered. But our organizations carry with them capabilities that are the result of their historical development. Consequently, organizations find themselves especially disrupted by changes in the environment, because these organizations have been so thoroughly adaptive in their pasts.

EIGHT

Some Implications of Red Queen Competition

RESEARCHERS AND MANAGERS alike will agree that competition is important to organizations. By understanding competition, we understand a powerful force affecting most organizations, either directly or indirectly, with life-or-death consequences. So, too, will all agree that we need to understand how organizations develop over time—and that the process of change and adaptation also is a matter of life and death for organizations. Yet the connection between competition and organizational development remains largely unexplored by researchers and ignored by managers. Researchers routinely study organizational learning without regard for the competitive context, or competition without noting the implications for learning. Managers just as routinely carve out strategies in an attempt to isolate themselves from competition, as prescribed by books on strategic management, without understanding the developmental consequences of such a move. Clearly, research and practice can gain by acknowledging the causal connection between competition and the development of organizations. To understand either, we need to understand the interplay of each on the other—the ongoing dynamic of competition and organizational learning in the Red Queen.

Armed with an awareness of Red Queen competition, we can better understand the implications of different approaches to organizational design and strategy. Consider, for example, the popular movement among organizations to engage in "strategic alliances." One of the primary reasons often given for these cooperative relationships is to help organizations learn from other organizations.[1] Of course, learning is explicitly stated as the reason for some alliances, such as research and development consortia. For instance, the Zirconium Alloy Tubing Corrosion Research and Development Program was registered under the U.S. National Cooperative Research Act to allow member organizations to conduct research on this topic while being protected from some of the more severe penalties that can result from antitrust prosecution.[2] By pooling their research efforts, organizations in such cooperative arrangements jointly share in whatever learning results from the research, and they take advantage of other coordination benefits such as standard setting. Yet by coordinating, the organizations involved in this consortium may have retarded learning by reducing competition in this arena. We do not know whether this unintended consequence did, in fact, result from this consortium. Without understanding Red Queen competition, those involved in creating this consortium would not even know to ask the question.[3]

In other cases, alliances among organizations are more targeted toward an operational goal, usually in situations where organizations are complementary in some way. For instance, Applied Materials and Komatsu formed an alliance in the 1990s to produce, in Japan, flat-panel display manufacturing equipment.[4] Applied was known as a technology powerhouse and wanted to establish its move into flat-panel display manufacturing equipment in Japan, which was central to technology developments in that area. Although Komatsu was typically associated with heavy machinery, it was an established Japanese institution and so could bring that positional advantage to the venture. So these organizations saw themselves as symbiotic, with Applied bringing technology know-how to the deal and Komatsu increasing the joint venture's status in Japanese labor markets, in relations with the Japanese government, and the like. Such examples abound and have fueled a large literature in organization theory on the ways that joint ventures and other such alliances enable organizations to learn from one another.[5]

In light of the Red Queen, however, one might question the underlying theory of learning behind the use of alliances as vehicles to further organization learning. Learning alliances presume that organizations learn through exposure to other organizations, from which information and understanding then may or may not be absorbed. If, however, organizations learn through the process of searching for solutions to problems, then the formation of an alliance with another organization may serve as the solution *instead* of learning. Komatsu, for instance, presumably had a lot to learn from Applied when it came to making the machinery that manufacturers semiconductor wafers and flat-panel displays. Yet, by establishing a joint venture with Applied for this purpose, Komatsu effectively outsourced the solving of any problems associated with such technologies, which may well have left it less capable over time when it comes to dealing with problems in this domain. As a result, by 1999, faced with a downturn in the joint venture's fortunes, Komatsu sold its rights to the alliance back to Applied, so that in the end Komatsu was left without any visible sign that it had participated in the venture. More generally, if organizations learn by confronting problems, then cooperative associations might, in fact, retard organizational learning by eliminating the imperative that drives the process of learning.

To some extent, whether alliances retard or accelerate learning depends on how they are structured and managed. In many cases, incentives and mechanisms for technology transfer are put in place to increase the likelihood that alliances promote knowledge sharing.[6] My point is not that such effective alliances do not occur. Rather, my point is that the formation of alliances among organizations create the potential for codependence among partners, wherein each partner passes off to the other precisely those problems that they can least deal with. Where this does occur, the struggles inherent in Red Queen evolution are essentially outsourced, so that such alliances leave organizations increasingly incapable in precisely the arenas where learning might have been greatest. More broadly, this example illustrates the very different outlook one might take when mindful of Red Queen competition and its effects on the development of organizations.

Managerial Implications of the Red Queen

Many regard research on the ecology of organizations as antithetical to managerial action. To some extent, this view is because the causes of organizational fates, in an ecological model, are external to the organization. Presumably, theories that shine a light on factors more immediately controllable by managers would be more useful as a guide to managerial action. Another reason for this view is somewhat more subtle. Ecological models characterize organizations without saying much regarding the actions of individual managers and so carry a connotation that action is not important. As with any structural explanation, an ecological model depicts individuals as driven by forces largely outside their immediate control. Obviously, such theory does not lend itself to heroic depictions of managers bucking the trend. One might admire Jack Welch and study the ecology of organizations, but probably not at the same moment.

But the ecology of organization becomes crucial to understanding effective versus ineffective organizations, if one allows for the theory of Red Queen competition. After all, the theory explains a set of persistent regularities that routinely perplex those who manage organizations. Competitors strengthen, even as your own organization improves, so you improve again but so do they. This is hardly the image of "competitive equilibrium" about which most of us learned in a basic economics course. In the Red Queen, by contrast, competition generates disequilibrium and ongoing change. When I speak to groups of executives from various industries, rarely if ever will a hand raise when I ask, "Who here is from an industry that is in equilibrium?" Far from being alien to this theory, most business executives find this theory to be descriptively accurate.

What's more, managers busily pursuing a strategy of isolation are especially challenged by this theory. If exposure to competition is what generates capabilities, then the strategy of differentiation in order to minimize competition is called into question. The problem with this strategy is not in terms of its immediate consequences; clearly, it is better today not to face competitors. The problem arises tomorrow, when an organization finally does confront competition, yet it has not had the benefit of dealing with competition in the past—nor the capabilities and alignment with the environment that a competitive history helps to bring about. If the Red Queen is the engine that drives the development of capabilities, then the strategic management of organizations should allow for this benefit of competition to be considered side-by-side with competition's obvious drawbacks.

One should be cautioned, however, to remain sober about the chances of managing organizational learning. Managers of organizations are confronted daily with inferential errors. Organizations are notoriously limited as information-processing systems, yet people in organizations are required to make inferences and act on them nonetheless. Waiting for performance feedback does not solve these problems, since selectivity bias then leaves us with organizations that systematically lack the full range of possible implications of action—the survivors. These various pathologies of organizational learning have long been the subject of the adaptive systems perspective as advanced by James March and his colleagues. These inferential hazards are magnified many times over under conditions of Red Queen competition. As organizations coevolve, inferential errors and misapplications of yesterday's lessons become magnified. Competition reinforces a given course of action when the Red Queen operates, since an organization is evaluated only relative to others who are, themselves, evaluated relative to the organization in question. This depiction of competition is a far cry from a force that corrects error, a role it often plays in economic models and among some who study the diffusion of information.

In light of the foibles possible under Red Queen competition, the implications for managers are both daunting and more important. If competition could be relied upon to remedy human error, then market competition could play the role of insurance in case those who manage our organizations fall victim to error. As a force reinforcing action that will turn maladaptive, however, competition becomes a dangerous safety net. Managers must understand that competition enhances the viability of organizations, but only when the logic of competition is relatively stable. Under conditions of changing competitive logics, however, relying on the Red Queen to improve one's organization is a dangerous misapplication of this theory. In such circumstances, organizations are likely to fall into competency traps, misapplying to new competitive realities lessons that were learned under different circumstances.

Ultimately the question of what managers can take away from the theory of Red Queen competition hinges on how we view the role of the manager. My view is that managerial expertise is greatest when an executive understands two things: why actions take place in organizations, and

232   CHAPTER EIGHT

why these actions lead to their consequences. Very often, organizations
take actions because of the competition they face, and people in organizations justify their actions by reference to competitors. And, similarly, the
consequences of actions often hinge on one's rivals, and on the actions of
one's rivals. Whenever actions and their consequences are triggered by
competition or affect one's competitiveness, the theory of Red Queen
evolution can help managers to make sense of these cause-effect relations.
In this way, understanding the Red Queen would be required for a manager to claim expertise in this most difficult profession.

Research Implications of the Red Queen

In an ecology of learning organizations, competition plays the role of triggering ongoing change. This outcome stands in stark contrast to the role
that competition plays in most other renderings, where it is typically seen
as a force that generates steady-state equilibrium. Across various theories,
two opposing forces often are identified as driving competitive systems to
steady state. First, it is widely thought that uniformity develops over time
across organizational populations. In neoclassical economics, and its evolutionary versions, efficient forms of organizations are expected to diffuse.[7]
Similarly, although conspicuously without the efficiency assumption, sociologists argue that organizations imitate competitors under conditions of
uncertainty.[8] Whether efficient or not, increasing uniformity is thought to
be the rule, especially in competitive contexts.

A second dynamic resulting from competition is a limit on imitation,
so that over time competition drives populations to steady state. Selection puts a ceiling on imitation[9] and stimulates organizations to differentiate,[10] so that the diffusion of strategies is balanced by selection and differentiation. Ecological models often predict such steady-state equilibrium,
albeit over a very long period.[11] Where disequilibrium occurs, this is from
exceptional oscillations, as in the theory of density delay,[12] from multipop-
ulation interactions,[13] or from attempts by organizations to strategically
differentiate.

One question worth asking is whether we ever see, in fact, organizational
populations that have achieved steady-state equilibrium. Asking managers
of organizations, one will virtually never hear that an industry is stable. If
you do, it is usually when someone claims that someone else's industry is
stable. Of course, such perceptions could be biased, influenced by selective
perceptions among those too close to the context to know when stability
has developed. Yet neither do our systematic studies of organizational populations tend to locate stable industries. New organizations enter, others
fail, some grow—all in a context of continuing change. I am not claiming

that change is happening faster than ever. I suspect, in fact, that organizational populations have been changing over much of modern history. I am claiming only that change is now, as it has always been, the rule rather than the exception. Given this, Red Queen theory, with its basic prediction that competition fuels disequilibrium, seems right on the mark.

As rendered here, Red Queen evolution generates dual, offsetting effects of historical competition. This formulation has the advantage that one can estimate such effects in any organizational population marked by competition over its history, regardless of the particular logics of competition, and corresponding capabilities, that arose in each particular historical time and social context. Two objections to this approach are common and are worthy of discussion. One objection is that modeling the Red Queen in terms of competitive hysteresis sacrifices too much in the way of contextual richness and idiographic detail. Proselytizing Mormons and innovating engineers are interesting—each in their own ways—and any model that boils down such varied organizational phenomena to a common underlying cause is requiring too much of a sacrifice.

I do not advocate that we ignore the particulars of context. In fact, the Red Queen model can only be well specified for any given context by attending to the details of history and place, and then building them into the model as best as one can—as I attempted to do here in two industries. More of a concern, I contend, is that organizational researchers have been too quick to see organizational capabilities as idiosyncratic. That very different capabilities in very different contexts might result from a common, measurable, and predictable historical process certainly is worth knowing, and such knowledge need not preclude further appreciation of the details of context. Furthermore, as I demonstrated for banks and computer manufacturers, many of the nuances of the Red Queen model will escape our notice if we fail to attend to institutional, political, technical, and other such developments in each particular time and place. In short, both ideographic and nomothetic analysis can further our knowledge of Red Queen evolution.

Organizational Learning Theory

In learning by competing, all one assumes about organizational processes is that people in organizations attempt to solve the problems for which they are accountable. A bank manager will be focused on increasing the number of loan applications, or improving cross-selling among banking services. Elsewhere in the organization, another employee may be focused on improving an information technology system's performance in some way, while another is concerned with cost control in materials acquisition, and yet another is focused on improving the yield on credit card advertising. Yet altogether, these efforts act to respond to competition, in that the problems confronted by each of these individuals are intensified by the actions of their rivals. Meanwhile, the solutions coming from the actions of each of these individuals, if effective, will in turn create more problems—albeit very indirectly—for those working within rival organizations. Over time, this back-and-forth of learning exciting competition, and then triggering more learning requires only that people in organizations attempt to do their jobs. By contrast, existing theories of organizational learning make subtly different assumptions about the underlying processes involved: learning by doing, and learning by observation.

One approach presumes that organizations learn by doing. In organizational ecology research, this approach appears in "age-dependent" models of organizational development.[14] In the organizational learning literature, this approach instead models learning as a function of cumulative output.[15] In either specification, the learning-by-doing approach assumes that organizations learn according to a process that unfolds regardless of circumstance. By contrast, the theory of Red Queen competition allows for the fact that isolated organizations can leave well enough alone, so it is not "automatic" that organizations improve over time or with cumulative activity. Instead, attempts to improve need to be triggered somehow, and a primary trigger for such attempts is the competitive contexts of organizations. Consequently, in contrast to age- and cumulative-output-dependent models, the Red Queen model distinguishes organizations according to whether they are in contexts that stimulate development.

The Red Queen also draws our attention to the fact that organizations do not initially know what it is that they will need to learn. In learning-by-doing models, the activities of organizations typically are known, and researchers then map how efficiently these activities are carried out as a function of cumulative output. This approach to learning begs the question of how the organization discovered what activities were important to begin with. Knowing this requires that the organization adapt to be aligned with the logic of competition that prevails in a given time and place. Learning about the organization's logic of competition, in turn, occurs through the process of Red Queen competition. Traditional models of learning curves have ignored this fundamental aspect of learning, since they do not consider the competitive contexts of organizations.

A second popular theoretical approach to learning presumes that organizations learn by observing other organizations. The arguments made are typically metaphorical. When organizations "see" other organizations doing things well, then it is expected that they will imitate such behavior. Of course, such behavior can and does occur. However, the assumptions behind this learning model are considerably more restrictive than what is needed for the Red Queen theory. In Red Queen evolution, individuals need not know what it is that triggers their search, and so indirect competition can act as a trigger. Imitation, however, requires explicit and direct knowledge of what is being imitated and portrays organizational action as akin to the social comparison processes that we see among socially aware humans.

Another variant of this approach is that organizations learn from the failure of others. From this perspective, organizations are inferentially complex, in that they see failures around them and make calculations about whether they might do something different—rather like a person or a smart animal.[16] My view is that surviving organizations may be more likely to make attributions that harm their ability to learn from the errors of others. Seeing that other organizations are failing, organizations might well simply make attributions that their own success is a sign of their greater abilities.[17] As for the empirical evidence in favor of this approach, the results in this study point to the pure-selection argument as a more compelling explanation. That is, organizations that have out-survived others are those with greater fitness to their environment's logic of competition. This explanation requires no resort to learning but is entirely consistent with the evidence presented by the learning-from-failure research.

Strategic Management Research

This evidence of Red Queen development among organizations highlights some unintended consequences of strategic behavior by organizations. A central theme in the field of strategic management is that organizations are better off if they can avoid competition. Much of the strategy literature aims at identifying ways that organizations can achieve "positional advantage," where they are shielded or differentiated from potential competitors. My work shows, however, that the more that such strategies succeed, the more they remove an organization from the Red Queen—depriving it of developmental benefits. In the short run, this trade-off yields higher survival chances, but over time organizations that experience competition become increasingly viable to the point where the survival-enhancing effects of the Red Queen more than offset the downside of current-time competition. By comparison, organizations kept isolated from competition suffer from increasing failure rates with age. These changes are not simply a function of organizational aging (as thought in most existing literatures), however, but hinge on whether organizations are exposed to competition and so enjoy the benefits of Red Queen development.

More generally, the theory of Red Queen evolution calls into question the standard claim that positional advantages and so-called capability-based advantages reinforce each other. Red Queen theory suggests that exposure to competition is one of the primary engines driving the development of organizational capabilities. Yet positional advantages shield organizations from competition (by definition), thereby depriving organizations of an important source of capabilities. In this way, positional advantage works against capability-based advantage, and over time we can expect to see the two sources of advantage inversely related. It is not surprising, in this light, that well-established market incumbents so often are displaced by previously unheard-of firms that lack any sort of positional advantage. These differences in adaptability are widely thought to be attributable simply to market incumbency effects. My work, however, suggests that these differences in competitiveness depend not simply on whether an organization is an incumbent, but rather on whether incumbents have attained a strategic position that isolates them from the Red Queen.

Essentially, the positional advantage school in strategic management advocates what I have called here the logic of predation. As discussed in chapter 2, under the logic of predation, competition loses its beneficial side effects—the "benefit to the third" mentioned in modern sociological theories that point to Simmel's essay on competition and conflict.[18] Gaining and maintaining institutional power is best served by destroying the other—either through infiltration and cooptation or by direct antagonistic action.[19] Simmel describes such actions as conflict, in contrast to competition, in that they have as their purpose the destruction of the rival and consequently can lead to a victory that has no beneficial implications for others. A strategy of predation can win, but it leads to market dominance without generating the organizational improvements that one would see if competition were to take place through the process of Red Queen evolution.

Appendix

Data Sources and Collection Methods

Commercial Banks

Commercial banking is an attractive study population for various reasons. As reviewed in chapter 5, the industry experienced an interesting contest among logics of competition. Furthermore, commercial banking in the United States was well documented, and the competitive context is well defined in both product and geographic space. Regulators required annual reporting of various data and carefully monitored the sizes, foundings, and failures of banks, so that comprehensive information about these organizations was available. Geographically, for most of the twentieth century, a commercial bank or bank branch competed within a limited radius of its physical location, with this constraint relaxing only after about 1985 with the proliferation of banking machines. In terms of products, over most of the twentieth century, U.S. commercial banks took deposits into personal and business accounts and lent money to consumers and organizations. Other financial service organizations, such as investment banks, brokerages, credit unions, and savings and loan associations, were related to but are not included in the commercial bank population.

Illinois was chosen for analysis because unit banks—banks without branches—remained the dominant form of commercial banking over the study period, permitting the distinct analysis of the many separate locales in that state. Nationally, after 1935, the number of bank branches increased dramatically across the United States, fueled by demographic shifts into suburban areas, and by technological changes that made it easier to coordinate multibranch systems.[20] But this overall trend concealed considerable persistence in differences across the states, with Illinois noteworthy as a bastion of unit banking. The Illinois Constitution of 1870 prohibited branch banking, and this prohibition remained absolute over most of the period that I study.[21] Because bank branching regulation has always been under state control, Illinois' firm prohibition on branch banking remained unchanged until 1982 even as other states liberalized their laws (with the exception of an allowance for a drive-up facility closely proximate to the bank, allowed in Illinois as of 1976). So-called multibank holding companies (MBHC), a legal device used since 1957 in some states to create de facto branch systems within a state, remained illegal in Illinois until 1982.[22] From 1900 through to 1982, then, bank branching was not possible in Illinois.

From 1982 through to the end of the study period, 1993, some very limited branching was gradually allowed in Illinois. During the period 1982 through 1985, Illinois banks could open two very limited facilities within ten miles of the bank or within a contiguous county. The year 1982 also saw the very limited allowance of in-state MBHCs in Illinois. In 1985 the number of branch facilities was increased to five, and these facilities were allowed to be full-service branches. As of 1991 the number of branches allowed was increased to ten, with no more than five in any one county, and with all remaining within ten miles of the main bank office. Yet through the end of the period I study, 1993, most Illinois banks remained unit banks.

Although data were collected on all Illinois commercial banks, Chicago was excluded from the analyses because it includes many banks that are not proximate. By contrast, one particularly attractive feature of the rest of the data is that banks within the same locale were sufficiently proximate that they could be assumed to be competitors of one another. The arrival of a second or third competitor was a significant event in most Illinois towns. In fact, once Chicago is excluded, the maximum number of banks in any one locale was only fourteen, and the mean number a mere two. Pooling Chicago with these other 1,182 locales would thus introduce a problem of analyzing mixed levels of aggregation.

Institutional Background

While the early twentieth century witnessed debates within states over intrastate branching, over the last half of the century the debate shifted to be about interstate branching. In the 1950s a wave of bank mergers and the rise of several multibank holding companies renewed concerns about concentration of the banking industry into a few multibranch systems. At issue was whether interstate branch systems could be allowed to form. In the 1956 Bank Holding Company Act (and the Douglas Amendment), multibank holding companies were prohibited from non-financial activities and from interstate expansion by acquisition unless explicitly permitted by state law.[23] (Few states gave such permission at that time.) Nevertheless, bank holding companies proliferated since that time, mostly in an effort to circumvent interstate branching prohibitions. Since 1957, when only 50 existed, bank holding companies grew to 3,702 by 1981.[24]

The overall trend, however, continued to be toward interstate banking. Among other allowances, the Depository Institutions Acts of 1980 and 1982 permitted bank holding companies to expand interstate by acquisition of large failing banks and all failing savings and loans (S&Ls).[25] Meanwhile, the spread of interstate ATM systems in the 1980s was triggered by a combination of technical developments and a 1983 court ruling. At the state level, the 1980s saw the passage of "reciprocal interstate banking" laws. These policies permitted bank holding companies to enter a state from a state that similarly permits entry, following the provisions of the Douglas Amendment.[26] By the late 1980s, most states permitted some degree of interstate ownership,[27] and finally the 1994 Riegle-Neal Interstate Banking and Branching Efficiency Act permitted interstate branching as of 1997—with some provisions for varying implementation depending on state regulations.

Meanwhile, nationally several policies have aimed to slow the trend toward industry concentration and interstate banking across the U.S. The Bank Merger Acts of 1960 and 1966 regulated, but did not stop, the consolidation of the industry begun in the 1950s.[28] In 1961 the Comptroller eased new-bank entry requirements, and many states followed suit in the 1970s. These changes led to a proliferation of new banks in many parts of the country and thus helped ease the trend toward industry concentration.[29] The Competitive Equality Banking Act of 1987 prohibited the chartering of new "nonbank banks"—the legal vehicle used by

holding companies for multistate and multiproduct operations.[30] These developments led to two opposing trends. Concentration has increased due to a dramatic
increase in mergers and acquisitions by branch systems and multibank holding
companies (with the timing of these changes depending on the laws of particular
states).[31] Yet the overall number of banks remained more or less stable due to a
concurrent surge in new bank foundings.[32]

Unlike most of the rest of the United States, Illinois continued to restrict interstate banking until 2004. Interstate banking of any form was prohibited in Illinois
until 1986. As of 1986, interstate multibank holding companies were allowed to
enter Illinois with the restriction that they obtain an already-existing charter—a
severe limitation when combined with Illinois' restrictions on bank acquisitions
by out-of-state banks. As of July 1986, Illinois allowed restricted interstate banking
on a reciprocal basis within the region including Iowa, Wisconsin, Indiana, Ken-
tucky, and Missouri. This meant that banks headquartered in these states could
establish banks and branches in Illinois, and vice versa, but the new bank needed
to use established charters of a certain age. Again this proved to be an effective
restriction. As of 1990, Illinois enacted legislation opening up the state to reciprocal interstate banking with fewer restrictions.[33] After the end of the study period,
Illinois continued to liberalize its interstate banking regulations, but not until
August 2004 was full interstate banking (including de novo bank openings) permitted in Illinois.

The 1980s also saw changes in the regulation of prices and products in commercial banking, nationwide across the United States as well as in Illinois. The changes
began in 1980 with the passage of the U.S. Monetary Control Act (DIDMCA),
triggering the six-year phase-out of "Regulation Q" and its regulation of the maximum interest rate that banks could pay on time and savings deposits. The act also
allowed, as of 1981, for banks to offer interest-bearing checking plans, as well as
automatic transfer services for overdraft coverage.[34] The act made other changes
as well, such as an increase in deposit insurance to $100,000 and the establishment
of a uniform reserve requirement. In 1982 the Garn-St. Germain Act continued
the deregulatory trend, eliminating borrowing limits, raising loan limits, and
phasing out interest rate ceilings and transaction limits from various interest-bearing accounts. DIDMCA and Garn-St. Germain also deregulated S&Ls, allowing
them to compete with commercial banks in commercial and consumer loans, credit
and debit cards, trust services, and interest-bearing accounts. By 1984 most of the
product and interest rate differences between the products from S&Ls and those
of banks were removed.[35] After the study period, deregulation continued, culminating in 1999 with the repeal of the Glass-Steagall restrictions against bank activities in brokerage and insurance.

Sample

Although banks existed in Illinois very early on, I begin the study period in 1900
because the quality of data available prior to that date was poor. In fact, I collected
data in raw form back as far as 1860, but examining these bankers' directories
showed them to include many organizations that were individual brokers rather
than banking organizations. Fortunately, the founding years of banks existing

prior to 1900 were recorded in the data source, so it was possible to accurately track the ages of these organizations from 1900 on. Starting in that year through to 1993, the data were coded including the sizes, times of founding and ending, and locations of every bank as recorded in the Rand McNally (and later Thompson) bankers' directories.

Asset size was coded for each bank in its first and last years of existence and in between at roughly five-year intervals. Assets were adjusted for inflation using the U.S. Bureau of Labor Statistics Consumer Price Index (CPI). In order to annualize the data, size as an independent variable was linearly interpolated to fill missing years between measurement panels.

Whenever a bank disappeared from the data, the bankers' directory recorded in text an explanation of the disappearance. These text entries occurred for several years after an event, so the occasional missing volume from the directories did not lead to a window during which a bank could appear and then disappear without being noted. Consequently, one can be confident that the data include every bank that existed in Illinois during the study period. Working with a team of coders, these textual reports were coded into types of events, with new types developed whenever an ending event appeared that did not fit into an existing event type. Over the period 1900–1993, the data came to include a variety of different types of events. When appropriate, these types were then grouped into three kinds of vital events: foundings, mergers, and failures. Other events, such as location changes or name changes, were not considered to be life-ending or life-starting events. Failure events included instances where regulators liquidated a failing bank but did so by distributing some or all of its assets and liabilities through another bank or banks. Merger or acquisition events that were not associated with failure were not coded as failures. Figures 5.1 through 5.4 show the frequencies of these events, and the number of banks in Illinois per year, over the study period.

The data were supplemented with variables representing exogenous forces likely to affect the carrying capacity for commercial banks. Both the size and the growth over time of the human population in each locale were coded decennially from the bankers' directories. Between censuses, values on these variables were linearly interpolated for each locale. The U.S. Census was used to obtain several measures of wealth and economic development at the county level.[36] These included the proportion of the population in urban areas, the number of manufacturing establishments, the number of farms, the number of retail establishments, the number of wholesale establishments, the average value of farms and farm buildings, and the average wage per manufacturing worker.

Data Structure for the Bank Founding and Failure Analyses

For the bank founding analysis, a history was created for each of the 1,182 localities in Illinois where a bank existed at any time from 1900 to 1993, excluding Chicago. Conceivably, some locales without banks were not at risk of experiencing a bank founding. Consequently, a locale was not entered into the risk set for experiencing a founding until after it had experienced a founding. In this way, for each locale, its history in the data began at the first founding of a bank in that locale, or as of 1900 for locales that already had a bank as of that year. (Thus, the first

founding in any locale was not modeled.) The history of each place was then seg-
mented into one-year observations in the data, so that independent variables could
be updated annually. The founding duration clock was started for each locale as of
the first founding of a bank and then reset to zero after any founding. For those
locales that had at least one bank as of 1900, the duration clock was started in
1900 to the number of years since the last founding event. In a small number of
instances, the number of banks in a locale fell to zero after having been greater
than zero. For these cases, the locale would be taken out of the risk set once the
number of banks fell to zero and then would reenter the risk set if and when
another founding occurred—but only after that new "first founding" event. So
constructed, the founding data for Illinois banks included 1,360 foundings (not
including first foundings) in 1,182 locales over 72,515 market-years. These data
are described in table 5.1.

For the analysis of organizational failure, the bank data were arranged with the
organization-year as the unit of analysis. Each bank's first record was the year of
its birth, or the year 1900 for banks in existence as of that year. The last record for
each bank was the year in which it ceased to exist, or 1993 for banks that remained
alive at least through that year. For every year in which a bank lived between its
year of birth and its year of death, an observation was created in order to update
independent variables annually. This approach led to a dataset describing the life
histories of 2,970 banks over 108,209 organization-years, with 1,444 of these
banks failing at some point from 1900 to 1993. Table 5.3 describes this dataset.

Computer Manufacturers

The computer industry data set includes a number of variables taken from the
coded data sources or from other sources.

Market tenure. Most discussions and estimates of organizational age in fact use
some measure of market tenure. For these data, this clock begins at the time that
an organization first entered into a given computer industry market and continues
to run until the organization exits the market or the study period ends. Because
the exact timing of market exits was typically not known, the midpoint for each
organization's last year was used instead. This approach minimizes bias that can
otherwise result from time aggregation.[37]

Organization size was not available in any single measure for each organization
for every year. Size was available, however, from the various sources of data measured in different ways for many years. The publication *Computers and Automation*
recorded an organization's number of employees for some years; *IDC* tracked the
number of products shipped in a given year for some organizations in some years;
and *Data Sources* listed the number of types of products sold in a given year for
some organizations. It was not possible simply to concatenate these different measures across years because their units of measurement could not be translated into
a single interval measure. Also complicating matters was the time-varying nature
of organizational size in this industry, where what constituted a large or small
company in 1955 was very different from the same distinction measured decades
later. Given these data limitations, I constructed a categorical measure for size—

small, medium, or large—for each organization for each year, measured in relative terms compared to other organizations that existed in the industry in a given year.

Organizations were designated as small, medium, or large first based on their numbers of employees. For years when this variable was not available, the size designation was made based on the measure of annual shipments if that measure was available. In cases were neither of these measures was available, information on the number of product types was used to estimate annual shipments. These estimates were obtained by regressing shipments on the number of product types within each market using data from observations that included information for both of these variables. The market-specific coefficients from these regressions were then used to create an estimated shipments value for organizations that lacked data on shipments but did have information on number of product types. These shipments estimates were then used to make a small, medium, or large categorical size assignment.

After constructing this annual categorical size variable, remaining gaps in the measure over the life of an organization were filled by linear interpolation of the underlying interval size measures. The interpolated values were then used to estimate the categorical size measure for years where that measure was missing, using the same sequence described above. For cases where size data were missing at the beginning or end of an organization's life history, linear extrapolation was used to complete the data series for up to four missing years forward or backward. After all these steps were followed, there remained 115 organizations for which no size data were available for any year, or for which we lacked any size measure for more than four years at the beginning or end of the organization's life history. Coders searched for descriptions of these organizations in archival documents to determine whether any of them were large or medium-sized organizations in a given year. Organizations that received scant attention were designated as "small."

Organizations were designated as *de novo* if they were born as computer manufacturers, and as *de alio* if they were born in another industry and then moved or diversified into the computer industry. This distinction was coded by Swanson using the following procedure.[38] Each organization's founding date was compared to its date of first operation in the computer industry. If an organization was founded prior to first appearing in the computer industry, it was individually researched to determine whether it was, in fact, a *de novo* computer manufacturer that was delayed between its year of founding and the release of its first product. When this search was indeterminant, the variable was coded based on whether there was a long time lag before the organization released a computer, by examining the organization's name over time, from searching the Internet, other online sources, and archival documents (Lexis/Nexis, *Who's Who in Electronics*, *U.S. Electronics Industry Directory*, and *Electronic Buyer's Guide*). This procedure led to the coding of 1,906 organizations as *de novo* and 696 as *de alio*.

Market exit refers to the event where an organization ceased to manufacture computers for sale or lease. Most market exits (93%) were exits from the entire computer industry because most computer manufacturers operated in only one market. Acquisitions were coded as exits only when a smaller organization was acquired by a considerably larger organization. Name changes, and mergers among organizations of roughly equal size, were not treated as exits for purposes of the statistical analyses. Determination of these events was made by researching every market exit in various archival documents and Lexis/Nexis. Using this procedure, only eleven disappearances were coded as mergers among equals. When these events occurred, the life of each merging organization was ended and coded as a right-censored event. The "new" organization created by the merger was given a new tenure clock. An organization was coded as experiencing *market entry* in the first year that it was reported in the various data sources as having offered for sale or lease a general-purpose, electronic, digital computer.

Organizational density in the current year was coded as the number of organizations in a given market at the start of a given year. The timing of entry and exit was known in most cases only to the year, so density at the start of any year was computed by adding entries and subtracting exits in the prior year from the prior year's starting density.

Historical competition was coded as the sum of the number of competitors faced in each year by an organization over its history, without including the current-year competition. This variable is denoted by T_j in the model. Also coded is the K_j, the number of distinct rivals faced by an organization historically up to a given year. The variable *recent historical competition* was coded by weighting each year's contribution to the organization's historical competition term by $1/\sqrt{\delta}$, where δ measures a year's distance back in time prior to the current year. *Distant-past historical* competition is the difference between an organization's overall historical competition (at each point in time) and its recent historical competition. *Rivals' historical competition* in a given market was computed by summing the historical competition term (T) across the organization's rivals.

The exogenous environmental conditions used as control variables include the *real gross domestic product in the U.S.* (in 1987 U.S. dollars).[39] Also included is the *prime interest rate* as of the last day of the prior year.[40]

Notes

Chapter 1: Why Are Some Organizations More Competitive than Others?

1. Van Valen, 1973.
2. Simon, 1945; March and Simon, 1958; Cyert and March, 1963; March 1988.
3. Vandenberghe, Nicolas, and William P. Barnett. 1995. *FITS Imaging, Inc.* Stanford Graduate School of Business case study.
4. Hannan and Freeman, 1989.
5. Ibid.
6. Barnett and McKendrick, 2004.
7. Wang, Irene, William P. Barnett, and David McKendrick. 2004. *Seagate 2004.* Stanford Graduate School of Business case study.
8. Friedland and Alford, 1991.
9. Ruef, 2000; Hannan, Pólós, and Carroll, 2007.
10. Carroll and Swaminathan, 2000.
11. Sigg, Keith, and William P. Barnett. 2000. *Webvan.*
12. Burgelman, 2002.
13. Porter, 1980.
14. Dutton, Lauren, and William P. Barnett. 1998. *Establishing Network Appliance.* Stanford Graduate School of Business case study.

Chapter 2: Logics of Competition

1. Scott, 1975.
2. Stinchcombe, 1965.
3. Friedland and Alford, 1991.
4. Dobrev and Carroll, 2003.
5. Barnett and Woywode, 2004.
6. Barnett et al., 2000.
7. Levitt and March, 1988.
8. Sigg and Barnett, *Webvan.*
9. Hannan and Freeman, 1989.
10. Barnett and Carroll, 1987.
11. Carroll and Swaminathan, 2000.
12. Harrington, Wendy, William P. Barnett, and Glenn R. Carroll. 1995. *Mendocino Brewing Company.* Stanford Graduate School of Business case study.
13. Leschly, Mark, and William P. Barnett. 1995. *Novo Nordisk.* Stanford Graduate School of Business case study.
14. Meyer and Rowan, 1977.
15. Tushman and Anderson, 1986; Christensen, 1997.

16. McVie, Cara, and William P. Barnett. 2003. *Qualcomm*. Stanford Graduate School of Business case study.

17. Schumpeter, 1950.

18. E.g. Nelson and Winter, 1982; Tushman and Anderson, 1986.

19. Chandler, 1962; Williamson, 1985.

20. Brittain and Freeman, 1980.

21. Selznick, 1957.

22. Meyer and Rowan, 1977.

23. Hannan and Freeman, 1989; Hannan and Carroll, 1992.

24. Carroll and Hannan, 2000.

25. Ruef, 2000.

26. Hannan et. al., 2007.

27. Ibid.

28. DiMaggio and Powell, 1983.

29. Carroll, 1984.

30. Ruef, 2000; Hannan et al., 2007.

31. Carroll, 1985; Dobrev et. al., 2001.

32. Reddy, Paul, and William P. Barnett. 1995. *Newell Company*. Stanford Graduate School of Business case study.

33. Pfeffer and Salancik, 1978.

34. Williamson, 1985.

35. Cumes, Terry, Roderick Morris, William P. Barnett, and William Durham. 2002. *Abercrombie and Kent: Pioneering Global Ecotourism*. Stanford Graduate School of Business case study.

36. Tirole, 1997.

37. Flanagan, Christopher S., and William P. Barnett. 2001. *Nextstage Entertainment*. Stanford Graduate School of Business case study.

38. Bresnahan and Reiss, 1991.

39. Hannan and Freeman, 1989; Hannan and Carroll, 1992.

40. Hannan and Carroll, 1992.

41. Podolny, 2004.

42. Benjamin and Podolny, 1999.

43. Merton, 1968; Podolny, 1993.

44. Burt, 1992; Pfeffer and Salancik, 1977.

45. Padgett and Ansell, 1993.

46. Barron, 1999.

47. Baker and Faulkner, 1993.

48. Ingram and Roberts, 2000.

49. Hansen et. al., 2000.

50. Zuckerman, 1999.

51. Wei, Jane, and William P. Barnett. 1997. *Varian, 1997*. Stanford Graduate School of Business case study.

52. Commons, 1924; North, 1981.

53. Barnett and Woywode, 2004.

54. McAdam et. al., 2001; Meyer and Staggenborg, 1996; Minkoff, 1997.

55. Honey, 2002.

56. Casillas, Gilbert, William P. Barnett, and William Durham. 2003. *Note on Ecotourism Certification Initiatives.* Stanford. Graduate School of Business case study.

57. Sigg and Barnett, *Webvan.*

58. O'Reilly and Tushman, 2002.

59. March, 1991.

60. O'Reilly and Tushman, 2007.

61. Meyer and Rowan, 1977.

62. Mukherjee, Pratap, William P. Barnett, and Jeffrey Chambers. 1999. *WR Hambrecht+Co.* Graduate School of Business case study.

63. McVie and Barnett, *Qualcomm.*

64. Levtov, Ilya, and William P. Barnett. 2004. *Napster 2.0.* Stanford Graduate School of Business case study.

65. Barnett and Carroll, 1993.

66. Streeck and Schmitter, 1985; Friedland and Alford, 1991.

67. Thornton and Ocasio, 1999; Friedson, 2001.

68. Scott et al., 2000.

69. Powell, 1991.

70. Zald, 1996.

71. Swidler, 1986; see also Hunt et al., 1994.

72. Friedland and Alford, 1991.

73. McAdam, 1996.

74. Chambers, Jeffrey. 2001. *McAfee.* Stanford Graduate School of Business case study.

75. Barnett and Woywode, 2004.

76. Tirole, 1997.

77. Ordover and Willig, 1991.

78. Farrell and Shapiro, 1990.

79. Simmel, 1908.

80. Burt, 1992.

81. Barnett and Carroll, 1993.

82. Searching the *Times*'s historical database, the earliest use of "natural monopoly" appears in a discussion of iron ore mining; see Frederick B. Hawley, "Letter to the Editor. The Tax on Pig Iron," March 7, 1883, p. 3. *New York Times (1857–current file).* But the bulk of the 189 uses of the term after 1883 come in the twentieth century, occurring typically in articles documenting debates of the possible legitimacy of monopoly in some instances.

83. "Small Company Wins Phone Line," *New York Times (1857–current file),* August 16, 1969, p. 47.

84. See, for example, "Court Asked to Ban Rival Clipper Line," *New York Times (1857–current file),* September 1, 1940, p. 13

85. E.g., Capron and Mitchell, 1999; Zollo and Singh, 2004.

86. Haleblian and Finkelstein, 1999.

87. March, Sproull, and Tamuz, 1991.

88. Porac, 1997.

89. McKendrick et al., 2003.

90. Levinthal and March, 1981; Dosi and Lovallo, 1997; Greve, 2003.

91. White, 1981.

92. See also Barney, 1986; Dosi and Lovallo, 1997.

93. Farashuddin, Asaf, and William P. Barnett. 1994. *DR Systems*. Stanford Graduate School of Business case study.

94. The relative frequency of competitions in a market resembles the theoretical construct of "niche grain" in Hannan and Freeman's (1977) original theory of organizational ecology, as well as the complexity theory idea of smooth fitness "landscapes" (Levinthal, 1997). In my usage, however, relative frequency refers specifically to the occurrence of competitive events.

95. Sitkin, 1992; Chuang and Baum, 2003.

96. Denrell, 2003.

97. Staw, 1975.

98. Miner and Haunschild, 1995.

99. Ingram and Baum, 1997.

100. Blau, 1955; Sinchcombe, 1965; Aldrich, 1999.

101. Freeman and Hannan, 1983; Amburgey et. al., 1993.

102. Lindblom, 1959; March, 1981; Burgelman, 2002.

103. Bendor, 1995.

104. Bannasch, Eric, Derek Butts, Andriy Shapowal, Jonathan Strike, Michael Wertheim, Charles A. O'Reilly, and William P. Barnett. 2006. *Trader Joe's*. Stanford Graduate School of Business case study.

105. Barron et. al., 1994.

106. Carroll and Hannan, 2000.

Chapter 3: The Red Queen

1. Hannan and Freeman, 1989.

2. Barnett and Carroll, 1987.

3. March and Simon, 1958; Cyert and March, 1963; March, 1988, 1994.

4. Simon, 1945.

5. Cyert and March, 1963.

6. March, 1988, 1994.

7. Levinthal and March, 1981.

8. March and Simon, 1958.

9. Levinthal and March, 1981.

10. March, 1988.

11. Levinthal and March, 1981.

12. Yong Suk Jang, Hokyu Hwang, Mooweon Rhee, and William P. Barnett. 2001. *Handysoft*. Stanford Graduate School of Business case study.

13. Cyert and March, 1963.

14. Thompson, 1967; Pfeffer and Salancik, 1978.

15. Tirole, 1988.

16. Burt, 1992.

17. Earle, Jamie, William P. Barnett, and Charles Holloway. 2003. *Network Appliance, 2003*. Stanford Graduate School of Business case study.

18. Van Valen, 1973.

19. Emery and Trist, 1965; Terreberry, 1968.
20. Selznick, 1960.
21. Barnett, 1997.
22. Wang and Barnett, *Seagate 2004.*
23. Mezias, Chen, and Murphy, 2002; Greve, 1998, 2003.
24. Cyert and March, 1963; March, 1988.
25. Lant, 1992; Greve, 1998.
26. Cyert and March, 1963; Lant, 1992; Mezias, Chen, and Murphy, 1997; Greve, 2003.
27. Alchian, 1950; Cyert and March, 1963; Nelson and Winter, 1982; Hannan and Freeman, 1984.
28. Cyert and March, 1963; Levinthal and March, 1981; Herriott, Levinthal, and March, 1985; Lant, 1992; Frank and Cook, 1995; Greve, 1998; Mezias et al., 2002; Frank, 2000.
29. Haveman, 1993.
30. Denrell, 2003.
31. Stinchcombe, 1965.
32. Barnett, 1997; Sorenson, 2000a. For a thorough, formal treatment of this idea, see Péli, 2007.
33. Lippmann and Rumelt, 1982.
34. Tushman and Anderson, 1986; Carroll and Teo, 1996; Christensen, 1997.
35. Vaupel et al., 1979.
36. March, 1981.
37. Levinthal, 1991.
38. Denrell, 2003.
39. Ibid.
40. Garud et al., 1997.
41. Dosi and Lovallo, 1997.
42. Hansen, Morten, Peter Zemsky, and William P. Barnett, 1994. *Launching a New Business at Hewlett Packard.* Stanford Graduate School of Business case study.
43. Benkard, 2000.
44. Stinchcombe, 1965.
45. Hannan and Freeman, 1984.
46. March, 1994: 91.
47. Berger and Luckmann, 1966.
48. Holland et al., 1989: 194.
49. Lorentzen, Peter, and William P. Barnett. 2002. *Stone Group.* Stanford Graduate School of Business case study.
50. Levinthal and March, 1981; Levitt and March, 1988.
51. Haveman, 1993; Mezias and Lant, 1994; Greve, 1996.
52. Friedman, 1953; see also Nelson, 1995; Miner and Haunschild, 1995.
53. Alchian, 1950.
54. Cole, 1996.
55. Barnett and Carroll, 1995.
56. See, for example, Wei and Barnett, *Varian, 1997*; and Wang and Barnett, *Seagate 2004.*

57. Barnett, 1990.
58. See Sorenson, 2003.
59. Kauffman, 1993.
60. Ansell and Padgett, 1993.
61. Kauffman, 1993.
62. Slatkin and Maynard Smith, 1979.
63. Swaminathan and Carroll, 1992; Barnett, 1993.
64. March, Sproull, and Tamuz, 1991.
65. Levinthal and March, 1993.
66. Denrell and March, 2001.
67. March, 1991; Greve, 2003.
68. Levinthal and March, 1993.
69. Powell, Greg, William P. Barnett, and Glenn R. Carroll. 2002. *Wind River Systems.* Stanford Graduate School of Business case study.
70. Miner and Haunschild, 1995; Aldrich, 1999.
71. Carroll and Swaminathan, 1992.
72. Stinchcombe, 1965.
73. Schumpeter, 1950; Tushman and Anderson, 1986; Carroll and Teo, 1996.
74. Barnett and Hansen, 1996; Barnett and Sorenson, 2002.
75. Tirole, 1997.
76. Porter, 1980.
77. Capron and Mitchell, 1999; Haleblian and Finkelstein, 1999; Zollo and Singh, 2004.
78. "Dead Firms Walking," *Economist*, September 23, 2004.
79. For example, see David Bank, "Oracle Hews to Acquisition Goals as It Fights for Peoplesoft Deal." *Wall Street Journal*, March 1, 2004.
80. Amburgey and Miner, 1992.

Chapter 4: Empirically Modeling the Red Queen

1. Barnett, 1997.
2. Hannan and Freeman, 1989.
3. Barnett and Carroll, 1987.
4. Hannan and Freeman, 1987, 1988; Hannan and Carroll, 1992.
5. E.g., McPherson, 1983; Burt, 1992; Baum and Singh, 1994; Podolny, Stuart, and Hannan, 1996.
6. E.g., Carroll, 1985; Baum and Mezias, 1992; Ruef, 2000.
7. Barnett and Amburgey, 1990.
8. Hannan and Ranger-Moore, 1986; Baum and Mezias, 1993.
9. Carroll and Swaminathan, 2000.
10. Levinthal and March, 1981; Levitt and March, 1988.
11. Vaupel et al., 1979.
12. See Swaminathan, 1996; Barnett, 1997.
13. See Tuma and Hannan, 1984.
14. See Barnett and Hansen, 1996; Barnett and Sorenson, 2002.
15. Hannan and Freeman, 1989; Carroll and Hannan, 2000.

16. Carroll and Hannan, 2000.
17. Hannan and Freeman, 1989; Carroll and Hannan, 2000.
18. Carroll and Hannan, 1989.
19. See Barnett, Swanson, and Sorenson (2003) for an alternative to density delay theory. Their theory of "asymmetric selection" notes that organizations in large birth cohorts may be less fit, in which case apparent evidence of density delay may in fact be spurious.
20. Swaminathan, 1996.
21. For example, Mezias and Lant, 1994; Miner and Haunschild, 1995; Ingram and Baum, 1997; Greve, 2003.

Chapter 5: Red Queen Competition among Commercial Banks

1. *New York Times*, December 20, 1900.
2. Rockoff, 2000.
3. Veblen, 1923.
4. Kolko, 1963.
5. Chapman and Westerfield, 1942.
6. Winerman, 2003.
7. Kolko, 1963.
8. Commons, 1924.
9. Fischer, 1968.
10. Southworth, 1928.
11. Bodenhorn, 2000.
12. Fischer, 1968.
13. Rothbard, 2002.
14. Wiebe, 1962.
15. Primm, 1989.
16. Kolko, 1963.
17. Hubbard and Davids, 1969; Kolko, 1963.
18. Warburg, 1930; Wiebe, 1962.
19. Kolko, 1963; Wiebe, 1962.
20. Primm, 1989.
21. U.S. Federal Reserve, 1959.
22. Fischer, 1968.
23. Klebaner, 1974.
24. Roussakis, 1984.
25. Ogilvie et. al., 1980.
26. Federal Reserve Bank of Atlanta, 1985.
27. See Kaufman, 1989.
28. Fischer, 1968.
29. Chernow, 1990.
30. Winningham and Hagan, 1980.
31. Mayer, 1974.
32. Pomeroy, 1914.
33. Rockoff, 2000.

34. Bodenhorn, 2000.
35. Primm, 1989.
36. See Kolko, 1963; Wiebe, 1962; Winerman, 2003.
37. Fraser and Kolari, 1985.
38. Fischer, 1968.
39. Klebaner, 1974.
40. Winningham and Hagan, 1980.
41. See Mayer, 1974.
42. See Knott and Posen, 2005.
43. Ranger-Moore et. al., 1991.
44. Barnett and Hansen, 1996.
45. Barnett and Sorenson, 2002.
46. Klebaner, 1974.
47. See Mayer, 1974.
48. Mizruchi and Stearns, 2001.
49. Mayer, 1974.
50. Burt, 1992.
51. Freeman and Audia, 2005.
52. Coal City Library, 1986.
53. Roussakis, 1984.
54. Mayer, 1974.
55. Mintz and Schwartz, 1985.
56. Calvani and Miller, 1993.
57. White, 1982.
58. Kolko, 1963.
59. See the "Statement of George W. Rogers, of the Bank of Commerce, Little Rock, Ark," in *Banking and Currency Hearings Before the Committee on Banking and Currency, United States Senate, Vol. 3, 1913*, p. 2248.
60. Ibid.
61. See Carroll and Hannan, 1992.
62. Carroll and Hannan, 1989.
63. Barnett and Amburgey, 1990.
64. Throughout the book, models are designated by the rate being analyzed (λ for founding models and r for failure models), the population being analyzed (B for banks, for example), and a model number. For instance, $\lambda_B 1$ denotes model 1 among the founding rate models for banks.
65. See Barnett, 1997.
66. See Barnett and Sorenson, 2002.
67. See Carroll and Hannan, 2002.
68. Each of models $\lambda_B 4$ through $\lambda_B 7$ are nested in model $\lambda_B 1$, and each strongly improves on the baseline model according to a comparison of their log-likelihoods ($p < 0.01$). Similarly, model $\lambda_B 6$ improves on the models that include only one or neither of the gini coefficients ($p < 0.01$).
69. Delacroix and Carroll, 1983.
70. Barnett and Amburgey, 1990.
71. Barnett and Sorenson, 2002.

72. The density of local rivals, as well as the number of "nonlocal" rivals (those in other locations) actually reduced a bank's survival chances according to the model estimates. These effects, however, were considerably lower in magnitude than the survival-enhancing consequences market share.

73. Based on the estimated coefficient of market share of -0.3406, a local monopolist's failure rate was 0.71 of what it would have been without this advantage, since $\exp[-0.3406] = 0.71$. This amounts to a multiplicative decrease in the failure rate of 0.29 due to having 100 percent local market share.

74. See Barnett and Hansen, 1996.

75. The coefficient estimate of 0.5288 implies a multiplier of the failure rate equal to $\exp[0.5288 \times 0.05] = 1.027$, or a 2.7 percent increase, at the observed mean. At the observed maximum of this variable, the multiplier is predicted to be $\exp[0.5288 \times 2] = 2.88$—nearly a three-fold increase in the failure rate for especially predatory organizations.

76. Barron et al., 1994.

77. See *Banking and Currency Hearings Before the Committee on Banking and Currency, United States Senate, 1913*

78. This theory is explained in Barnett et. al., 2003.

Chapter 6: Red Queen Competition among Computer Manufacturers

1. Lee Gomes. "Passage of Y2K May Unlock Tech Spending—Smooth Changeover to Free Resources for Backlog of Projects Put on Hold," *New York Times,* January 3, 2000, p. A3.

2. Hayes and Ulrich, 1998: 39.

3. See Bardini, 2000.

4. Ibid.

5. Freiberger and Swaine, 1984.

6. Roberts, 1967: 3.

7. Bell and Newell, 1971: 505.

8. Phister, 1979.

9. Ibid., 520.

10. Pugh et al., 1991.

11. Luckoff, 1979: 83.

12. Ibid., 185.

13. Larrowe, 1964.

14. See Stern, 1981.

15. Hall, 1996.

16. Fischer et al., 1983.

17. Pugh, 1984; Ceruzzi, 1998.

18. See Bell and Newell, 1971; Stern, 1981.

19. See Ceruzzi, 1998.

20. Grosch, 1953.

21. See, for example, Davis, 1973.

22. See, for example, Rosen, 1969.

23. Phister, 1979.

24. Mendelson, 1987.
25. Knuth and Pardo, 1980.
26. Cerruzi, 1998.
27. Backus, 1980.
28. Halstead, 1962.
29. Osborn, 1954.
30. Ceruzzi, 1998.
31. Bell and Newell, 1971: 37.
32. Pugh, 1984; Fisher et al., 1983.
33. Deitel, 1990.
34. Ibid.; Ceruzzi, 1998.
35. Armer, 1980.
36. Rifkin and Harrar, 1988.
37. Deitel, 1990; Stewart, 2005.
38. *Punched Card Data Processing*, 1959.
39. Fisher et al., 1983.
40. Langlois, 1997.
41. Fisher et al., 1983.
42. Blumberg, 1964: 8.
43. Fisher et al., 1983.
44. Reddy and Barnett, *Newell Company (A)*.
45. Phister, 1979.
46. Shigeru, 2005.
47. Pugh et al., 1991; see also Brooks, 1984, on the exaggerated stock market reaction to these companies.
48. Quoted in Fisher et al., 1983: 249.
49. Gilder, 2000.
50. Sorenson, 2000b.
51. ERP refers to "enterprise resource planning," a type of software system used by large organizations to rationalize, plan, track, and otherwise control the deployment of people and use of materials throughout the organization. Although software running on mainframes has carried out such functions in limited ways since the 1960s, the term "ERP" was not commonly used until relatively recently. A Lexus search shows use of the term by industry experts no earlier than 1991. More commonplace use of the term came later; searches of the *New York Times* and *Wall Street Journal* historical archives show first appearances in those journals no earlier than 1996.
52. Personal communication with Dave Hitz, founder of Network Appliance, December 15, 2005.
53. *Proceedings of the ACM/IEEE Conference on Supercomputers*, 1988.
54. Fisher et al., 1983.
55. Galbraith 1971; Williamson, 1985; Chandler, 2001.
56. Early on, IBM and then some of the other large mainframe manufacturers vertically integrated often because markets for high-quality components, software, or peripherals did not yet exist. See Pugh, 1984, and more generally, see Stigler, 1951.
57. Fisher et al., 1983.

58. Scientific Data Systems annual report, quoted in Fisher et al., 1983: 175.
59. Brock, 1981.
60. Rosen, 1969, Lukoff, 1979.
61. Bresnahan and Greenstein, 1999.
62. Pugh, 1984.
63. Brooks, 1984; Pugh et al., 1991.
64. Pugh et. al., 1991.
65. Greenstein and Wade, 1998.
66. Levy, 1984.
67. Ornstein, 2002.
68. Bell and Newell, 1971.
69. Ibid.
70. Weitzman, 1974.
71. Mendelson, 1987.
72. Everett, 1980.
73. Ceruzzi, 1998.
74. Levy, 1984: 11.
75. Tushman and Anderson, 1986.
76. Bell and Newell, 1971.
77. Rifkin and Harrar, 1988.
78. Bell and Newell, 1971.
79. Blanton et al., 1967.
80. Brynjolfsson and Hitt, 1996.
81. Blanton et al., 1967.
82. Rifkin and Harrar, 1988.
83. Brown and Eisenhardt, 1997.
84. Eisenhardt and Tabrizi, 1995.
85. Sorenson, 2000b.
86. The earliest discovery of such a renewal processes was in Delacroix and Carroll, 1983.
87. McGlynn, 1982.
88. Freiberger and Swaine, 1984.
89. Ibid., 106.
90. Levy, 1984.
91. Freiberger and Swaine, 1984: 104.
92. Poole et al. (eds), 1999.
93. Bothner, 2003.
94. Bardini, 2000.
95. Langlois, 1992.
96. Freiberger and Swaine, 1984.
97. Isshiki, 1982; McGlynn, 1982.
98. Porac, 1997.
99. Dietel, 1990.
100. See, for example, Savage et. al., 1986.
101. Henderson, 1999.

102. E.g., Stross, 1993. This fall from grace would be temporary. Jobs would regain his vision later, with the highly public successes of Pixar, the iMac, and the ipod.

103. Anderson, 1995; Henderson and Stern, 2004.

104. Carroll, 1985.

Chapter 7: The Red Queen and Organizational Inertia

1. Kang, Soong Moon, William Shen, William Barnett, and Glenn R. Carroll. 1998. *American Craft Brewing International.* Stanford Graduate School of Business case study.

2. Morimoto, Sakuya, Erik Weitzman, and William Barnett. 1998. *Atlus Corporation.* Stanford Graduate School of Business case study.

3. Barnett and Carroll, 1995.

4. Hannan and Freeman, 1984; Tushman and Anderson, 1986; Henderson and Clark, 1990.

5. Amburgey et al., 1993; Levinthal, 1997; Hannan et al., 2007.

6. Levitt and March, 1988.

7. Stinchcombe, 1965; Hannan and Freeman, 1984.

8. Rhee, Mooweon, William P. Barnett, and James March. 2003. *Hyundai Motor Company.* Stanford Graduate School of Business case study.

9. Hannan et al., 2007.

10. Rao et al., 2003.

11. Miner and Haunschild, 1995.

12. Greve, 1999.

13. Barnett and Carroll, 1995.

14. Interview with former Data General engineer, October 25, 2005.

15. Backus, 1980.

16. Anderson, 1995.

17. Hannan and Freeman, 1984; Barnett and Carroll, 1995.

18. Tushman and Anderson, 1986; Christensen, 1997.

19. Peters, 1992.

20. Hannan and Freeman, 1984; Hannan et al., 2007.

21. Barnett and Freeman, 2000.

22. Tushman and Romanelli, 1985.

Chapter 8: Some Implications of Red Queen Competition

1. Khanna et. al., 1998.

2. Barnett, Mischke, and Ocasio, 2000.

3. Powell et. al., 1996.

4. Stuart, Toby, William P. Barnett, and Charles A. O'Reilly. 1994. *Applied Materials, 1992.* Stanford Graduate School of Business case study.

5. Kogut, 1988.

6. Argote, 1999.

7. Stigler, 1968; Nelson, 1995.

8. DiMaggio and Powell, 1983; Burt, 1987; Haveman, 1993; Miner and Haunschild, 1995; Greve, 1996.

9. Hannan and Freeman, 1989; Mezias and Lant, 1994.

10. White, 1981; Carroll, 1985; Delacroix et al., 1989; Amburgey et al., 1994; Dobrev et al., 2001.

11. Carroll and Harrison, 1994.

12. Carroll and Hannan, 1989.

13. May, 1974.

14. Carroll and Hannan, 2000.

15. Argote, 1999.

16. See Ingram and Baum, 1997; Baum and Ingram, 1998; Miner and Haunschild, 1995; Sorenson, 2000a.

17. Denrell, 2003.

18. Simmel, 1908; Hannan and Freeman, 1989; Burt, 1992.

19. See Selznick, 1948.

20. Saunders and White, 1986.

21. See Rand-McNally, 1983, 1986; Thomson Bank Directory, 1992; Amel, 1988.

22. Rose, 1987.

23. Krooss, 1969.

24. Roussakis, 1984.

25. Federal Reserve Bank of Chicago, 1983.

26. Savage, 1987.

27. Kaufman, 1989.

28. Roussakis, 1984.

29. Rhoades, 1982.

30. Kaufman, 1989.

31. See Amel, 1993, and Kroszner and Strahan, 1999.

32. Amel and Jacowski, 1989.

33. Rose, 1989.

34. Vrabac, 1983.

35. Ibid.

36. U.S. Department of Commerce, 1988, 1992.

37. Petersen, 1991.

38. Swanson, 2002.

39. U.S. Department of Commerce, 2001.

40. Federal Reserve, 2002.

References

Akerlof, George A. 1976. "The Economics of Caste and of the Rat Race and Other Woeful Tales." *Quarterly Journal of Economics* 90: 599–617.

Alchian, Armand. 1950. "Uncertainty, Evolution, and Economic Theory." *Journal of Political Economy* 58: 211–221.

Aldrich, Howard. 1999. *Organizations Evolving.* London: Sage.

Amburgey, Terry, and Anne S. Miner. 1992. "Strategic Momentum: The Effects of History, Strategic Position and Structure on Merger Activity." *Strategic Management Journal* 13:335–348.

Amburgey, Terry L., Dawn Kelly, and William P. Barnett. 1993. "Resetting the Clock: The Dynamics of Organizational Transformation and Failure." *Administrative Science Quarterly* 38: 51–73.

Amel, Dean F. 1988. "State Laws Affecting Commercial Bank Branching, Multibank Holding Company Expansion, and Interstate Banking." Federal Reserve Board of Governors, working paper.

———. 1993. "State Laws Affecting the Geographic Expansion of Commercial Banks," ms., Board of Governors of the Federal Reserve System.

Amel, Dean F., and Michael J. Jacowski 1989. "Trends in Banking Structure since the Mid-1970s." *Federal Reserve Bulletin* (March): 120–133.

Anderson, Philip. 1995. "Microcomputer Manufacturers," pp. 37–58 in Glenn R. Carroll and Michael T. Hannan, eds., *Organizations in Industry: Strategy, Structure, and Selection.* New York: Oxford University Press.

Argote, Linda. 1999. *Organizational Learning: Creating, Retaining, and Transferring Knowledge.* Norwell, MA: Kluwer.

Armer, Paul. 1980. "SHARE—A Eulogy to Cooperative Effort." *Annals of the History of Computing* 2: 122–129.

Backus, John. 1980. "Programming in America in the 1950s—Some Personal Recollections," pp 125–135 in Nicholas Metropolis, Jack Howlett, and Giancarlo Rota, eds., *A History of Computing in the Twentieth Century.* New York: Academic Press.

Baker, Wayne E., and Robert R. Faulkner. 1993. "The Social Organization of Conspiracy: Illegal Networks in the Heavy Electrical Equipment Industry." *American Sociological Review* 58:837–860.

Bardini, Thierry. 2000. *Bootstrapping: Douglas Engelbart, Coevolution, and the Origins of Personal Computing.* Stanford: Stanford University Press.

Barnett, William P. 1990. "The Organizational Ecology of a Technological System." *Administrative Science Quarterly* 35:31–60.

———. 1993. "Strategic Deterrence Among Multipoint Competitors." *Industrial and Corporate Change* 2: 249–278.

———. 1997. "The Dynamics of Competitive Intensity." *Administrative Science Quarterly* 42: 128–160.

Barnett, William P., and Terry L. Amburgey. 1990. "Do Larger Organizations Generate Stronger Competition?" pp. 78–102 in Jitendra Singh, ed., *Organizational Evolution: New Directions.* Beverly Hills: Sage.

Barnett, William P., and Glenn R. Carroll. 1987. "Competition and Mutualism among Early Telephone Companies." *Administrative Science Quarterly* 32: 400–421.

———. 1993. "How Institutional Constraints Affected the Organization of Early U.S. Telephony." *Journal of Law, Economics and Organization* 9: 98–126.

———. 1995. "Modeling Internal Organizational Change" in John Hagan, ed., *Annual Review of Sociology* 21: 217–236.

Barnett, William P., and John Freeman. 2001. "Too Much of a Good Thing? Product Proliferation and Organizational Failure." *Organization Science* 12: 539–558.

Barnett, William P., Henrich R. Greve, and Douglas Y. Park. 1994. "An Evolutionary Model of Organizational Performance." *Strategic Management Journal* 15: 11–28.

Barnett, William P., and Morten T. Hansen. 1996. "The Red Queen in Organizational Evolution." *Strategic Management Journal* 17: 139–157.

Barnett, William P., and David McKendrick. 2004. "Why Are Some Organizations More Competitive Than Others? Evidence from a Changing Global Market." *Administrative Science Quarterly.*

Barnett, William P., Gary A. Mischke, and William Ocasio. 2000. "The Evolution of Collective Strategies among Organizations." *Organization Studies* 21: 325–354.

Barnett, William P., and Olav Sorenson. 2002. "The Red Queen in Organizational Creation and Development." *Industrial and Corporate Change* 11: 289–325.

Barnett, William P., Aimee Noelle Swanson, and Olav Sorenson. 2003 "Asymmetric Selection among Organizations." *Industrial and Corporate Change* 12, 4: 673–695.

Barnett, William P., and Michael Woywode. 2004. "From Red Vienna to the Anschluss: Ideological Competition among Viennese Newspapers during the Rise of National Socialism." *American Journal of Sociology* 109: 1452–1499.

Barney, Jay B. 1986. "Strategic Factor Markets: Expectations, Luck, and Business Strategy." *Management Science* 32: 1231–1241.

Barney, Jay B., and Edward J. Zajac. 1994. "Competitive Organizational Behavior: Toward an Organizationally-Based Theory of Competitive Advantage." *Strategic Management Journal* 15: 5–9.

Barron, David N. 1999. "The Structuring of Organizational Populations." *American Sociological Review* 64: 421–445.

Barron, David N., Elizabeth West, and Michael T. Hannan. 1994. "A Time to Grow and a Time to Die: Growth and Mortality of Credit Unions in New York City, 1914–1990." *American Journal of Sociology* 100: 381–421.

Baum, Joel A. C., and Paul Ingram. 1998. "Survival-enhancing Learning in the Manhattan Hotel Industry, 1898–1990." *Administrative Science Quarterly* 37: 580–604.

Baum, Joel A. C., and Stephen J. Mezias. 1993. "Competition, Institutional Linkages, and Organizational Growth." *Social Science Research* 22: 131–164.

Baum, Joel A. C., and Jitentra V. Singh. 1994. "Organizational Niches and the Dynamics of Organizational Mortality." *American Journal of Sociology* 100: 346–380.

Bell, C. Gordon, and Allen Newell. 1971. *Computer Structures: Readings and Examples.* New York: McGraw-Hill.

Bendor, Jonathan. 1995. "A Model of Muddling Through." *American Political Science Review* 89: 819–840.

Benjamin, Beth A., and Joel M. Podolny. 1999. "Status, Quality, and Social Order in the California Wine Industry." *Administrative Science Quarterly* 44: 563–589.

Benkard, C. Lanier. 2000. "Learning and Forgetting: The Dynamics of Aircraft Production." *American Economic Review* (September).

Berger, Peter L., and Thomas Luckmann. 1966. *The Social Construction of Reality.* New York: Doubleday.

Bernheim, B. Douglas, and Michael D. Whinston. 1990. "Multimarket Contact and Collusive Behavior." *Rand Journal of Economics* 21: 1–26.

Blanton, Alexander M., Joseph Traut, and Associates. 1967. *Computers and Small Manufacturers.* New York: Computer Research and Publications Associates.

Blau, Peter M. 1955. *The Dynamics of Bureaucracy.* Chicago: University of Chicago Press.

Blumberg, Donald F. 1964. "New Directions for Computer Technology and Applications: A Long-Range Prediction." *Computers and Automation* (January): 8.

Bodenhorn, Howard. 2000. *A History of Banking in Antebellum America: Financial Markets and Economic Development in an Era of Nation-Building.* Cambridge: Cambridge University Press.

Bothner, Matthew S.. 2003. "Competition and Social Influence: The Diffusion of the Sixth-Generation Processor in the Global Computer Industry." *American Journal of Sociology* 108: 1175.

Bresnahan, Timothy F., and Shane Greenstein. 1999. "Technological Competition and the Structure of the Computer Industry." *The Journal of Industrial Economics* 47: 1–40.

Bresnahan, Timothy F., and Peter C. Reiss. 1991. "Entry and Competition in Concentrated Markets." *Journal of Political Economy* 99: 997–1009.

Brittain, Jack, and John Freeman. 1980. "Organizational Proliferation and Density-Dependent Selection," pp. 291–338 in John Kimberly and Robert Miles, eds., *Organizational Life Cycles.* San Francisco: Jossey-Bass.

Brock, Gerald. 1981. *The Telecommunications Industry: The Dynamics of Market Structure.* Cambridge, MA: Ballinger.

Brooks, John. 1984. *The Go-Go Years.* New York: Dutton.

Brown, Shona L., and Kathleen M. Eisenhardt. 1997. "The Art of Continuous Change: Linking Complexity Theory and Time-paced Evolution in Relentlessly Shifting Organizations." *Administrative Science Quarterly* 42: 1–34.

Brüderl, Josef, and Rudolf Schüssler. 1990. "Organizational Mortality: The Liability of Newness and Adolescence." *Administrative Science Quarterly* 35: 530–547.

Brynjolfsson, Eric, and Lorin M. Hitt. 1996. "Paradox Lost? Firm-level Evidence on the Returns to Information Systems." *Management Science* 42: 4.

Burgelman, Robert A. 2002. *Strategy Is Destiny: How Strategy-Making Shapes a Company's Future.* New York: Free Press.

Burt, Ronald S. 1992. *Structural Holes.* Cambridge: Harvard University Press.

Calvani, Terry, and W. Todd Miller. 1993. "Antitrust Analysis of Bank Mergers: Recent Developments." *The Review of Banking & Financial Services* 9: 127.

Capron, Laurence, and Will Mitchell. 1999. "Bilateral Resource Deployment and Capabilities Following Horizontal Acquisitions." *Industrial and Corporate Change* 7: 453–484.

Carroll, Glenn R. 1984. "The Specialist Strategy." *California Management Review* 26: 126–137.

———. 1985. "Concentration and Specialization: Dynamics of Niche Width in Populations of Organizations." *American Journal of Sociology* 90: 1262–1283.

Carroll, Glenn R., and Michael T. Hannan. 1989. "Density Delay in the Evolution of Organizational Populations: A Model and Five Empirical Tests." *Administrative Science Quarterly* 34: 411–430.

———. 2000. *The Demography of Corporations and Industries.* Princeton:Princeton University Press.

Carroll, Glenn R., and J. Richard Harrison. 1994. "On the Historical Efficiency of Competition between Organizational Populations." *American Journal of Sociology* 100: 720–749.

Carroll, Glenn R., and Anand Swaminathan. 1992. "The Organizational Ecology of Strategic Groups in the Brewing Industry from 1975 to 1990." *Industrial and Corporate Change* 1: 65–97.

———. 1993. "On Theory, Breweries, and Strategic Groups (A Reply to Tremblay)." *Industrial and Corporate Change* 2: 99–106.

———. 2000. "Why the Microbrewery Movement? Organizational Dynamics of Resource Partitioning in the American Brewing Industry after Prohibition." *American Journal of Sociology* 106: 715–762.

Carroll, Glenn R., and Albert C. Y. Teo. 1996. "Creative Self-Destruction among Organizations: An Empirical Study of Technical Innovation and Organizational Failure in the American Automobile Industry, 1885–1982." *Industrial and Corporate Change* 6: 619–644.

Ceruzzi, Paul E. 1998. *A History of Modern Computing.* Cambridge: MIT Press.

Chandler, Alfred D., Jr. 1962. *Strategy and Structure: Chapters in the History of the American Industrial Enterprise.* Cambridge: MIT Press.

———. 2001. *Inventing the Electronic Century: The Epic Story of the Consumer Electronics and Computer Industries.* New York: Free Press.

Chapman, John M., and Ray B. Westerfield. 1942. *Branch Banking.* New York: Harper & Bros.

Charlton, W. E. 1958. "Rental vs. Purchase." *Machine Accounting and Data Processing* 1: 9.

Chernow, Ron. 1990. *The House of Morgan: An American Banking Dynasty and the Rise of Modern Finance.* New York: Atlantic Monthly Press.

Christensen, Clayton M. 1997. *The Innovator's Dilemma: When New Technologies Cause Great Firms to Fail.* Cambridge: Harvard Business School Press.

Chuang, You Ta, and Joel A. C. Baum. 2003. "It's All in the Name: Failure-induced Learning by Multiunit Chains." *Administrative Science Quarterly* 48:33–59.

Coal City Library. 1986. *Souvenir Edition 75th Anniversary Affiliated Bank/Coal City National Bank.*

Cole, Robert E. 1999. *Managing Quality Fads: How American Business Learned to Play the Quality Game*. New York: Oxford University Press.

Commons, John R. 1924. *Legal Foundations of Capitalism*. New York: Macmillan.

Cyert, Richard M., and James G. March. 1963. *A Behavioral Theory of the Firm*. Engelwood Cliffs, NJ: Prentice-Hall.

Davis, Gordon B. 1973. *Computer Data Processing* 2nd edition. New York: McGraw-Hill.

Deitel, Harvey M. 1990. *Operating Systems*, 2nd edition. New York: Addison-Wesley.

Delacroix, Jacques, and Glenn R. Carroll. 1983. "Organizational Foundings: An Ecological Study of the Newspaper Industries of Argentina and Ireland." *Administrative Science Quarterly* 28: 274–291.

Denrell, Jerker. 2003. "Vicarious Learning, Undersampling of Failure, and the Myths of Management." *Organization Science* 14: 243.

Denrell, Jerker, and James G. March. 2001. "Adaptation as Information Restriction: The Hot Stove Effect," *Organization Science* 12: 523–538.

DiMaggio, Paul J., and Walter W. Powell. 1983. "The Iron Cage Revisited: Institutional Isomorphism and Collective Rationality in Organizational Fields." *American Sociological Review* 48: 147–160.

Dosi, Giovanni, and Dan Lovallo. 1997. "Rational Entrepreneurs or Optimistic Martyrs? Some Considerations on Technological Regimes, Corporate Entries, and the Evolutionary Role of Decision Biases," pp. 41–68 in Raghu Garud, Praveen R. Nayyar, and Zur Shapira, eds., *Technological Innovation: Oversights and Foresights*. Cambridge: Cambridge University Press.

Dosi, Giovanni, and Franco Malerba, eds., 2002. *Industrial and Corporate Change, Special Issue on Industrial Dynamics*. New York: Oxford.

Dobrev, Stanislav, and Glenn R. Carroll. 2003. "Size (and Competition) among Organizations: Modeling Scale-based Selection among Automobile Producers in Four Major Countries, 1885–1981." *Strategic Management Journal* 24: 541–558.

Dobrev, Stanislav, Tai-Young Kim, and Michael T. Hannan. 2001. "Dynamics of Niche Width and Resource Partitioning." *American Journal of Sociology* 106: 1299–1337.

Eisenhardt, Kathleen M., and Behnam N. Tabrizi. 1995. "Accelerating Adaptive Processes: Product Innovation in the Global Computer Industry." *Administrative Science Quarterly* 40: 84–110.

Emery, Fred E., and Eric L. Trist. 1965. "The Causal Texture of Organizational Environments." *Human Relations* 18: 21–32.

Evans, Bob O. 1984. "SPREAD Report: The Origin of the IBM System/360 Project." *Annals of the History of Computing* 5: 4–44.

Everett, Robert R. 1980. "Whirlwind," pp. 365–384 in Nicholas Metropolis, Jack Howlett, and Giancarlo Rota, eds., *A History of Computing in the Twentieth Century*. New York: Academic Press.

Farrell, Joseph, and Carl Shapiro. 1990. "Horizontal Mergers: An Equilibrium Analysis," *American Economic Review* 80: 107–126.

Federal Reserve Bank of Chicago. 1983. *Leveling the Playing Field: Review of the DIDMCA of 1980 and the Garn-St Germain Act of 1982*. Chicago: Federal Reserve Bank of Chicago.

Federal Reserve Bank of Atlanta. 1985. "Interstate Banking Laws." *Economic Review*, Federal Reserve Bank of Atlanta.

Federal Reserve Statistical Release: Annual bank prime loan. 2002. http://www.federalreserve.gov/release/H15/data.htm.

Fischer, Gerald C. 1968. *American Banking Structure*. New York: Columbia University Press.

Fisher, Franklin M., James W. McKie, and Richard B. Mancke. 1983. *IBM and the U.S. Data Processing Industry: An Economic History*. New York: Praeger.

Frank, Robert H. 2000. *Luxury Fever: Money and Happiness in an Era of Excess*. Princeton: Princeton University Press.

Frank, Robert H., and Phillip J. Cook. 1995. *The Winner Take All Society*. New York: Free Press.

Fraser, Donald R., and James W. Kolari. 1985. *The Future of Small Banks in a Deregulated Environment*. Cambridge, MA: Ballinger.

Freeman, John, and Pino Audia. 2005. "Community Context and Founding Processes of Banking Organizations." Ms., Haas School of Business Administration.

Freeman, John, and Michael T. Hannan. 1983. "Niche Width and the Dynamics of Organizational Populations." *American Journal of Sociology* 88: 1116–1145.

Freiberger, Paul, and Michael Swaine. 1984. *Fire in the Valley: The Making of the Personal Computer*. Berkeley: Osborne/McGraw-Hill.

Freidson, Eliot. 2001. *Professionalism: The Third Logic*. Chicago: University of Chicago Press.

Friedland, Roger, and Robert R. Alford. 1991. "Bringing Society Back In: Symbols, Practices, and Institutional Contradictions," pp. 232–263 in Walter W. Powell and Paul J. DiMaggio, eds., *The New Institutionalism in Organizational Analysis*. Chicago: University of Chicago Press.

Friedman, Milton. 1953. *Essays in Positive Economics*. Chicago: University of Chicago Press.

Galbraith, John Kenneth. 1971. *The New Industrial State*, 2nd ed. New York: New American Library.

Garud, Raghu, Praveen R. Nayyar, and Zur Shapira. 1997. "Technological Choices and the Inevitability of Errors," pp. 20–40 in Raghu Garud, Praveen R. Nayyar, and Zur Shapira, eds., *Technological Innovation: Oversights and Foresights*. Cambridge: Cambridge University Press.

Gilder, George. 2000. *Telecosm*. New York: Free Press.

Greenstein, Shane M., and James B. Wade. 1998. "The Product Life Cycle in the Commercial Mainframe Computer Market, 1968–1982." *RAND Journal of Economics* 29: 772–789.

Greve, Henrich R. 1996. "Patterns of Competition: The Diffusion of a Market Position in Radio Broadcasting." *Administrative Science Quarterly* 41: 29–61.

———. 1998. "Performance, Aspirations, and Risky Organizational Change." *Administrative Science Quarterly* 43: 58–86.

———. 2002. "Sticky Aspirations: Organizational Time Perspective and Competitiveness." *Organization Science* 13: 1–17.

———. 2003. Organizational Learning from Performance Feedback: A Behavioral Perspective on Innovation and Change. Cambridge: Cambridge University Press.

Grosch, Herbert R. J. 1953. "High Speed Arithmetic: The Digital Computer as a Research Tool," *Journal of the Optical Society of America* 43: 4.

Haleblian, Jerayr, and Sydney Finkelstein. 1999. "The Influence of Organizational Acquisition Experience on Acquisition Performance: A Behavioral Perspective." *Administrative Science Quarterly* 44: 29–56.

Hall, Eldon C. 1996. *Journey to the Moon: The History of the Apollo Guidance Computer.* Reston, VA: AIAA.

Halstead, Maurice H. 1962. *Machine-Independent Computer Programming.* Washington, DC: Spartan Books.

Hannan, Michael T., and Glenn R. Carroll. 1992. *Dynamics of Organizational Populations: Density, Legitimation, and Competition.* New York: Oxford University Press.

Hannan, Michael T., and John Freeman. 1977. "The Population Ecology of Organizations." *American Journal of Sociology* 82: 929–964.

———. 1984. "Structural Inertia and Organizational Change." *American Sociological Review* 49: 149–164.

———. 1989. *Organizational Ecology.* Cambridge: Harvard University Press.

Hannan, Michael T., László Pólos, and Glenn R. Carroll. 2007. *Social Codes and Ecologies: Logics of Organization Theory.* Princeton: Princeton University Press.

Hannan, Michael T., and James Ranger-Moore. 1990. "The Ecology of Organizational Size Distributions: A Microsimulation Approach." *Journal of Mathematical Sociology* 15: 67–89.

Hansen, Morten T., Henry W. Chesbrough, Nitin Nohria, and Donald Sull. 2000. "Networked Incubators: Hothouses of the New Economy." *Harvard Business Review* (September): 74–84.

Haunschild, Pamela R., and Bilian N. Sullivan. 2002. "Learning from Complexity: Effects of Prior Accidents and Incidents on Airlines' Learning." *Administrative Science Quarterly* 47: 609–643.

Haveman, Heather. 1993. "Organizational Size and Change: Diversification in the Savings and Loan Industry after Deregulation." *Administrative Science Quarterly* 38: 20–50.

Hayes, Ian S., and William M. Ulrich. 1998. *The Year 2000 Software Crisis: The Continuing Challenge.* Upper Saddle River, NJ: Yourdon Press.

Henderson, Andrew D. 1999. "Firm Strategy and Age Dependence: A Contingent View of the Liabilities of Newness, Adolescence, and Obsolescence." *Administrative Science Quarterly* 44: 281–314.

Henderson, Rebecca M., and Kim B. Clark. 1990. "Architectural Innovation: The Reconfiguration of Existing Product Technologies and the Failure of Established Firms." *Administrative Science Quarterly* 35: 9–30.

Henderson, Andrew D., and Ithai Stern. 2004. "Selection-based Learning: The Coevolution of Internal and External Selection in High-velocity Environments." *Administrative Science Quarterly* 49: 39–75.

Herriott, Scott R., Daniel Levinthal, and James G. March, 1985. "Learning from Experience in Organizations," *American Economic Review* 75: 298–302.

Holland, John H., Keith J. Holyoak, Richard E. Nisbett, and Paul R. Thagard. 1989. *Induction: Processes of Inference, Learning, and Discovery.* Cambridge: MIT Press.

Honey, Martha, ed., 2002. *Ecotourism and Certification: Setting Standards in Practice*. Washington, D.C.: Island Press.

Hubbard, Timothy William, and Lewis E. Davids. 1969. *Banking in Mid-America*. Washington, D.C.: Public Affairs Press.

Hunt, Scott A., Robert D. Benford, and David A. Snow. 1994. "Identity Fields: Framing Processes and the Social Construction of Movement Identities," pp. 185–208 in Enrique Laraña, Hank Johnston, and Joseph R. Gusfield, eds., *New Social Movements: From Ideology to Identity*. Philadelphia: Temple University Press.

Iansiti, Marco, and Kim B. Clark. 1994. "Integration and Dynamic Capability: Evidence from Product Development in Automobiles and Mainframe Computers." *Industrial and Corporate Change* 3: 557–605.

Ingram, Paul, and Joel A. C. Baum. 1997. "Opportunity and Constraint: Organizations' Learning from the Operating and Competitive Experience of Industries." *Strategic Management Journal* 18: 75–98.

Ingram, Paul, and Peter W. Roberts. 2000. "Friendships among Competitors in the Sydney Hotel Industry." *American Journal of Sociology* 106: 387–423.

Isshiki, Koichiro R. 1982. *Small Business Computers: A Guide to Evaluation and Selection*. Englewood Cliffs, NJ: Prentice-Hall.

Kaufman, George G. 1989. *The U.S. Financial System (Fourth edition)*. Englewood Cliffs, NJ: Prentice-Hall.

Kauffman, Stuart A. 1993. *The Origins of Order: Self-Organization and Selection in Evolution*. New York: Oxford University Press.

Khanna, Tarun, Ranjay Gulati, and Nitin Nohria. 1998. "The Dynamics of Learning Alliances: Competition, Cooperation, and Relative Scope." *Strategic Management Journal* 19: 193–210.

Kidder, Tracy. 1981. *The Soul of a New Machine*. New York: Avon Books.

Klebaner, Benjamin 1974. *Commercial Banking in the United States: A History*. Hinsdale, IL: Dryden Press.

Knott, Anne Marie, and Hart Posen. 2005. "Is Failure Good?" *Strategic Management Journal* 26: 617–641.

Knuth, Donald E., and Luis Trabb Pardo. 1980. "The Early Development of Programming Languages," pp 197–273 in Nicholas Metropolis, Jack Howlett, and Giancarlo Rota, eds., *A History of Computing in the Twentieth Century*. New York: Academic Press.

Kogut, Bruce. 1988."Joint Ventures: Theoretical and Empirical Perspectives." *Strategic Management Journal* 9: 319–332.

Kolko, Gabriel. 1963. *The Triumph of Conservatism: A Reinterpretation of American History, 1900–1916*. New York: Free Press.

Krooss, Herman E., ed., 1969. *Documentary History of Banking and Currency in the United States, Vol. 4*. New York: McGraw-Hill.

Kroszner, Randall S., and Philip E. Strahan. 1999. "What Drives Deregulation: Economics and Politics of the Relaxation of Bank Branching Restrictions." *Quarterly Journal of Economics* 114: 1437–1467.

Langlois, Richard N. 1992. "External Economies and Economic Progress: The Case of the Microcomputer Industry." *Business History Review* 66: 1–50.

———. 1997. "Cognition and Capabilities: opportunities Seized and Missed in the History of the Computer Industry," pp. 71–94 in Raghu Garud, Praveen R. Nayyar, and Zur Shapira, eds., *Technological Innovation: Oversights and Foresights*. Cambridge: Cambridge University Press.

Lant, Theresa K. 1992. "Aspiration Level Adaptation: An Empirical Exploration." *Management Science* 38: 623–644.

Larrowe, Vernon L. 1964. "Hybrid Computers," pp. 69–74 in Richard Goodman, ed., *Computer Yearbook and Directory*. Detroit: American Data Processing Inc.

Lerner, Josh. 1997. "An Empirical Exploration of a Technology Race." *RAND Journal of Economics* 28: 228–247.

Levi, Steven. 1984. *Hackers: Heroes of the Computer Revolution*. New York: Anchor/Doubleday.

Levinthal, Daniel A. 1991 "Random Walks and Organizational Mortality." *Administrative Science Quarterly* 36: 397–420.

———. 1997. "Adaptation on Rugged Landscapes." *Management Science* 43: 934–950.

Levinthal, Daniel A., and James G. March 1981. "A Model of Adaptive Organizational Search." *Journal of Economic Behavior and Organization* 2: 307–333.

———. 1993. "The Myopia of Learning." *Strategic Management Journal* 14: 95–112.

Levitt, Barbara, and James G. March. 1988: "Organizational Learning." *Annual Review of Sociology* 14: 319–340.

Levy, Steven. 1984. *Hackers: Heroes of the Computer Revolution*. New York: Anchor/Doubleday.

Lindblom, Charles E. 1959. "The Science of Muddling Through." *Public Administration Review* 38: 232–239.

Lippman, S., and Richard Rumelt. 1982. "Uncertain Imitability: An Analysis of Interfirm Differences in Efficiency under Competition." *Bell Journal of Economics* 13: 418–438.

Luckoff, Herman. 1979. *From Dits to Bits: A Personal History of the Electronic Computer*. Portland, OR: Robotics Press.

March, James G. 1981. "Footnotes to Organizational Change." *Administrative Science Quarterly* 26: 563–577.

———. 1988. *Decisions and Organizations*. Cambridge, MA: Basil Blackwell.

———. 1991. "Exploration and Exploitation in Organizational Learning." *Organization Science*, 2: 71–87.

———. 1994. *A Primer on Decision Making: How Decisions Happen*. New York: Free Press.

March, James G., and Herbert A. Simon. 1958. *Organizations*. New York: John Wiley.

March, James G., Lee S. Sproull, and Michal Tamuz. 1991. "Learning from Samples of One or Fewer." *Organization Science* 2: 1–13.

May, Robert M. 1974. *Stability and Complexity in Model Ecosystems*. 2nd ed. Princeton: Princeton University Press.

Mayer, Martin. 1974. *The Bankers*. New York: Weybright and Talley.

McAdam, Doug. 1996. "Movement Strategy and Dramaturgic Framing in Democratic States." *Research on Democracy and Society* 3: 155–176. Greenwich, CT: JAI Press.

McAdam, Doug, Sidney Tarrow, and Charles Tilly. 2001. *Dynamics of Contention.* Cambridge: Cambridge University Press.

McGlynn, Daniel, R. 1982. *Personal Computing,* 2nd Edition. New York: Wiley.

McKendrick, David G., Jonathan Jaffee, Glenn R. Carroll, and Olga M. Khessina. 2003. "In the Bud? Disk Array Producers as a (Possibly) Emergent Organizational Form." *Administrative Science Quarterly* 48: 60–93.

McPherson, J. Miller. 1983. "An Ecology of Affiliation." *American Sociological Review* 48: 519–535.

Mendelson, Haim. 1987. "Economies of Scale in Computing: Grosch's Law Revisited." *Communications of the ACM* 30: 1066–1072.

Merton, Robert K. 1968. "The Matthew Effect in Science." *Science* 159: 56–63.

Meyer, David S., and Suzanne Staggenborg. 1996. "Movements, Countermovements, and the Structure of Political Opportunity." *American Journal of Sociology* 101: 1628–60.

Meyer, John W., and Brian Rowan. 1977. "Institutionalized Organizations: Formal Structure as Myth and Ceremony." *American Journal of Sociology* 83: 340–363.

Mezias, Stephen J., Ya Ru Chen, and Patrice R. Murphy. 2002. "Aspiration-level Adaptation in an American Financial Services Organization: A Field Study." *Management Science* 48:1285–1300.

Mezias, Stephen J., and Theresa K. Lant. 1994. "Mimetic Learning and the Evolution of Organizational Populations," pp. 179–198 in Joel A.C. Baum and Jitendra V. Singh, eds., *Evolutionary Dynamics of Organizations.* New York: Oxford University Press.

Miner, Anne S., and Pamela Haunschild. 1995. "Population-level Learning." *Research in Organizational Behavior* 17: 115–166.

Minkoff, Debra C. 1997. "The Sequencing of Social Movements." *American Sociological Review* 62: 779–799.

Mintz, Beth, and Michael Schwartz. 1985. *The Power Structure of American Business.* Chicago: University of Chicago Press.

Mizruchi, Mark S., and Linda Brewster Stearns. 2001. "Getting Deals Done: The Use of Social Networks in Bank Decision-Making." *American Sociological Review* 66: 647–671.

Musil, Robert, trans. 1996. *The Man without Qualities.* Vol. 1: *A Sort of Introduction and Pseudo Reality Prevails.* New York: Vintage.

Nelson, Richard R. 1995. "Recent Evolutionary Theorizing about Economic Change." *Journal of Economic Literature* 1995, 33: 48–90.

Nelson, Richard R., and Sidney G. Winter. 1982. *An Evolutionary Theory of Economic Change.* Cambridge, MA: Belknap Press.

New York Times. "Big Bankers Feast and Make Merry," December 20, 1900, p. 1.

North, Douglass C. 1981. *Structure and Change in Economic History.* New York: W.W. Norton.

Ogilvie, Nigel R. 1980. "Foreign Banks in the US and Geographic Restrictions on Banking." *Journal of Bank Research,* 11: 72.

Ordover, Janusz, and Robert Willig. 1991 "An Economic Definition of Predation: Pricing and Product Innovation." *Yale Law Journal* 91: 8–53.

Ornstein, Severo M. 2002. *Computing in the Middle Ages: A View from the Trenches 1955–1983.* Minneapolis: Tandem Library.

O'Reilly, Charles A., and Michael L. Tushman. 2007. "Ambidexterity as a Dynamic Capability: Resolving the Innovator's Dilemma." Working paper.

Osborn, Roddy. 1954. "GE and UNIVAC: Harnessing the High-Speed Computer." *Harvard Business Review* (July–August): 99–107.

Padgett, John F., and Christopher K. Ansell. 1993. "Robust Action and the Rise of the Medici, 1400–1434. *American Journal of Sociology* 98: 1259–1319.

Parker, George G. C. 1981. "Now Management Will Make or Break the Bank." *Harvard Business Review* (November).

Péli, Gábor. 2007. "Fit by Founding, Fit by Adaptation: Reconciling Conflicting Theories with Logical Formalizaton." Working paper.

Peters, Tom. 1992. *Liberation Management: Necessary Disorganization for the Nanosecond Nineties.* New York: Knopf.

Peterson, Trond. 1991. "Time-Aggregation Bias in Continuous-Time Hazard-Rate Models," in Peter Marsden, ed., *Sociological Methodology 1991.* Cambridge: Blackwell.

Pfeffer, Jeffrey, and Gerald R. Salancik. 1978. *The External Control of Organizations.* New York: Harper and Row.

Phister, Montgomery Jr. 1979. *Data Processing Technology and Economics,* 2nd edition. Santa Monica, CA: Digital Press.

Podolny, Joel M. 1993. "A Status-Based Model of Market Competition." *American Journal of Sociology* 98: 829–872.

———. 2004. *Status Signals: A Sociological Study of Market Competition.* Princeton, NJ: Princeton University Press, in press.

Podolny, Joel M., Toby E. Stuart, and Michael T. Hannan. 1996. "Networks, Knowledge, and Niches: Competition in the Worldwide Semiconductor Industry, 1984–1991." *American Journal of Sociology* 102: 659–689.

Pomeroy, J. S. 1914. Address to the Minnesota Bankers Association, quoted in 1989 Minnesota Bankers Association documents.

Poole, Hilary, Tami Schuyler, Theresa M. Senft, and Christos J.P. Moschovitis, eds., 1999. *History of the Internet: A Chronology, 1843 to the Present.* Oxford, UK: ABC-Clio.

Porac, Joseph F. 1997. "Local Rationality, Global Blunders, and the Boundaries of Technological Choice: Lessons from IBM and DOS," pp. 129–146 in Raghu Garud, Praveen R. Nayyar, and Zur Shapira, eds., *Technological Innovation: Oversights and Foresights.* Cambridge: Cambridge University Press.

Porac, Joseph F., Howard Thomas, Fiona Wilson, Douglas Paton, and Alaina Kanfer. 1995. "Rivalry and the Industry Model of Scottish Knitwear Producers." *Administrative Science Quarterly* 40: 203–227.

Porter, Michael E. 1980. *Competitive Strategy,* New York: Free Press.

Porter, Michael E. 1990. *The Competitive Advantage of Nations.* New York: Free Press.

Powell, Walter. 1991. "Expanding the Scope of Institutional Analysis," pp. 183–203 in Walter Powell and Paul DiMaggio, eds., *The New Institutionalism in Organizational Analysis*. Chicago: University of Chicago Press.

Powell, Walter W., Kenneth W. Koput, and L. Smith-Doerr. 1996. "Interorganizational Collaboration and the Locus of Innovation: Networks of Learning in Biotechnology." *Administrative Science Quarterly* 41: 116–145.

Primm, James Neal. 1989. *A Foregone Conclusion: The Founding of the Federal Reserve Bank of St. Louis*. St. Louis: Federal Reserve Bank.

Proceedings of the ACM/IEEE Conference on Supercomputers. 1988. Los Alamitos, CA: IEEE Computer Society Press.

Pugh, Emerson W. 1984. *Memories That Shaped an Industry*. Cambridge: MIT Press.

Pugh, Emerson, Lyle R. Johnson, and John H. Palmer. 1991. *IBM's 360 and Early 370 Systems*. Cambridge: MIT Press.

Punched Card Data Processing. 1959. New York: Gille Associates.

Rand-McNally & Company. Various years. *The Rand-McNally Bankers Directory*. Chicago: Rand-McNally & Company.

Ranger-Moore, James, Jane Banaszak-Holl, and Michael T. Hannan 1991. "Density Dependence in Regulated Industries: Founding Rates of Banks and Life Insurance Companies." *Administrative Science Quarterly* 36: 36–65.

Rao, Hayagreeva, Philippe Monin, and Rodolphe Durand. 2003. "Institutional Change in Toque Ville: Nouvelle Cuisine as an Identity Movement in French Gastronomy." *American Journal of Sociology* 108: 795–843.

Rhoades, Stephen A. 1982. "Size and Rank Stability of the 100 Largest Commercial Banks, 1925–1978." *Journal of Economics and Business* 34: 123–128.

Richardson, Lewis Fry. 1960. *Arms and Insecurity: A Mathematical Study of the Causes and Origins of War*. Pittsburgh: Boxwood Press.

Rifkin, Glenn, and George Harrar. 1988. *The Ultimate Entrepreneur: The Story of Ken Olsen and Digital Equipment Corporation*. Chicago: Contemporary.

Roberts, Lawrence G. 1967. "Multiple Computer Networks and Intercomputer Communication." *ACM Symposium on Operating System Principles*, Gatlinburg, Tenn.

Rockoff, Hugh. 2000. "Banking and Finance, 1789–1914," pp. 643–684 in Stanley L. Engerman and Robert E. Gallman, eds., *The Cambridge Economic History of the United States. Vol. 2. The Long Nineteenth Century*, New York: Cambridge University Press.

Rose, P. S. 1987. *The Changing Structure of American Banking*. New York: Columbia University Press.

Rosen, Saul. 1969. "Electronic Computers: A Historical Survey." *Computing Surveys* 1: 7–36.

Rothbard, Murray N. 2002. *A History of Money and Banking in the United States: The Colonial Era to World War II*. Auburn, AL: Ludwig von Mises Institute.

Roussakis, Emmanuel N. 1984. *Commercial Banking in an Era of Deregulation*. New York: Praeger.

Ruef, Martin. 2000. "The Emergence of Organizational Forms: A Community Ecology Approach." *American Journal of Sociology* 106: 658–714.

Saunders, Anthony, and Lawrence J. White, eds. 1986. *Technology and the Regulation of Financial Markets*. Lexington, MA: Lexington Books.

Savage, Donald, T. 1987. "Interstate Banking Developments." *Federal Reserve Bulletin* (February): 79–92.

Savage, John E., Susan Magidson, and Alex M. Stein. 1986. *The Mystical Machine: Issues and Ideas in Computing*. Reading, MA: Addison-Wesley.

Schumpeter, Joseph A. 1950. *Capitalism, Socialism, and Democracy*. 3rd ed. New York: Harper and Row.

Scott, W. Richard. 1975. "Organizational Structure." *Annual Review of Sociology* 1: 1–20.

Scott, W. Richard, Martin Ruef, Peter J. Mendel, and Carol A. Caronna. 2000. *Institutional Change and Healthcare Organizations: From Professional Dominance to Managed Care*. Chicago: University of Chicago Press, 2000.

Selznick, Philip. 1957. *Leadership in Administration*. New York: Harper and Row.

———. 1960. *The Organizational Weapon*. Glencoe, IL: Free Press.

Shigeru, Takahashi. 2005. "The Rise and Fall of Plug-Compatible Mainframes." *IEEE Annals of the History of Computing* 27 (January–March): 4–16.

Simmel, Georg. 1908. *Conflict*. 1955 tr. New York: Free Press.

Simon, Herbert A. 1945. *Administrative Behavior*. New York: Macmillan.

Simon, Herbert A. 1969. *The Sciences of the Artificial*. Cambridge: MIT Press.

Sitkin, Sim B. 1992. "A Strategy of Learning through Failure: The Strategy of Small Losses," pp. 231–266, in B. M. Staw and L. Cummings, eds., *Research in Organizational Behavior*, vol. 14. Greenwich, CT: JAI Press.

Slatkin, Montgomery, and John Maynard Smith. 1979. "Models of Coevolution." *Quarterly Review of Biology* 18: 151–159.

Sorenson, Olav. 2000a. "The Effect of Population-Level Learning on Market Entry: The American Automobile Industry." *Social Science Research* 29: 307–327.

———. 2000b. "Letting the Market Work for You: An Evolutionary Perspective on Product Strategy." *Strategic Management Journal* 21: 277–292.

———. 2003. "Interdependence and Adaptability: Organizational Learning and the Long-Term Effect of Integration." *Management Science* 49: 446–463.

Sorenson, Olav, and Jesper Sorensen B. 2001. "Finding the Right Mix: Franchising, Organizational Learning, and Chain Performance." *Strategic Management Journal* 22: 713–725.

Southworth, Shirley D. 1928. *Branch Banking in the United States*. New York: McGraw Hill.

Souvenir Edition Affiliated Bank/Coal City National 75th Anniversary. 1986. Coal City, IL: Bailey's Printing and Publishing.

Staw, Barry M. 1975. "Attributions of the 'Causes' of Performance: A New Alternative Interpretation of Cross-sectional Research in Organizations." *Organizational Behavior and Human Performance* 13: 414–432.

Stern, Nancy. 1981. *From ENIAC to UNIVAC: An Appraisal of the Eckert-Mauchly Computers*. Bedford, MA: Digital Press.

Stewart, Daniel. 2005. "Social Status in an Open-Source Community." *American Sociological Review* 70: 823–842.

Stigler, George. 1951. "The Division of Labor Is Limited by the Extent of the Market." *Journal of Political Economy* 59: 185–193.

———. 1968. *The Organization of Industry.* Homewood, IL: Irwin.

Stinchcombe, Arthur L. 1965. "Social Structure and Organizations," pp. 142–193 in James G. March, ed., *Handbook of Organizations.* Chicago: Rand McNally.

Streeck, Wolfgang, and Philippe C. Schmitter. 1985. "Community, Market, State-and Associations? The Prospective Contribution of Interest Governance to Social Order." *European Sociological Review* 1: 119–139.

Stross, Randall E. 1993. *Steve Jobs and the NeXT Big Thing.* New York: Atheneum.

Swaminathan, Anand. 1996. "Environmental Conditions at Founding and Organizational Mortality: A Trial-by-Fire Model." *Academy of Management Journal* 39: 1350–1377.

Swanson, Aimee Noelle. 2002. "Form Coherence and the Fates of De Alio and De Novo Organizations in the U.S. Digital Computer Industry: 1951–1994." Ph.D. Dissertation, Department of Sociology, Stanford University.

Swidler, Ann. 1986. "Culture in Action: Symbols and Strategies." *American Sociological Review* 51: 273–286.

Thompson, James D. 1967. *Organizations in Action.* New York: McGraw-Hill.

Thomson Bank Directory. Various years. Skokie, IL: Thomson Financial Publishing.

Thornton, Patricia H., and William Ocasio. 1999. "Institutional Logics and the Historical Contingency of Power in Organizations: Executive Succession in the Higher Education Publishing Industry, 1958–1990." *American Journal of Sociology* 105: 801–843.

Tirole, Jean. 1988. *The Theory of Industrial Organization.* Cambridge: MIT Press.

———. 1997. *The Theory of Industrial Organization.* Cambridge: MIT Press.

Tuma, Nancy Brandon, and Michael T. Hannan. 1984. *Social Dynamics: Models and Methods.* New York: Academic Press.

Tushman, Michael L., and Philip Anderson. 1986. "Technological Discontinuities and Organizational Environments." *Administrative Science Quarterly* 31: 439–465.

Tushman, Michael L., and Charles A. O'Reilly. 2002. *Winning through Innovation: A Practical Guide to Leading Organizational Change and Renewal.* Boston: Harvard Business School Publishing.

Tushman, Michael L., and Elaine Romanelli. 1985. "Organizational Evolution: A Metamorphosis Model of Convergence and Reorientation." In Lawrence L. Cummings and Barry M. Staw, eds., *Research in Organizational Behavior*, 7: 171–222. Greenwich, CT: JAI Press.

U.S. Department of Commerce. 1975. *Historical Statistics of the United States.* Washington, DC: U.S. Government Printing Office.

———. 1988. *County and City Data Book.* Washington, DC: U.S. Department of Commerce, Social and Economic Statistics Administration, Bureau of the Census.

———. 1992. *USA County Statistics* [CD-ROM database]. Washington, DC: U.S. Department of Commerce, Social and Economic Statistics Administration, Bureau of the Census.

————. 2001. "Real Gross Domestic Product." Washington, DC: U.S. Department of Commerce, Bureau of Economic Analysis.

U.S. Federal Reserve, Board of Governors. 1959. *All Bank Statistics, 1896–1955.* Washington, DC: U.S. Government Printing Office.

————. 1976. *Banking and Monetary Statistics, 1941–1970.* Washington, DC: U.S. Government Printing Office.

Van Valen, L. 1973. "A New Evolutionary Law." *Evolutionary Theory* 1: 1–30.

Vaupel, James W., Kenneth G. Manton, and Eric Stallard. 1979. "The Impact of Heterogeneity in Individual Frailty on the Dynamics of Mortality." *Demography* 16: 439–454.

Veblen, Thornstein. 1923. *Absentee Ownership and Business Enterprise in Recent Times: The Case of America.* New York: Huebsch.

Vrabac, Daniel J. 1983. "Recent Developments at Banks and Nonbank Depository Institutions," *Federal Reserve Board of Kansas Economic Review* 983: 33–45.

Warburg,. Paul M. 1930. *The Federal Reserve System: Its Origin and Growth.* New York: Macmillan.

Weitzman, Cay. 1974. *Minicomputer Systems: Structure, Implementation and Application.* Englewood Cliffs, NJ: Prentice Hall.

White, Eugene Nelson. 1982. "The Political Economy of Banking Regulation, 1864–1933." *Journal of Economic History* 42 (March): 33–42.

White, Harrison. 1981. "Where Do Markets Come From?" *American Journal of Sociology* 87: 517–547.

Wiebe, Robert H. 1962. *Businessmen and Reform: A Study of the Progressive Movement.* Cambridge: Harvard University Press.

Williamson, Oliver F. 1985. *The Economic Institutions of Capitalism.* New York: Free Press.

Winerman, Marc. 2003. "The Origins of the FTC: Concentration, Cooperation, Control, and Competition." *Antitrust Law Journal* 71: 1–97.

Winningham, Scott, and Donald G. Hagan. 1980. "Regulation Q: An Historical Perspective." *Economic Review,* Federal Reserve Bank of Kansas City (April) 3–17.

Zald, Mayer N. 1990. "History, Sociology, and Theories of Organizations," pp. 81–108. In J. E. Jackson, ed., *Institutions in American Society: Essays in Market, Political, and Social Organizations.* Ann Arbor: University of Michigan Press.

————. 1996. "Culture, Ideology, and Strategic Framing," pp. 261–274 in Doug McAdam, John D. McCarthy, and Mayer N. Zald, eds., *Comparative Perspectives on Social Movements.* Cambridge: Cambridge University Press.

Zollo, Maurizio, and Harbir Singh. 2004. "Deliberate Learning in Corporate Acquisitions: Post-Acquisition Strategies and Integration Capability in US Bank Mergers." *Strategic Management Journal* 25: 1233–1256.

Zuckerman, Ezra W., 1999. "The Categorical Imperative: Securities Analysts and the Illegitimacy Discount." *American Journal of Sociology* 104: 1398–1438.

Zuckerman, Ezra W., and Tai-Young Kim. 2003. "The Critical Trade-off: Identity Assignment and Box-Office Success in the Feature Film Industry." *Industrial and Corporate Change* 12:27–67.

Index